AF660796

EMPOWERMENT OF WOMEN IN NORTH EAST INDIA

The Editors

Harendra Sinha obtained his MA (Political Science) and Ph.D. degrees from Gauhati University, Guwahati, Assam. He is presently working as Associate Professor and Head of the Department of Political Science, Government J. Buana College Lunglei, Mizoram. He has authored the book "Bureaucracy and Rural Development in Mizoram" (2011), published by Concept Publishing Company Pvt. Ltd., New Delhi and contributed number of research papers and regularly contributes papers to various journals and presents papers at seminars. He is currently a member of Mizoram Academic Forum, Mizoram Political Science Association and North East Political Science Association.

J. Zorema obtained his MA (History) and Ph.D. degrees from NEHU, Shillong. He is presently the Principal, Government J. Buana College Lunglei, Mizoram. He has authored the book "Indirect Rule in Mizoram—1890-1954" (2007) published by Mittal Publications, New Delhi and contributed a number of research papers and regularly contributes papers to various journals and presents papers at seminars. He is a life member of North East India History Association and Mizo History Association. He is actively involved in social work and had been the President of YMA Sub-Headquarters for two consecutive terms.

Empowerment of Women in North East India

Socio-economic Perspectives

Edited by
Harendra Sinha
J. Zorema

CONCEPT PUBLISHING COMPANY PVT. LTD.,
NEW DELHI-110059

© Editors

All rights reserved. No part of this work may be reproduced, stored, adapted, or transmitted in any form or by any means, electronic, mechanical, photocopying, micro-filming recording or otherwise, or translated in any language, without the prior written permission of the copyright owner and the publisher. The book is sold subject to the condition that it shall not, by way of trade or otherwise, be lent, resold, hired out, or otherwise circulated without the prior publisher written consent in any form of binding or cover other than that in which it is published.

The views and opinions expressed in this book are author(s) own and the facts reported by him/her have been verified to the extent possible, and the publishers are not in any way liable for the same.

ISBN-13: 978-81-8069-907-8

First Published 2012

Published and Printed by :

Concept Since 1974

Concept Publishing Company Pvt. Ltd.
A/15-16, Commercial Block, Mohan Garden
New Delhi-110059 (India)
T: 25351460, 25351794, *F*: 091-11-25357109
E: publishing@conceptpub.com, W: www.conceptpub.com
Editorial Office: H-13, Bali Nagar, New Delhi-110 015, India.

Cataloging in Publication Data--Courtesy: D.K. Agencies (P) Ltd. <docinfo@dkagencies.com>

Empowerment of women in North East India : socio-economic perspectives / edited by Harendra Sinha, J. Zorema.

p. cm.
Contributed articles.
Includes bibliographical references and index.
ISBN 9788180699078

1. Women in development—India, Northeastern. 2. Women in development Government policy—India, Northeastern. I. Sinha, Harendra. II. Zorema, J.(James), 1960-

DDC 305.4209541 23

Acknowledgements

We express our sincere thanks to the contributors who kindly accepted our request to include their papers and rendered necessary information, assistance and cooperation during the edition of this volume.

During the course of editing the book, the teaching and non-teaching members of Government J. Buana College, Lunglei, Mizoram rendered kind help and support in compiling the book. We gratefully acknowledge their kind cooperation.

We also deeply express our heartfelt gratitude to our family members for supporting us during this work.

We wish to pass on our sincere thanks to many scholars worldwide whose valuable works have been consulted and drawn upon during the compilation work. The blessings of information technology are highly acknowledged through which much information, data and study materials were gathered.

Finally, we are deeply obliged to Mr. A.K. Mittal of Concept Publishing Company Pvt. Ltd., New Delhi for accepting the manuscript and for their kind help, support and cooperation in publishing this volume in a short period and in elegant manner.

We are responsible for all the shortcomings in the book, if any, and would welcome suggestions for future guidance.

Lunglei, Mizoram
29th November, 2011

Harendra Sinha
J. Zorema

Contents

SECTION III
POLITICAL EMPOWERMENT AND WOMEN OF MIZORAM

SECTION IV
SOCIAL AND ECONOMIC EMPOWERMENT: PERSPECTIVES ON MIZORAM

Introduction

The empowerment, equality and autonomy of women are globally recognized as a key factor to achieve progress in socio-economic and political spheres. It is one of the eight Millennium Development Goals to which world leaders agreed at the Millennium Summit held in New York in 2000. Empowerment of women leads in raising women's self-awareness, skill development, creative decision-making and shaping as better citizens. It presents a way towards dignity and security for women, their families and the entire community. Political empowerment is valued as the most important one of all empowerments. It is regarded as the key driver for the economic and social empowerments. Their enhanced participation in governance structures is viewed as key to redress the inherent gender inequalities in different societies.

The Universal Declaration of Human Rights affirms that everyone has the right to take part in the government of his or her country and the right of equal access to public service. The International Covenant on Civil and Political Rights also states, *inter alia*, that every citizen shall have the right and opportunity to take part in the conduct of public affairs, directly or through freely-chosen representatives, to vote and to be elected at genuine periodic elections and to have access, on general terms of equality, to public service in his or her country. The provision for political empowerment of women got international attention with the Declaration of 'Convention on the Political Rights of Women' which states that women shall be on equal terms with men and without any discrimination entitled to vote in all elections, eligible for election to all publicly-elected bodies, entitled to hold public office and to exercise all public functions established by national law.

In India, the principle of gender equality is enshrined in the Indian Constitution in its Preamble, Fundamental Rights, Fundamental Duties and Directive Principles. The Constitution not only grants equality to women, but also empowers the States to adopt positive measures in favour of women. However, the demand for greater representation of women in political institutions was taken up in a systematic way with the setting up of the Committee on the Status of Women in India (CSWI) which published its report in 1976. The Committee was set-up with a view to make recommendations for improvement of the socio-economic position of women. The CSWI report suggested that women's representation in political institutions, especially at the grass roots level, needed to be increased through a policy of reservation of seats for them in Legislatures.

Since then, the empowerment of women has been accepted as the essential subject in determining the status of women. Various legislations, development plans and policies have been made aiming women's development in all spheres. Setting up of National Commission for Women by an Act of Parliament in 1990 to safeguard the rights and legal entitlements of women, provision for at least 33 per cent reservation of seats in the local bodies (now most of the States in India passed legislation for 50 per cent of seats reserved for women at the grass roots bodies following the Union Cabinet's decision, to bring a bill to amend Article 243(D) of the Constitution) of Panchayats and Municipalities by the Constitution of India 73rd and 74th Amendment (1993) which enables women's participation at the grass roots level and the proposed Bill of 33 per cent Reservation for Women in Parliament and State Legislatures if passed will usher a new chapter towards women's participation in decision making at all levels. The National Policy for the Empowerment of Women 2001 sets the goal to bring about the advancement, development and empowerment of women. The Policy disseminated so as to encourage active participation of all stakeholders for achieving its goals in creating an environment through positive economic and social policies for full development of women and to enable them to realize their full potential. Since women comprise the majority of the population below the poverty line and are very often in situations of extreme poverty, given the harsh realities of intra-household and social discrimination, macroeconomic policies and poverty eradication programmes will specifically address the needs and problems of such women. Special measures are being taken to eliminate discrimination, universalize education, eradicate illiteracy, create a gender-sensitive educational system, increase enrolment and retention rates of girls and improve the quality of education to facilitate life-long learning as well as development of occupation/vocation/technical skills by women.

However, in spite of the various legislations and provisions in the Constitution of India through various articles (Art. 14, 15, 23, 29, 30, 42, 45 etc.) for equal rights of women, Indian women continue to remain oppressed and struggle over everything from survival to resources. While women have made considerable progress in some areas such as education and employment, they continue to be subjected to the influence of the existing patriarchal attitudes in Indian society. The dilemma for Indian women today is that despite the liberal provisions of the Constitution and various laws, serious inequalities remain.

Women of North East India have no exception and face multiple hurdles in the overall backward economy of the region. The North East India comprises of eight small states (Arunachal Pradesh, Assam, Manipur, Meghalaya, Mizoram, Nagaland, Tripura and Sikkim) comprising the total area of the region of 2,55,036 sq. km of which 70 per cent is hilly terrain and deep valley. It represents about 7.5 per cent of India's landmass and 3.5 per cent of India's population (2001). Its population density of 143 per sq. km is much lower than the all-India figure of 313. Significantly, it accounts for 26 per cent of the national forest cover. About 90 per cent of the regions boundaries form India's international border with Bangladesh, Bhutan, China and Myanmar. The region is extremely rich in terms of mineral and natural resources, yet suffers with low economic indicators. The document prepared by the National Institute of Public Finance and Policy for North East Council says the per capita Gross State Domestic Product (GSDP) of North East India is 31 per cent less than the national average. In 2004-05, the entire region's GSDP, a measure of the standard of living for people, was Rs. 18,027 against the national average of Rs. 25,968. Even within the region, there are vast differences in the plains and hills. To reach all-India level of per capita income in 2020, the GSDP of the North East region will have to grow at 11.8 per cent annually on an average (East Vision 2020 Document Paper). Women have been the victims of poverty, unemployment, exploitation, inequality and find it difficult to participate in the political process that has hitherto been a male bastion. There is lack of participation of women from grass roots level and political marginalization of women at the national, state and village level has always been prevailing in the region including Mizoram. Mizo society, being patriarchal, right from the beginning, attributed to the reigning of very few female chiefs. Some of the women chiefs were mostly successors of their husbands and were stand-bys, until their sons were old enough to occupy the throne. It is sad to find out that there has never been a female Lok Sabha and Rajya Sabha member from the State of Mizoram. The State never had a female Chief Minister and even a Speaker of the State Assembly till date.

The present work is an attempt in the aforesaid direction. The book "*Empowerment of Women in North East India: Socio-Economic Perspectives*" is a collection of twenty-three papers, mainly those presented in the ICSSR Sponsored State Level Seminar organized by Government J. Buana College, Lunglei, Mizoram. The papers presented in this volume have covered various dimensions concerning socio-economic and political empowerment of women in India and North East with special focus on Mizoram. We have divided the entire book into five sections. A section-wise highlight of this book is presented below.

The first section deals with the "*Empowerment of Women in India*". In this section, the paper entitled '*The Challenge of Empowering Women in India: The Current Dynamics*' presented by Hazra, observes that in spite of various initiatives insisting on women's rights, women in India are still much more likely to be poor, malnourished and illiterate and have less access than their counterparts to medical care, property ownership, credit, training and employment. Women are far less likely than men to be politically active and are vulnerable to domestic violence. His paper reiterates that role and participation of women must be given high priority both because women have a fundamental right to enjoy equality with men in all aspects of life as well as their capacity in playing a crucial role in the sustainable development process. Debnath in his paper, '*Women in India: A Historical Perspective*' attempts to analyse the status of women in India from historical perspective and observed that women enjoyed equal status and rights during the early Vedic period but in the later periods, the status of women began to decline with the Smritis and with the Islamic invasion of Babur and the Mughal empire and later British Rule in India curtailed women's freedom and rights. Post-independence, democratic India marks a difference in the status of women where they participate in all activities such as education, politics, media, art and culture, service sectors, science and technology. Datta Roy in his attempt '*Panchayati Raj System: A Road to Women's Empowerment in India*' recommends that New Panchayati Raj Institutions can bring effective changes in women's life in respect of their social and political status and economic well-being, for which there is need for effective local-self governance where Indian women have to be more aware about their potentialities, responsibilities and rights and empowerment.

Women Empowerment is an integral part of rural development strategies in India and various programmes were initiated to ensure that women can get equal access to health, education and decision making in their households. Sanyal in her paper '*Women's Right to Health Care: Some Reflections from Cachar District, Assam, India*' made a case study on rural women and their health care decision making capacities in villages near Silchar, Assam. Roy and Vanlalveni in their paper '*Voice, Gender and Space in Time of Five Year Plans in India: The Idea of Lata Mangeshkar and Lalrindiki Khiangte*' attempted to explore on how, through the career of India's most famous female 'playback' singers—Lata Mangeshkar and Lalrindiki Khiangte (Mizoram) over previous two decades or so, a particular female singing voice with its characteristic tonality and modulation—became an expression of gender identity in India. Lata Mangeshkar is the conjunctional site and that of modern 'territorialised' understanding of 'culture' whereas Daduhi, in contrast, is the meeting site of fantasy of sound, orality, religious traditions along with identity and ethnicity.

The *"Women's Empowerment: North East India Perspective"* has been presented in section two. This includes the studies entitled '*Women Empowerment through MNREGS: A North East India Perspective*' by Singh and Zote examines the impact of MGNREGA on the North East women. The emergence of women workers through MGNREGA infused among women to play greater role in decision making in the family, confident about their role as contributors to family expenditures and control the use of their earnings and confidence to earn without support. They conclude that despite numerous problems, MNREGA is a programme that has begun to make a difference in the lives of women and there is a massive demand for MNREGA work. The administration needs to respond to it by increasing the scale of women employment. Majumder in her paper, '*Women in Panchayats: A Tripura Perspective*' highlights the changing role of women in panchayats and the evolution of panchayats and the New Panchayati Raj in the State of Tripura. She suggested that women should participate in the political process but at the same time they should be properly empowered economically. Education plays a vital role and the women leaders at the grass roots level should be trained and qualified so that they can perform their assigned responsibilities in a proper way.

Women are the prime targets of programmes that aim at improving maternal and child health and achieving other desired demographic goals. This is not surprising since women are the ones that bear children and are typically the primary caregivers in households. An understanding of the status and empowerment of women in society and within their households is thus critical to promoting change in reproductive attitudes and behaviour, especially in patriarchal societies. The National Population Policy 2000, specifically identified the low status of women in India as an important barrier to the achievement of population and maternal and child welfare goals. Sinha and Datta in their paper, '*Status of Women Empowerment and Health: An Analytical Study of Tripura*' made an attempt to analyze the status of women empowerment through participation of household decision making especially on mean ages of marriage and maternal healthcare indicators in Tripura. The study recorded that a good progress was made in some aspects and in some others it has to take corrective actions.

'*Political Empowerment and Women of Mizoram*' is the theme of section three. In this section, the paper entitled '*Religion and Political Empowerment: A Study on the Impact of Christianity on the Empowerment of the Tribal Women of Mizoram*' Paul examines the role of religion—Christianity in particular, in women's empowerment. Many aspects of life of the Mizo society are influenced by modernization/Westernization and this began particularly after the early part of 20th century when the Mizos came in contact with the British and the Christian Missionaries. Although traditional cultures were re-defined, patriarchy still continues to influence the Mizo society. Religion is the supreme factor that cannot only free women from the dominance of their complementary counterpart (man) but can also ensure the creation of a mindset wherein people are not discriminated on the basis of sex, caste, creed or colour but on the basis of one's ability and performance. The author hopes that the Mizo intellectuals, scholars, activists and Church leaders will come forward and take up the challenge in addressing the issue of gender discrimination in Mizoram. In their paper, '*Political Empowerment and Women of Mizoram: An Overview*' Pathak and Vanlalsiammawia stressed that real empowerment may be achieved by womenfolk only when they get political access, social recognition and economic development. Women in Mizoram possess nothing even though they did most of the work within and outside the house. They suggest effective democratization of the socio-economic and political structures in Mizoram to promote women's empowerment. The enhanced and effective political representation will be very important for equitable share in decision-making. Lalrinchhani in her paper, '*Political Empowerment in Patriarchic Society: A Study in Mizoram*' focuses on the participation of women in the patriarchic society in

Mizoram and try to look into the various problems which hindered women to take an active role at the decision making level particularly in the public elected offices. She argues that despite the abolition of the traditional institutions traditional values still lingers among the people. The patriarchal values reside not only in the minds of the men but strangely among the women also. The concept of patriarchy has to be questioned because as long as these norms exist, women would always be marginalized. *Lalzahawma* in his paper, *'Participation of Women in Contemporary Mizo Politics: An Analysis'* examines the participation of women in contemporary Mizo politics. Despite women's wings in almost every Church with several activities ranging from attending separate Church ceremony, rehabilitation, and spiritual rejuvenation and every political party also have 'mahila' or 'women wings' yet, their participation in the national, state and local politics is minimal. There are various factors leading to their marginalization in politics and there are different solutions, which, however, are delayed and neglected for long. He suggested for women's empowerment through legislation and reservation.

The fourth section deals with the "*Social and Economic Empowerment of Women: Perspectives on Mizoram*". In this section, the paper entitled '*Socio-Economic Empowerment of Women: A Study with Special Reference to Mizoram*' Sundaram made an analysis on women's empowerment programmes and its implementation and utilizations with special reference to Mizoram. He stressed on the effective implementation and utilization of Women Empowerment Programme in India and Mizoram in particular which will safeguard the interests of women. '*Empowerment and Women in the Sixth Schedule Area of Mizoram with Special Reference to Lai Autonomous District Council (LADC)*' presented by Doungel analyses the role and status of women in the Sixth Schedule areas of Mizoram with a case study of the LADC area. Women in the study area seem to be fairly empowered in the field of government service, economic sector and in Church activities. Yet, their present involvement in politics seems to be not up to the mark which required further empowerment and suggested for a balanced growth with evolutionary process without disturbing the social norms and not in a revolutionary process. In her paper, '*Economic Contribution of Women in Mizoram*', Colbert analyses the economic participation of women in Mizoram. Her paper identified that Mizo women although contribute immensely to the economy of the State but does not control properties acquired through their hard earned labour resulting in very unsound economic conditions. Women rendered their services in the *jhum* or office and all the responsibilities of the home like washing, buying and preparing food, cleaning and beautifying of houses and campus, fetching water and collecting fuelwood, caring for domestic animals like pigs and poultry, kitchen gardening, rearing of children—feeding, clothing, studies, medicating, looking after husband and his belongings, and so on and so forth which are never ending, right from early morning till late at night but without having authority and decision making in the family. The paper entitled '*Role of Mizo Women in Economy*' by Zorema examines how far; in a patriarchal Mizo society women are involved in the economy of the State. He analyzed the factors that hinder women's development and to bring light on how women are affected by programmes, projects and policies. He suggested for women's cooperatives as a strategy to expand their access to information, increase their comparative bargaining power, and create opportunities for collective actions to access economic inputs. Vanlalkulhpuia and Singh in their paper '*Socio-Economic Empowerment of Mizo Women through Rashtriya Mahila Kosh: An Analysis*' made an attempt to analyse the socio-economic empowerment of Mizo women through Rashtriya Mahila Kosh (RMK). They found that Mizoram is far behind with regards to the performance and achievements of the RMK in comparison with other States of the North East and suggested that effective implementation part should be taken by creating awareness regarding the workings and benefits of RMK with regular trainings and workshops. In his paper '*Empowerment of Women through Entrepreneurship: A Study of Mizo Women*', Singha made an attempt to highlight the various aspects of women entrepreneurs and the challenges and opportunities of Mizo women entrepreneurs in the era of globalization. He found that the growth of women entrepreneurship is slow in Mizoram due to various constraints such as lack of education, dual role of women, lack of aptitudes and training, lack of freedom to choose a job according to ability, custom and family burden, small market, financial problem and suggested various aspects like infrastructure, initiative to promote investment and entrepreneurship with proper marketing strategy and focus on business opportunities on trade with neighbouring countries, agro and food processing, sericulture, handloom and handicrafts to develop.

Section five has presented the "*Women's Empowerment: Barriers and Strategies*". In this section, Ahmed in an attempt '*Political Empowerment of Women in Mizoram: Barriers and Strategies*' observed that women in Mizoram are largely educated and they have attained an honoured place in the economy and society, but in politics they are miserably lagging behind. He suggested for a combined strategy along

Contributors

A. Sundaram (Dr.), Associate Professor, Department of Economics, Government Saiha College, Saiha, Mizoram.

Andrew H. Vanlaldika (Dr.), District Civil Supply Officer, Lunglei, Mizoram.

Anuj Kanchan Datta Roy, Research Scholar, Department of Political Science, Assam University, Silchar, Assam.

Anupam Hazra, Assistant Professor, Department of Social Work, Assam University, Silchar, Assam.

B. Lalrinchhani (Dr.), Assistant Professor, Department of History, Government J. Buana College, Lunglei, Mizoram.

Bilal Ahmed, Assistant Professor, Department of History, Government Mamit College, Mamit, Mizoram.

C. Vanlalkulhpuia, Research Scholar, Department of Management, Mizoram University, Aizawl.

Chandrika Basu Mazumder (Dr.), Associate Professor and Head, Department of Political Science, Tripura University, Agartala.

Debasish Paul, Lecturer, Department of Education, Kamalanagar College, Lawngtlai, Mizoram.

Elangbam Nixon Singh (Dr.), Reader, Department of Management, Mizoram University, Aizawl.

H. Vanlalveni, Lecturer, Department of English, Kamalanagar College, Kamalanagar, Lawngtlai, Mizoram.

Harendra Sinha (Dr.), Associate Professor, Department of Political Science, Government J. Buana College, Lunglei, Mizoram.

Irene Colbert (Dr.), Associate Professor, Department of Political Science, Government J. Buana College, Lunglei, Mizoram.

J. Zorema (Dr.), Principal, Government J. Buana College, Lunglei, Mizoram.

Jangkhongam Doungel (Dr.), Reader, Department of Political Science, Government Lawngtlai College, Lawngtlai, Mizoram.

K. Zohra (Dr.), Associate Professor, Department of History, Govt. Saiha College, Mizoram.

Lalramdinpuii Chhangte, Assistant Professor, Department of Public Administration, Government J. Buana College, Lunglei, Mizoram.

Lalzahawma, Research Scholar, Department of Political Science, Mizoram University, Aizawl.

M. Pathak (Dr.), Associate Professor, Department of Chemistry, Lunglei Government College, Lunglei, Mizoram.

Pankaj Roy, Lecturer, Department of English, Kamalanagar College, Kamalanagar, Lawngtlai, Mizoram.

Pulak Chandra Devnath, Lecturer, Department of Education, Kamalanagar College, Lawngtlai, Mizoram.

R.K. Vanlalsiammawia, Assistant Professor, Department of Botany, Government College, Lunglei, Mizoram.

R.K.P.G. Singha (Dr.), Head, Department of Commerce, Pachhunga University College, Aizawl, Mizoram.

Sanjay Sinha, Research Scholar, Department of Economics, Assam University, Silchar, Assam.

Subhashree Sanyal, Assistant Professor, Department of Social Work, Assam University, Silchar, Assam.

Sumanash Datta (Prof.), Professor, Department of Economics, Assam University, Silchar, Assam.

Zonunsanga Zote, Research Scholar, Department of Management, Mizoram University, Aizawl.

SECTION I

Empowerment of Women in India

1

The Challenge of Empowering Women in India:

The Current Dynamics

Anupam Hazra

Introduction

Current framework of international development recognizes women empowerment as an immense effective stratagem for the all-round development of the society. The empowerment of women is a contemporary issue regardless of the country in which a social planner tries to bring a sustainable development. Though women empowerment is not a sufficient condition but it is being regarded as a necessary condition in order to stabilize and in turn to have sustainability of the development process. In the current context of development, empowerment is now increasingly being regarded as a process by which one has without power gain greater control over their lives. This means control over material assets, intellectual resources and ideology. It involves power to, power with and power within. Some define empowerment as a process of awareness and conscientization, of capacity building leading to greater participation, effective decision making power and control leading to transformative action. Kabeer (1999) defines empowerment as 'the expansion in people's ability to make strategic life choices in a context where this ability was previously denied to them.' For her, empowerment is inescapably bound with the condition of disempowerment and refers to the processes by which those who have been denied the ability to make choices acquire such ability. In other words, empowerment entails a process of change and women themselves must become agents of that change if empowerment has to take place.

Thus, empowering women implies enhancing women's ability to do, their capability to accomplish tasks, their command over events and their ability to exercise influence. In essence, it is power that stems from new

Table 1.1: A Model Exploring the Dynamics of Women Empowerment from Multi–dimensional Perspectives

Dimension	*At Family Level*	*At Society/Community Level*	*At State/National Level*
Economic	Self-employment opportunities for women; Women's involvement in income-generating activities; Contribution to family income; Access to and control of family resources.	Women's access to employment opportunities; Access to credit facilities; Ownership of land and assets; Women's association and involvement in microenterprises.	Strong framework for gender budgeting; Enhancement in allocation for gender budgeting; Representation of women's economic interests in macro-economic policies, Non-discrimination in payment of wages at work places on the basis of gender.
Socio-cultural	Women's freedom of movement; Non-discriminatory treatment to daughters; Initiatives towards educating girl child.	Space for women's participation in social sphere; Symbolic representation of the female in myth and ritual; Existence of women's association in society; Shift in patriarchal norms such as preference to male child.	Affirmative media-representation for women highlighting their roles and contributions for the nation; Women's literacy and access to a broad range of educational options.
Familial/Interpersonal	Active involvement in decision making process of family; Control over sexual relations; Ability to make childbearing decisions; Freedom from domestic violence.	Societal values and norms emphasising greater importance and autonomy for women e.g. self-selection of spouses; Removal of the practice of dowry; Acceptability of divorce; Campaign against domestic violence.	Systems providing easy access to reproductive health services.

Dimension	*At Family Level*	*At Society/Community Level*	*At State/National Level*
Legal	Knowledge about women's basic rights; Family support and encouragement for exercising women's rights.	Ensuring Right to enjoy equality with men in all aspects of life; Community consciousness about women's rights; Social advocacy for ensuring women's rights; effective local enforcement of legal rights.	Strict enforcement of legislations protecting women's rights and promoting women empowerment, Media support for ensuring proper implementation of Acts and legislations ensuring women welfare; Active judicial system to address women's rights' violations.
Political	Knowledge of political as well as democratic system and means of access to it; Domestic support for political involvement.	Representation in local bodies of government; Women's involvement or mobilization in the local political system/campaigns.	Women's representation in regional and national decision making bodies of government e.g. Lok Sabha, State Legislative Assemblies; Representation of women's interests in effective lobbies and interest groups.
Psychological	Respect from every member of the family; An increase in self-esteem; A feeling of self-efficacy and psychological well-being.	A well-accepted social identity and social status; Women's sensitivity and collective awareness about gender-based injustice and discrimination.	Women's sense of inclusion in the process of national development.

Source: Author's articulation based on Siwal (2005).

knowledge and skills acquired, action taken and inner strength gained from educational experiences.

Women Empowerment: A Key to the Millennium Commitments

Since the early 90s, women have been identified as key agents of sustainable development and women's equality and empowerment are seen as central to a more holistic approach towards establishing new patterns and processes of development that are sustainable. The Fourth World Conference on Women in Beijing (1995) and the Beijing Platform for Action have provided new impetus for governments and civil society organisations to address women empowerment and gender inequalities in society at all levels. It was recognized that without active participation of women and the incorporation of women's perspectives at all levels of decision making process—the goals of equality, development and peace for women and men cannot be achieved. The World Bank has suggested that empowerment of women should be a key aspect of all social development programmes. Societies that discriminate on the basis of gender have greater poverty, slower economic growth, weaker governance, and a lower standard of living. Women's empowerment, lies at the heart of development and the achievement of the Millennium Development Goals. (World Bank, 2001).

Women Empowerment and the Millennium Development Goals

Goal 1. Eradicate extreme poverty and hunger.	• Need-based capacity-building and a better access to livelihood opportunities for women will provide a major boost to family-income, accelerating country's economic growth and ensuring a stronger platform for poverty eradication for the nation. • Equal investment in women's health and nutritional status reduces chronic hunger and malnourishment, which increases productivity and well-being.
Goal 2. Achieve universal primary education.	• Educated girls and women have greater control over their fertility and participate more in public life. • A mother's education is a strong and consistent determinant of her children's school enrolment and attainment of their health and nutrition outcomes.
Goal 3. Promote gender equality and empowerment.	• Women's empowerment which ultimately leads to gender equality lies at the heart of sustainable development and the achievement of the Millennium Development Goals. Though women empowerment is not a sufficient condition but it is still a necessary condition in order to stabilize and in turn to have sustainability of the development process.

(Contd.

Goal 4. Reduce child mortality.	• Research-based evidences proved that a mother's education, income, and empowerment have a significant impact on lowering child mortality.
Goal 5. Improve maternal health.	• Studies revealed that a mother's education, income, and empowerment have a significant impact on lowering maternal mortality.
Goal 6. Combat HIV/AIDS, malaria, and other diseases.	• Greater economic independence for women, increased ability to negotiate safe sex, greater awareness of the need to alter traditional norms around sexual relations, better access to treatment, and support for the care function that women perform are essential for halting and reversing the spread of HIV/AIDS and other epidemics.
Goal 7. Ensure environmental sustainability.	• Women are often regarded as primary users of environmental resources and if they are educated and empowered enough, they can manage the environmental resources in a more sustainable manner in comparison to men.
Goal 8. Develop a global partnership for development.	• Greater space in the political sphere for women may lead to higher investments in development cooperation.

The MDG goal to ensure women empowerment and to achieve gender equality recognizes the costs to society of continued female disadvantage. As compared to the other goals in the MDGs, the goal to reduce gender disparities is unique because it is not specific to any one sector or issue, such as health, education, or access to water; instead it cuts across all the sectors and issues addressed in the MDGs and its success depends on the extent to which it is addressed within each of the other sector-specific goals. Moreover, the goal of gender equality is pre-eminent among the MDGs because if it is not achieved, none of the other goals can be fully met.

The Global Gender Gap Index introduced by the World Economic Forum (WEF) in 2006, is a framework for capturing the magnitude and scope of gender-based disparities and tracking their progress. The Global Gender Gap Index examines the gap between men and women in four fundamental categories: economic participation and opportunity, educational attainment, health and survival and political empowerment. World Economic Forum in its latest Global Gender Gap Index for the year 2009, ranked India in the bottom half among 134 countries, placing it in the 114th position in terms of gender equality. As per the report, India performed very poorly on the economic, education and health sub-indexes; the overall scores are partially bolstered by relatively good performances in the sphere of political empowerment of women. (WEF, 2009) Contemporary Indian society has been exposed to the broad processes of social transformation, agricultural modernization and economic development, urbanization and globalization. However, these processes have generated regional imbalances, sharpened class inequalities and augmented the gender disparities. Hence, women have become critical symbols of these growing imbalances. All these have affected adversely the various aspects of women's empowerment in the contemporary Indian society. In India women are nearly 50 per cent of the total population but their representation in public life is very low. Women bear the major load of the household work. Her primary role is often viewed by the society as housewife. The plight of women in India ranges from domestic disparity to societal oppression. In most of the areas in India, a strong cultural bias favours sons over daughters. Female children frequently suffer neglect in terms of health care and education. Studies reveal that boys receive health care more often than girls, and the average amount spent on treatment was also significantly higher for boys (Coonrod, 1998). Subordination of women in society acts a structural constraint to their participation in political activities. This constraint operates more or less for all classes and communities of women. Prevalent culture which is very complicated and often decisions are taken behind the scene may be regarded as another constraint in this regard. Recognising women's rights and believing their ability are essential for women's empowerment and development. Females should realize their own capabilities and potentials which will strengthen their self-image and foster them with confidence to take action in life. Political empowerment does not imply just a right to role silently but to discuss, share and empower politics by knowing its pros and cons and thereby to influence policies and decision-making.

Welfare Measures for Women in India

Over the past three decades, women's empowerment has been increasingly recognized as a crucial factor for any country's holistic and sustainable development. Several programmes and projects across the world have been launched and are currently in progress to bring social, economic and political equity and broader access to basic livelihood needs. In order to bring women into the mainstream and to encourage their participation in the process of national development has, therefore, been a major concern of the Government. Since independence, the Government of India has always given great importance to the protection and promotion of the human rights of women and has been committed towards achieving it. Within the framework of a democratic polity, India's laws, development policies, plan and programmes have aimed at women's advancement in different spheres. The Constitution is firmly grounded in the principles of liberty, fraternity, equality and justice. It contains a number of provisions for the empowerment of women. Women's right to equality and non-discrimination are defined as justiciable fundamental rights. The Constitution explicitly clarifies that affirmative action programmes for women are not incompatible with the principle of non–discrimination on the grounds of sex. Drawing the strength from the constitutional commitments, the Government of India has been engaged in the continuous endeavour of concretely translating all the rights, commitments and safeguards incorporated in the Indian Constitution for women.

Constitutional Safeguards for Women

- Article 14 – Equal rights and opportunities for men and women in political, economic and social spheres.
- Article 15(1) – Prohibits discrimination against any citizen on the grounds of religion, race, caste, sex etc.
- Article 15(3) – Empowers the state to make affirmative discrimination in favour of women.
- Article 16 – Provides equality of opportunity for all citizens in matters relating to employment or appointment to any office under the State.
- Article 39(a) – The State shall direct its policy towards securing all citizens men and women, equally, the right to means of livelihood.
- Article 39(d) – Equal pay for equal work for both men and women.
- Article 42 – Directs the state to ensure provisions for just and humane condition of work and maternity relief.
- Article 46 – The State to promote with special care the educational and economic interests of the weaker sections of the people and to protect them from social injustice and all forms of exploitation.
- Article 47 – The State to raise the level of nutrition and the standard of living of its people and the improvement of public health.
- Article 51(A)(e) – Mandates every citizen to renounce practices derogatory to the dignity of women.
- Article 243 D(3) – Not less than one-third (including the number of seats reserved for women belonging to the Scheduled Castes and the Scheduled Tribes) of the total number of seats to be filled by direct election in every Panchayat to be reserved for women and such seats to be allotted by rotation to different constituencies in a Panchayat.
- Article 243 D(4) – Not less than one-third of the total number of offices of Chairpersons in the Panchayats at each level to be reserved for women.

The approach on women development changed from viewing women as beneficiaries of social services to contributors of social and economic development process in nation building. Development approach has attempted to address not only women's immediate needs but also their strategic gender interests addressing inequalities in employment, political participation and cultural and legal status. In the last few decades, a significant shift has been apparent in the planning process of the country. Approach towards empowering women, which was started with 'welfare' in the fifties, shifted to 'development' in the seventies and has been successfully continuing with the approach of 'empowerment' from the nineties onwards under different Five Year Plans–which is evident from Table 1.2.

Table 1.2: How the Issue of 'Women Empowerment' has been Addressed in Different Five Year Plans

The First Five Year Plan (1951–1956)	...Central Social Welfare Board was set-up in 1953 to promote activities leading to women welfare through funding to voluntary organisations, charitable trusts and philanthropic agencies etc.
The Second Five Year Plan (1956–1961)	...Recognised special needs of women at work place such as ensuring maternity benefits, crèche facilities for the children of working women and provision of equal pay for equal work etc.
The Third Plan (1961–1966)	...A major focus was given on women's education, pre-natal and child health services, supplementary feeding for children, nursing and expectant mothers.
The Interim plans (1966–1969) & The Fourth Plan (1969–1974)	...Continued with its emphasis on gender mainstreaming. The basic approach was to promote women's welfare within the family as the basic unit of operation. The outlay on family planning was stepped up.
The Fifth Plan (1974–1979)	...Identified areas of health, family planning, nutrition, education, employment, legislation and social welfare for formulating and implementing action programmes for women and called for planned intervention towards women empowerment. This plan marked a major shift in the approach towards women, from welfare towards development.

(Contd

The Sixth Plan (1980–85)	...Accepted women's development as a separate economic agenda. The Multi-disciplinary approach with three-pronged thrust on health, education and employment. The Sixth Five Year Plan onwards, the plan document has been including a separate chapter on women and children.
The Seventh Plan (1985–1990)	...Declared as its objective to bring women into the mainstream of national development. During this period, the Department of Women and Child (DWCD) was established within the Ministry of Human Resource Development of Govt. of India. The Seventh Plan introduced the concept of monitoring of 27 beneficiary oriented schemes for women by DWCD. The exercise continues and number of schemes covered is being expanded.
The Eighth Plan (1992–1997)	...Highlighted for the first time a gender perspective and the need to ensure a definite flow of funds from the general developmental sectors to women. The Plan document states that "....the benefits to development from different sectors should not bypass women and special programmes on women should be complement to the general development programmes. The latter, in turn, should reflect greater gender sensitivity". This plan projected paradigm shift, from development to empowerment and promised to ensure flow of benefits to women in the core sectors of education, health and employment. Outlay for women rose from 4 crores in the First Plan to Rs. 2000 crores in the Eighth Plan.
The Ninth Plan (1997– 2002)	...Adopted 'Women Component Plan' as one of the major strategies and directed both the Central and State Governments to ensure not less than 30 per cent of the funds/benefits are earmarked in all the women's related sectors. Special vigil was advocated on the flow of the earmarked funds or benefits through ... effective mechanism to ensure that ... proposed strategy brings forth a ... approach towards empowering wom... National Policy for Empowerment ... 2001 of GoI adopted during ... envisaged introduction of ... perspective in the budgeting ... operational strategy.

The Tenth Five Year Plan (2002–2007)	....Suggested specific strategies, policies and programmes for empowerment of women. They are as follows: Measurement of development has to go beyond achievement of GDP growth to indicators of distributive justice and their monitoring. Women headed households have to be specifically targeted, identifying added disadvantages in the rural and urban locations with reference to different parameters of deprivation. Formulation of Gender Development Indicators to measure Human Development and their use as a tool for monitoring development needs to be hastened. It appreciated efforts at ensuring gender-just and gender-sensitive budget and promised to continue the process of dissecting the government budget to establish its gender-differential impact and to translate gender commitment to budgetary commitments. It made provision of outlay of Rs. 13,780 crores. It accepted that Women Component Plan and Gender Budget play complimentary role for effective convergence, proper utilization and monitoring of fund from various developmental sectors. The Ministry of Women and Child Development was established during this plan period.
The Eleventh Five Year Plan (2007–2012)	The Approach Paper of this plan mentions..."gender equity requires adequate provisions to be made in policies and schemes across Ministries and Departments." It also entails 'strict adherence to Gender Budgeting across the board.' It promises special focused efforts for creation of 'an enabling environment for women to become economically, politically and socially empowered'.

Source: Five Year Plan Documents.

The Government of India has shown increasing concern for women's issues through a variety of legislation also promoting the socio-economic status of women. Among the major legislations—the Hindu Succession Act was enacted to give daughters equal rights as sons in ancestral property. The Immoral Traffic Prevention Act has been amended to strengthen its provisions, enforce more stringent punishment for traffickers and prevent re-victimisation of victims. States are being requested to set-up anti-human trafficking units. In recent times, the Mahatma Gandhi National Rural Employment Guarantee Act (MGNREGA) seeks to provide for the enhancement of livelihood security of the households in rural areas of the country by providing at least one hundred days of guaranteed wage employment in a financial year to every household whose adult members volunteer to do unskilled manual work; under MGNREGA, priority has been given to women by reserving at least one-third of the jobs for women who have registered and requested for work under this Act.

Besides these legislative measures, India has ratified various international conventions and human rights instruments committing to secure equal rights of women. At the same time, the Ministry of Women and Child Development has been implementing a number of schemes, which strive towards both economic and social empowerment of women. The Ministry has set-up support systems like working women hostels and crèches to help employed women in their struggle towards economic empowerment. *Swadhar* and short stay homes have been set-up to provide shelter and care services for women in distress. Considering the increasing need of shelter homes, it is proposed to set-up one *Swadhar* home per district. The scheme for construction of working women's hostel has also been revamped. The Ministry also implements laws and legislations for women including Sati Prevention Act, Dowry Prohibition Act, the Protection of Women from Domestic Violence Act etc. The Protection of Women from Domestic Violence Act, 2005 is first of its kind in the country to get into the private sphere of a household. For the first time, the term 'domestic violence' has been widened in meaning and scope from the culture specific restriction of 'dowry deaths' and penal provisions to positive civil rights of protection and injunction. A Scheme for Relief and Rehabilitation of Victims of Rape has also been formulated to assist the rape victims in restoring their dignity and self-confidence. For economic empowerment *Rashtriya Mahila Kosh* (RMK) was established in 1993 under Department of Women and Child Development to ensure micro-credit facilities through micro-credit organizations such as NGOs and Voluntary Organisations, women development corporations, women co-operative societies, suitable Govt. or local bodies etc. Flagship schemes like *Swayamsiddha* and *Swa-Shakti* were introduced and taking into consideration the success of the programmes, the Ministry proposes to take up the second phase of *Swayamsiddha* during the Eleventh Plan. The lessons learnt in *Swayamsiddha*, Phase-I and *Swa-Shakti* has been proposed to be incorporated in the next phase giving an integrated set of training inputs relating to social and economic empowerment, including skill development and training in traditional and non-traditional sectors.

Empowering Women: Filling the Gaps

Despite of these efforts, women in India still continue to be discriminated and their current status still causes concern. Although the constitution provides legal equality for men and women but social and economic equality is yet to achieve. This is the fact why Indian women continue to be recipients of welfare and remain at a lower status with low literacy and poor access to resource and facilities. The problem persists despite the vibrant resistance by the women's movement to this over the past several decades. In most parts of India today, women constitute a disproportionate share of the chronically poor population. Indian women face gender discrimination throughout their life within the family, society and at workplace that runs common across the country along all class, caste and religion with varying degrees. Gender division of labour prevails in all sectors of employment. Gender discrimination starts from the foetus, in terms selection of sex, childrearing, feeding, education, employment, control over property and resources, participation and influencing decision-making in public and political spheres etc. Women need self-confidence to fight against all the atrocities against her and to live self-esteemed life. Hence, boosting the morale and self-confidence of the women, is the key to eliminate their inferior complex. Women also have all the potential and empowering women will help to use her full capability and mitigate the economic dependency of women. Empowering women with decision-making aptitude, education and employment will make the society to accept the women as an equal gender like male.

Women's political participation has been considered a major measure of women's empowerment; but in India, attempts to secure political representation particularly in higher political arenas have not been so successful. Fresh impetus is required with a modern approach. Indian democracy is 60 years old now, yet the participation of women in politics has actually declined since the days of the freedom movement, both in quantity and quality. Having a high participation of women at the local self-Government level can create an environment which is enabling for other women, receptive to the idea of gender based initiatives and can serve to monitor and implement community and gender based programmes of the government related to education, nutrition and health. It is also now often pointed out that women's empowerment must be seen as a process wherein we must consider women's awareness consciousness, choices with live alternatives, resources at their disposal, voice, agency and participation. These are all related to enhancement of women's capabilities and decisions they take individually or collectively for themselves. An overview on the role of position of women in these institutions indicates that women have entered these institutions for the first time by introduction of the policy of reservation but, yet they have to go a long way to prove that they are equally capable as men. The policy of reservation provided for women is important not as an end in itself but a step forward in promoting women's participation in the grass roots of democracy.

Dowry has always been an important part of marriages in India, especially of Hindu marriages. Although dowry was legally prohibited in 1961 by Dowry Prohibition Act but it continues to be highly institutionalized. It is ridiculous to notice that even among highly educated sections; the articles of dowry are proudly exhibited in the marriage as a status symbol. In some parts of the country particularly in rural India, dowry still remains the major reason for all the discrimination and injustice shown to women. On the other hand, the changing socio-economic scenario and the phasing out of the joint family system along with poor community based protection systems are some of the reasons why women are becoming increasingly prone to violence and abuse. The weak law enforcement and gender insensitivity of the various functionaries fail to check the growing violence against women. At the same time, the extremely poor levels of awareness amongst women themselves on their rights also perpetuate violence against them. The lack of adequate rehabilitation and reintegration facilities is another crucial factor that finds victimized women further victimized or ostracized by the community. The media too does not reflect gender issues with sympathy and sensitivity; instead there is a tendency to glorify patriarchal traditions or to depict women as objects of sexual entertainment.

On the other hand, though more than 40 Gender Cells have been set-up in various Departments and Ministries but studies suggested that the following few factors like: (i) Gender budgeting statement covers only the specifically targeted programmes for women and pro-women programmes, which constitute less than 5 per cent of total budget. The real challenge of gender budgeting is to explore the rest 95 per cent of the budget through gender lens, (ii) Officers of the Gender Budgeting Cell are rarely consulted at the time of formulation of the Annual Plan/ Budget of the Department, (iii) There is a significant deviation between the budget allocations and the revised estimates and in turn actual spending, (iv) Unavailability of sex-disaggregated data, (v) The problem of proliferation of too many programmes with too little money continues over the years, and (vi) Senior officers involved in policy formulation of the Department are still not fully aware of the concepts of gender budgeting as such workshops are generally attended by lower level officers or officers in Gender Budgeting Cells etc.—creating obstacles in mainstreaming the gender budget initiatives in India. (Hazra, 2010)

Keeping into consideration the hindering factors—there is an urgent need to build the capacity of the Gender Budgeting Cells that have been set-up in various Ministries. In fact, the Central Government and the Planning Commission should take strong measures for getting the Ministries and Departments to implement WCP, and collect and report gender disaggregated data on their programmes and schemes. Gender Budgeting cannot be seen in isolation from the overall economic-political scenario. Identifying and listing resource allocations for women is only a part of the whole approach of Gender Budgeting. The crux of the issue is the overall economic policy framework in which we operate. If the overall economic framework continues to be driven by a philosophy of withdrawal of the state from important social and economic sectors, its impact on women would be much more harmful than what some additional resource allocations or schemes for women here or there—can mitigate. Gender Budgeting must be adopted to address socio-economic discrimination against women because many policy commitments can only be achieved if sufficient funds are allocated for their implementation. Women's and men's needs, concerns and priorities differ due to their different roles in society and in case these differences are not recognized—the way a government raises and spends money can have a negative impact on women by perpetuating the existing inequalities. Taking into consideration the contemporary scenario, following initiatives may be effective to provide an impetus to the process of women empowerment:

How to Strengthen Efforts towards Women Empowerment: Some Suggestive Measures

- Women's groups, civil society, and government agencies need to push for change in the rules, structures, and processes that specify how resources are allocated and how tasks, responsibilities, and values are assigned in institutions as well as in the society more broadly.

- Promote participatory democracy and decentralise planning processes.
- Need of an increased consultation with women's groups in the planning process, especially at the grass roots level.
- Provisioning more financial resources and power to make decisions directly to Panchayat to empower them; women representatives at *panchayat* level should get more autonomy.
- Ensuring provision of vocational training in traditional sector, suitable employment and income-generation activities with the ultimate objective of making all potential women economically independent and self-reliant.
- Movement towards experiments in gender responsive budgeting. However, one cannot ignore the challenges that face the process but gender budgeting must be implemented across all Ministries and all machineries, including at the state and *panchayat* levels.
- Engendering social audits and making gender audits mandatory for all the Government schemes.
- Measures to improve the status, role and participation of women must be given high priority both because women have a fundamental right to enjoy equality with men in all aspects of life and because women can play a crucial role in and must fully participate in the sustainable development process. It is therefore essential to integrate gender perspectives in policies, projects and programmes that can be achieved by gender analysis.
- Adopting policies to reduce women's vulnerability to violence; ensure adequate infrastructure and budgets for the Implementation of Domestic Violence Act and for safe environs outside home.
- Adopting a comprehensive life-cycle approach towards women's health and malnourishment; from cradle to the grave, with women-centred health initiatives to reduce the maternal mortality rate.
- There is a marked lack of sensitivity to gender issues at all levels, be it government or bureaucracy or media or the mainstream civil society; these issues need to be acknowledged and should be given due attention to be addressed.
- Immediate steps need to be taken to control the declining child sex ratio by regulating medical practitioners and giving due emphasis to the implementation of the PCPNDT Act.
- Initiatives should be taken to enact a comprehensive gender

specific law on sexual violence with an expanded definition of rape, with gender neutral provisions to address child sexual abuse.

- Leaders and policy-makers seem to require more intense technical expertise and knowledge of how to mainstream gender concerns into development policies and programmes, so suitable provision for their knowledge-building and need-based training regarding this issue needs to be arranged.
- Government and non-governmental organizations need adequate funding for direct interventions and to build capacity in collecting data and evaluating programmes and policies for gender equality and women's empowerment.

Empowering women is being considered as the basic to the basics of human rights where she wants neither to beg for power nor search for power hierarchy to exercise power against others. On the contrary, she demands to be accepted as human first of all. Measures to improve the status, role and participation of women must be given high priority both because women have a fundamental right to enjoy equality with men in all aspects of life as well as because women are capable of playing a crucial role in the sustainable development process. In order to bring women into the mainstream and to encourage their participation in the process of national development, therefore, should remain the priority of the Government.

REFERENCES

Coonrod, C.S. (1998): Chronic hunger and the status of women in India. Condition of women in India. Retrieved from http://www.thp.org/reports/indiawom.htm (accessed November 21, 2009).

Grown, C. *et al.* (2005): Taking action: achieving gender equality and empowering women. UN Millennium Project Task Force on Education and Gender Equality. London: Earthscan.

Hazra, Anupam. (2009): "Gender Disparity in Education". *Yojana*. Vol. 53..

Hazra, Anupam. (2010): "Gender Budgeting and Development: The Indian Scenario". *A Journal of Social Focus*, Vol. 1 (2).

Hazra, Anupam (2011): "Protection of The Rights of Girl Child". *Social Welfare*, Vol. 57 (1).

Kabeer N. (1999): "Resources, Agency, Achievements: Reflections on the Measurement of Women's Empowerment". *Development and Change*, Vol. 30 (3).

Narayan, D. (ed). (2002): *Empowerment and Poverty Reduction: A Sourcebook.* Washington D.C., USA: World Bank.

Planning Commission. Five Year Plan Documents. Retrieved from www.planningcommission.nic.in (accessed November 21, 2009).

Siwal, B.R. (2005): *Basic Framework and Strategy for Gender Training.* New Delhi, India: National Institute of Public Cooperation and Child Development (NIPCCD).

World Bank. (2001): *Engendering Development: Through Gender Equality in Rights, Resources, and Voice.* New York, U.S.A: Oxford University Press.

World Economic Forum (WEF). (2009): *The Global Gender Gap Report 2009.* WEF. Geneva. Switzerland.

2
Women in India:
A Historical Perspective

Pulak Chandra Devnath

Women in Ancient India

In ancient India, the women enjoyed equal status with men in all fields of life. However, some others hold contrasting views. Works by ancient Indian grammarians such as Patanjali and Katyayana suggest that women were educated in the early Vedic period. Rigvedic verses suggest that the women married at a mature age and were probably free to select their husband. Scriptures such as Rig Veda and Upanishads mention several women sages and seers, notably Gargi and Maitreyi. Some kingdoms in the ancient India had traditions such as *nagarvadhu* ("bride of the city"). Women competed to win the coveted title of the *nagarvadhu*. Amrapali is the most famous example of a *nagarvadhu*. According to studies, women enjoyed equal status and rights during the early Vedic period. However, later (approximately 500 B.C.), the status of women began to decline with the Smritis (esp. Manusmriti) and with the Islamic invasion of Babur and the Mughal empire and later Christianity curtailing women's freedom and rights. Although reformatory movements such as Jainism allowed women to be admitted to the religious order, by and large, the women in India faced confinement and restrictions. The practice of child marriages is believed to have started from around sixth century.

Women in Medieval Period

The Indian woman's position in the society further deteriorated during the medieval period when *Sati*, *child marriages* and a ban on widow remarriages became part of social life in India. The *Muslim conquest in the Indian subcontinent* brought the *purdah* practice in the Indian society. Among the *Rajputs* of Rajasthan, the *Jauhar* was practised. In some parts of India, the *Devadasis* or the temple women were sexually exploited. Polygamy was widely practised especially among Hindu Kshatriya rulers. In many Muslim families, women were restricted to *Zenana* areas. In spite of these conditions, some women excelled in the fields of politics, literature, education and religion. *Razia Sultana* became the only woman monarch to have ever ruled *Delhi*. The *Gond* queen *Durgavati* ruled for fifteen years, before she lost her life in a battle with Mughal emperor *Akbar*'s general Asaf Khan in 1564. *Chand Bibi* defended *Ahmednagar* against the mighty *Mughal* forces of Akbar in 1590s. *Jehangir*'s wife *Nur Jehan* effectively wielded imperial power and was recognized as the real force behind the Mughal throne. The Mughal princesses Jahanara and Zebunnissa were well-known poets, and also influenced the ruling administration. *Shivaji*'s mother, *Jijabai* was deputed as queen regent, because of her ability as a warrior and an administrator. In South India, many women administered villages, towns, divisions and heralded social and religious institutions.

The Bhakti movements tried to restore women's status and questioned some of the forms of oppression. Mirabai, a female saint-poet, was one of the most important Bhakti movement figures. Some other female saint-poets from this period include Akka Mahadevi, Rami Janabai and Lal Ded. Bhakti sects within Hinduism such as the Mahanubhav, Varkari and many others were principle movements within the Hindu fold to openly advocate social justice and equality between men and women. Shortly after the Bhakti movement, Guru Nanak, the first Guru of Sikhs also preached the message of equality between men and women. He advocated that women be allowed to lead religious assemblies; to perform and lead congregational hymn singing called Kirtan or Bhajan; become members of religious management committees; to lead armies on the battlefield; have equality in marriage, and equality in *Amrit* (Baptism). Other Sikh Gurus also preached against the discrimination against women.

Women in British Period

European scholars observed in the 19th century that Hindu women are "naturally chaste" and "more virtuous" than other women. During the British Raj, many reformers such as Ram Mohan Roy, Ishwar Chandra Vidyasagar, Jyotirao Phule etc. fought for the upliftment of women. While this list might suggest that there was no positive British contribution during the Raj era, that is not entirely so, since missionaries' wives like Martha Mault née Mead and her daughter Eliza Caldwell née Mault are rightly remembered for pioneering the education and training of girls in south India—a practise that initially met with local resistance, as it flew in the face of tradition. Raja Rammohan Roy's efforts led to the abolition of the Sati practice under Governor—General William Cavendish—Bentinck in 1829. Ishwar Chandra Vidyasagar's crusade for the improvement in condition of widows led to the Widow Remarriage Act of 1856. Many women reformers such as Pandita Ramabai also helped the cause of women upliftment.

Kittur Chennamma, the queen of the princely state Kittur in Karnataka, led an armed rebellion against the British in response to the Doctrine of lapse. Abbakka Rani the queen of coastal Karnataka led the defence against invading European armies notably the Portuguese in 16th century. Rani Lakshmi Bai, the Queen of Jhansi, led the Indian Rebellion of 1857 against the British. She is now widely considered as a nationalist hero. Begum Hazrat Mahal, the co-ruler of Awadh, was another ruler who led the revolt of 1857. She refused the deals with the British and later retreated to Nepal. The Begums of Bhopal were also few of the notable female rulers during this period. They did not observe purdah and were trained in martial arts. Chandramukhi Basu, Kadambini Ganguly and Anandi Gopal Joshi were few of the earliest Indian women to obtain educational degrees.

In 1917, the first women's delegation met the Secretary of State to demand women's political rights, supported by the Indian National Congress. The All India Women's Education Conference was held in Pune in 1927. In 1929, the Child Marriage Restraint Act was passed, stipulating fourteen as the minimum age of marriage for a girl through the efforts of Mahomed Ali Jinnah. Though Mahatma Gandhi himself married at the age of thirteen, he later urged people to boycott child marriages and called upon the young men to marry the child widows.

Women played an important part in India's independence struggle. Some of the famous freedom fighters include Bhikaji Cama, Dr. Annie Besant, Pritilata Waddedar, Vijayalakshmi Pandit, Rajkumari Amrit Kaur, Aruna Asaf Ali, Sucheta Kriplani and Kasturba Gandhi. Other notable names include Muthulakshmi Reddy, Durgabai Deshmukh etc. The Rani of Jhansi Regiment of Subhash Chandra Bose's Indian National Army consisted entirely of women including Captain Lakshmi Sahgal. Sarojini Naidu, a poet and a freedom fighter, was the first Indian woman to become the President of the Indian National Congress and the first woman to become the Governor of a state in India.

Women in Independent India

Women in India now participate in all activities such as education, politics, media, art and culture, service sectors, science and technology, etc. Indira Gandhi, who served as Prime Minister of India for an aggregate period of fifteen years is the world's longest serving woman Prime Minister. The Constitution of India guarantees to all Indian women equality (Article 14), no discrimination by the State [Article 15(1)], equality of opportunity (Article 16), equal pay for equal work [Article 39(d)]. In addition, it allows special provisions to be made by the State in favour of women and children [Article 15(3)], renounces practices derogatory to the dignity of women [Article 51(A) (e)], and also allows for provisions to be made by the State for securing just and humane conditions of work and for maternity relief. (Article 42).

The feminist activism in India picked up momentum during later 1970s. One of the first national level issues that brought the women's groups together was the Mathura rape case. The acquittal of policemen accused of raping a young girl in Mathura in a police station, led to a wide-scale protests in 1979-80. The protests were widely covered in the national media, and forced the Government to amend the Evidence Act, the Criminal Procedure Code and the Indian Penal Code and introduce the category of custodial rape. Female activists united over issues such as female infanticide, gender bias, women health, and female literacy.

Since alcoholism is often associated with violence against women in India, many women groups launched anti-liquor campaigns in Andhra Pradesh, Himachal Pradesh, Haryana, Orissa, Madhya Pradesh and other states. Many Indian Muslim women have questioned the fundamental leaders' interpretation of women's rights under the Shariat law and have criticized the triple talaq system.

In 1990s, grants from foreign donor agencies enabled the formation of new women-oriented NGOs. Self-help groups and NGOs such as Self Employed Women's Association (SEWA) have played a major role in women's rights in India. Many women have emerged as leaders of local movements. For example, Medha Patkar of the Narmada Bachao Andolan. The Government of India declared 2001 as the Year of Women's Empowerment (*Swaṣhakti*). The National Policy for the Empowerment of Women was passed in 2001. In 2006, the case of a Muslim rape victim called Imrana was highlighted in the media. Imrana was raped by her father-in-law. The pronouncement of some Muslim clerics that Imrana should marry her father-in-law led to widespread protests and finally Imrana's father-in-law was given a prison term of 10 years. The verdict was welcomed by many women's groups and the All India Muslim Personal Law Board. In 2010, March 9, one day after International Women's day, Rajya Sabha passed Women's Reservation Bill, ensuring 33 per cent reservation to women in Parliament and state legislative bodies.

Women at a Glance

We can conclude by looking at what has been achieved by women in the country:

- 1879: John Elliot Drinkwater Bethune established the Bethune School in 1849, which developed into the Bethune College in 1879, thus becoming the first women's college in India.
- 1883: Chandramukhi Basu and Kadambini Ganguly became the first female graduates of India and the British Empire.
- 1886: Kadambini Ganguly and Anandi Gopal Joshi became the first women from India to be trained in Western medicine.
- 1905: Suzanne R.D. Tata was the first Indian woman to drive a car.
- 1916: The first women's university, SNDT Women's University, was founded on June 2, 1916 by the social reformer Dhondo Keshav Karve with just five students.
- 1917: Annie Besant became the first female President of the Indian National Congress.
- 1919: For her distinguished social service, Pandita Ramabai became the first Indian woman to be awarded the Kaiser-i-Hind by the British Raj.
- 1925: Sarojini Naidu became the first Indian born female President of the Indian National Congress.
- 1927: The All India Women's Conference was founded.
- 1944: Asima Chatterjee became the first Indian woman to be conferred the Doctorate of Science by an Indian university.
- 1947: On August 15, 1947, following independence, Sarojini Naidu became the Governor of the United Provinces, and in the process became India's first woman Governor.

- 1951: Prem Mathur of the Deccan Airways became the first Indian women commercial pilot.
- 1953: Vijaya Lakshmi Pandit became the first woman (and first Indian) President of the United Nations General Assembly.
- 1959: Anna Chandy become the first Indian woman judge of a High Court (Kerala High Court)
- 1963: Sucheta Kriplani became the Chief Minister of Uttar Pradesh, the first woman to hold that position in any Indian state.
- 1966: Captain Durga Banerjee become the first Indian woman pilot of the state airline, Indian Airlines.
- 1966: Kamaladevi Chattopadhyay won Ramon Magsaysay award for community leadership.
- 1966: Indira Gandhi become the first woman Prime Minister of India.
- 1970: Kamaljit Sandhu become the first Indian woman to win a Gold in the Asian Games.
- 1972: Kiran Bedi become the first female recruit to join the Indian Police Service.
- 1979: Mother Teresa won the Nobel Peace Prize, becoming the first Indian female citizen to do so.
- 1984: On May 23, Bachendri Pal became the first Indian woman to climb Mount Everest.
- 1989: Justice M. Fathima Beevi become the first woman Judge of the Supreme Court of India.
- 1997: Kalpana Chawla become the first India-born woman to go into space.
- 1992: Priya Jhingan become the first lady cadet to join the Indian Army (later commissioned on March 6, 1993).
- 1994: Harita Kaur Deol become the first Indian woman pilot in the Indian Air Force (IAF), on a solo flight.
- 2000: Karnam Malleswari became the first Indian woman to win an Olympic medal (bronze medal in the 2000 Summer Olympics at Sydney).
- 2002: Lakshmi Sahgal became the first Indian woman to run for the post of President of India.
- 2004: Punita Arora became the first woman in the Indian Army to get the highest rank of Lieutenant General.
- 2007: Pratibha Patil become the first woman President of India.
- 2009: Meira Kumar became the first woman Speaker of Lok Sabha, the Lower House in Indian Parliament.

REFERENCES

Bader, Clarisse (2001): *Women in Ancient India*, Trubner's Oriental Series, Routledge.

Jayapalan (2001). *Indian Society and Social Institutions*. Atlantic Publishers & Distributors.

Kamat, Jyotsna (2006): "Gandhi.and Status of Women" http://www.kamat.com/mmgandhi/gwomen, accessed on 2nd August, 2011.

"Info Change women: Background & Perspective", http://www.infochangeindia.org/, accessed on 2nd August, 2011.

Majumdar, R.C. and A.D. Pusalker (ed.): *The History and Culture of the Indian People*. Volume I, *The Vedic age*. Bombay: Bharatiya Vidya Bhavan 1951.

Menon, Kalyani Sen, A.K. Shiva Kumar (2001): "Women in India: How Free? How Equal?" United Nations, http://www.un.org.in/wii.htm, accessed on 5th August, 2011.

Mishra, R.C. (2006). *Towards Gender Equality*. Authorspress., https://www.vedamsbooks.com/no43902.htm, accessed on 2nd August, 2011.

Pruthi, Raj Kumar; Rameshwari Devi and Romila Pruthi (2001). *Status and Position of Women: In Ancient, Medieval and Modern India*. Vedam Books.

"Rajya Sabha Passes Women's Reservation Bill". *The Hindu*. http://hindu.com/2010/03/10/stories/2010031050880100.htm, accessed on 5th August, 2011.

Rai, B.C. (2003), *History of Indian Education*, Prakashan Kendra, Lucknow.

"The Dowry Prohibition Act, 1961". http://www.wcd.nic.in/dowryprohibitionact.htm, accessed on 5th August, 2011.

"The World's Most Beautiful Woman?" *cbsnews.com,* 5th August, 2011.

"The Commission of Sati (Prevention) Act, 1987". http://www.wcd.nic.in/commissionofsatiprevention.htm, accessed on 5th August, 2011.

"Vedic Women: Loving, Learned, Lucky!". http://hinduism.about.com/library/weekly/aa031601c.htm, accessed on 5th August, 2011.

"Women in History". National Resource Centre for Women. http://nrcw.nic.in/, accessed on 9th August, 2011.

3

Panchayati Raj System:

A Road to Women's Empowerment in India

Anuj Kanchan Datta Roy

The term 'empowerment' connotes a process through which people realize in themselves their full potentials and achieve control over their own lives. It ensures people the freedom to make choices and accept responsibility; valuing self and thereby, is a helping process in the development of people's self-esteem. Empowerment is also considered as the ability to make decisions about personal or collective circumstances, to access information and resources for decision-making, to exercise assertiveness in collective decision-making, to learn and access skills for improving personal or collective circumstances, to increase one's self-image and worth and to involve in the ongoing process of development. Empowerment helps to measure people's psychological development. It is also seen as a methodology of people's capacity building leading to greater contributions and gains in matters surrounding them. In short, the concept of empowerment indicates increasing the political, social, economic and other strength of individuals and communities. However, the term has a broad range of meanings and definitions and its meanings may vary in relation to different concepts. The concept of empowerment has gained greater relevance and visibility when it is associated with women. As concept women's empowerment means having their contributions recognized and valued by themselves and by the society. It promotes women's inherent strength and self-image. The concept should not be misunderstood that to empower women we have to give women more power to dominate, abuse and exploit others. It only demands equal partnership and due recognition in the participation of development process of the society. Simply, it refers to ability of women to assert themselves in matters relating to their lives. Women's empowerment in

India is one of the most important concerns among the scholars, academicians and government. Mahatma Gandhi also believed that full and balanced development of the nation and establishment of a just society is possible only when women participate actively and fully in the political deliberations of the nation.[1] Thus, women's political participation has been considered as a major measure of women's empowerment. Now, the question may arise that why the question of women's empowerment in political arena has become so crucial in India? Indian women have been part of politics since pre-independence period. They acted as freedom fighters, leaders and volunteers. After independence the Indian Constitution guarantees equal rights to all citizens without making any discrimination on the ground of sex. Women in India have been granted equal political rights too along with men. But in spite of these, the political representation and participation of women in India is definitely below the mark.[2] According to the Document on Women's Development (1985) women's role in the political process has virtually remained unchanged since independence. Broad-based political participation of women has been severely limited due to various traditional factors such as caste, religion, feudal attitude and family status.[3] Thus, women's empowerment in political arena has become an important issue of concern due to the magnitude of women's powerlessness and subordination in society. In this regard, the Government of India's initiative to empower women through Panchayati Raj System needs a special mention. It has provided scope to rural women to empower themselves politically through their participation in local self-government.

Panchayati Raj is a model of government at the local level that advocates for decentralization of power. The basic concept of Panchayati Raj is that the villagers themselves should act for their own socio-economic development. They should think and decide about their village self-governance and should act for their collective interest. Gandhiji and Nehru also advocated for Panchayati Raj system. Gandhiji considered it as the foundation of India's political system. He expressed the term "*Gram Swaraj*" or Village Self-governance for the concept. And Jawaharlal Nehru, the first Prime Minister of India stated, "India is poor because the villages of India are poor. India will be rich if the villages of India are rich. Panchayats should be given greater power; for we want the villagers to have a greater measure of real swaraj [self-government] in their own villages."[4] Panchayati Raj fulfils the conditions of a true democracy. It reflects the needs and aspirations of rural people without any discrimination on the grounds of sex in the village governance. The development of Panchayati Raj system in India has a long evolutionary history since ancient periods. After independence the concept of Panchayati Raj found expression in Article 40 of the Indian Constitution where it stated, "The State shall take steps to organize village Panchayats and endow them with such powers and authority as may be necessary to enable them to function as units of self-government."[5] The system gained momentum with gaining constitutional status. The 73rd Constitutional Amendment Act was passed in 1992 and was incorporated in the part IX of the Indian Constitution. The Act provides provisions for devolution of powers and responsibilities to the Panchayats to deal with both economic development and social justice and for implementation of certain subjects listed in the eleventh schedule of the constitution. The Act is a crucial one regarding the political empowerment of Indian women. It has provided opportunity to rural women to participate in the rural decision-making process and to share the fruits along with their counterparts in society through reservation of seats in Panchayati Raj Institutions. The Act has provided reservations for women in two respects—for the office of the members and for that of the chairpersons. According to sub-clause (2) of Article 243(d), not less than one-third of the total number of seats reserved under clause (1)[6] shall be reserved for women belonging to the Scheduled Castes or, as the case may be, the Scheduled Tribes.[7] Sub clause (3) of the same article states, "Not less than one-third (including the number of seats reserved for women belonging to the Scheduled Castes and the Scheduled Tribes) of the total number of seats to be filled by direct election in every Panchayat shall be reserved for women and such seats may be allotted by rotation to different constituencies in a Panchayat."[8] And the provision that sub-clause (4) of Article 243 (d) contains is that "...not less than one-third (including the number of offices of chairperson reserved for women belonging to the SCs and STs) of the total number of offices of chairpersons in the Panchayat at each level shall be reserved for women, provided also that the number of offices reserved under this clause shall be allotted by rotation to different Panchayats at each level."[9] Reservations for women in Panchayati Raj Institutions indicate that women, through their participation in politics, can make use of power and resources to bring about the necessary changes in society. The Balwant Rai Mehta Committee on Panchayati Raj System also emphasized that rural women should not become mere beneficiaries of development but should be made equal partners in its affairs as contributors.[10]

The Government of India has adopted some programmes focusing on the empowerment of rural women. In 1988, a scheme known as

Swashakti–the Rural Women Development and Empowerment Project was introduced. In 2001, the government launched *Swayamsiddha*—the Integrated Women Empowerment Scheme which aims at empowerment of women by generating awareness. Beside these, *Streeshakti* and *Balika Samrudhi Yojana* were also brought for women's empowerment. The year 2001 was declared as Women's Empowerment Year in India and in 2002 *Swadhar* was launched to make rural women economically strong. Under the Ninth Plan (1997–2002) women's empowerment was one of the important objectives of development. And under the provisions of 'The Women (Empowerment for Equal Participation) Bill, 2005, it is stated that "reservation for women in local bodies like village Panchayats, municipalities etc. is not enough. They should have equal participation in the governance of the nation—legislative, executive and judiciary on the basis of their numerical strnegth."[11]

Panchayati Raj system can be a good mechanism to empower Indian women. It can bring effective changes in women's life in respect of their social and political status and economic well-being. Moreover, political participation of women not only leads to women's empowerment and development but also brings about awareness and helps to mobilize other women to participate in the process and thereby to promote their socio-economic and other interests too. It is also necessary to mention here that to become more effective with local-self governance Indian women have to be more aware about their potentialities, responsibilities and rights and empowerment would become more relevant if women are more educated. However, more efforts should be directed towards the empowerment of each and every stratum of women by giving them their due recognition.

NOTES

1. Ajit Pal Singh, "Women's participation at grass roots level: An Analysis", *Mainstream*, XLVII, No. 12 (2009): accessed 5th September, 10, www.mainstreamweekly.net
2. Bharti Chhibber, "Women and the Indian Political Process", *Mainstream*, XLVIII, No.18 (2010): accessed 5th September,10, www.mainstream weekly.net
3. "State Pulse: Orissa: Empowerment of women at ground level", (14, July, 2010): accessed 21st September, 2010, http://www.centralchronicle.com/viewnews.asp?articleID=41465
4. R. Kannan, "Rural Development—Panchayati Raj System in Independent India", personal website of R. Kannan, accessed 7th September, 10, http://kannanpersonal.com/learning/banking2/panchayat-raj.html

5. A.S. Narang. "Indian Government and Politics". New Delhi: Gitanjali Publishing House, 2000, 286-287.
6. Seats shall be reserved for the Scheduled Castes; and the Scheduled Tribes, in every Panchayat and the number of seats so reserved shall bear, as nearly as may be, the same proportion to the total number of seats to be filled by direct election in that Panchayat as the population of the Scheduled Castes in that Panchayat area or of the Scheduled Tribes in that Panchayat area bears to the total population of that area and such seats may be allotted by rotation to different constituencies in a Panchayat.
7. Part IX, The Panchayats, Constitution of India, (n.d), accessed 23rd September,10, http://www.commonlii.org/in/legis/const/2004/12.html
8. *Ibid.*
9. Ajit Pal Singh, *op. cit.*
10. *Ibid.*
11. *Ibid.*

REFERENCES

Ball, Alan R. and Guy Peters. *Modern Politics and Government*, Palgrave, China, 2000.

Chakraborty, Biswanath. *People's Participation in West Bengal Panchayat System*, Mitram, Kolkata, 2008.

Chaturvedi, Archana. *Indian Government and Politics*, Commonwealth, New Delhi, 2006.

Chhibber, Bharti. "Women and the Indian Political Process." *Mainstream*, XLVIII. No. 18 (2010): accessed 5th September, 10. www.mainstream weekly.net

Jena, K.N. *Globalised India and Development Issues*, Abhijeet Publication, Delhi, 2009.

Kannan, R. "Rural Development–Panchayati Raj System in Independent India." personal website of R. Kannan, accessed 7th September,10. www.kannanpersonal.com

Narang, A.S. *Indian Government and Politics*. New Delhi: Gitanjali Publishing House, 2000.

Singh, Ajit Pal. "Women's participation at grass roots level: An Analysis." Mainstream XLVII. No. 12 (2009): accessed 5th September, 10. www.mainstreamweekly.net

State Pulse: Orissa: Empowerment of women at ground level. (2010): accessed 21st September, 2010. http://www.centralchronicle.com

4
Women's Right to Health Care:
Some Reflections from Cachar District, Assam, India

Subhashree Sanyal

Introduction

Development paradigm largely focuses on "rural attention" in India. It is said that the heart of sustainable development lies in our villages. Elimination of poverty, ignorance, disease and inequality of opportunities and providing a better and higher quality of life are the basic premises upon which all the plans and blueprints of development were built. For India, rural development implies both the improved quality of life in rural areas as well as greater social transformation. In order to provide rural people with better prospects for development, increased participation of people in the rural development programmes, decentralization of planning, better enforcement of land reforms and greater access to credit are envisioned time and again by policy makers and bureaucrats. Even the civil society is working hand-in-hand with the State in its initiatives for rural welfare.

Women Empowerment is an integral part of rural development. Different schemes and programmes have been launched to ensure that women have equal access to health, education and decision-making in their households. Even NGOs especially in the North Eastern States are working focusing on different agendas ensuring rights of women in all spheres. Socio-economic development of a nation depends upon the development of its human resources. Women, like men, contribute significantly in this process. Statistical information on the status of women and men in all spheres of a society is vitally important as it enables in evaluation of gender imbalance and also helps in planning for equitable distribution of resources and opportunities. Women's right to decision-making and health care is a key concern among the policy makers, states and civil societies in India.

Health is a priority goal in its own right and a central input into economic development and poverty reduction. Significant achievements have been made in a number of areas which include health parameters, legislation, research and technology and disease control. India made its first health policy document 35 years since Independence. It can be well concluded that such a Health Policy emerged after the Alma Ata Declaration in 1978 for Health for All by 2000 for which India too is a signatory nation. Different public health care programmes aimed both at rural and urban regions of the country have been launched in view of the goal by Government of India from time to time.

When we speak about Health Care, the "Health Status" of women and reproductive health becomes an integral component of it. Even the Millennium Development Goals speaks of reducing maternal mortality as a individual separate goal realizing the importance of women and health care. In India, Health care is not a medical phenomenon; it is governed by socio-economic and cultural factors. A woman's access to health care and decision-making in terms of matters related to it are governed by her capacity to exercise her decision making powers and her position and status in her micro and macro environment. Therefore, reproductive health care and decision-making in health care is a key indicator of Women Empowerment.

The present research paper reflects on women's decision-making in reproductive health care and awareness about health care services in urban village of Cachar District, Assam. Primary data reveals facts on health and empowerment status of women in Cachar, Assam.

Major Health Schemes for Women in India

National Policy on Empowerment of Women

The policy for women empowerment focuses on women's health issues. It has highlighted the importance of reduction of infant mortality and maternal mortality, which are sensitive indicators of human development. The Policy highlighted that women should have access to comprehensive, affordable and quality health care. Government will take measures will be adopted that take into account the reproductive rights of women to enable them to exercise informed choices, their vulnerability to sexual and health problems together with endemic, infectious and communicable diseases such as malaria, TB, and water borne diseases as well as hypertension and cardio-pulmonary diseases. The social, developmental and health consequences of HIV/AIDS and other sexually transmitted diseases will also be tackled from a gender perspective. Intra-household discrimination in nutritional matters *vis-à-vis* girls and women will be sought to be ended through appropriate strategies. Widespread use of nutrition education would be made to address the issues of intra-household imbalances in nutrition and the special needs of pregnant and lactating women. Women's participation will also be ensured in the planning, superintendence and delivery of the system. Therefore, we can see how health is an integral component in building women empowerment in Assam. (MOWCD, 2011)

Indira Gandhi Matri Sahyog Yojana: Conditional Maternity Benefit Scheme

A new scheme for pregnant and lactating women has been approved by the Government initially on pilot basis in 52 selected districts across the country. The scheme would contribute to better enabling environment by providing cash incentives for improved health and nutrition to pregnant and lactating mothers. The scheme is to be implemented through the ICDS platform and Aanganwadi workers get incentive under this scheme to implement and transfer cash to beneficiary. The scheme also encourages family planning and safe health for women by providing benefits for 2 children only (MOWCD, 2011).

Janani Suraksha Yojana

Janani Suraksha Yojana (JSY) is a safe motherhood intervention under the National Rural Health Mission (NRHM) being implemented with the objective of reducing maternal and neo-natal mortality by promoting institutional delivery among the poor pregnant women. JSY is a 100 per cent centrally sponsored scheme and it integrates cash assistance with delivery and post-delivery care. The success of the scheme would be determined by the increase in institutional delivery among the poor families. The government has specially provisioned ASHA, the accredited social health activist as an effective link between the Government and the poor pregnant women in 10 low performing states, namely the 8 EAG states, Assam, J&K and the remaining NE States.

Kishori Shakti Yojana

Kishori Shakti Yojana was launched with the objective of improving the nutritional and health status of adolescent girls between 11–18 years of age, to train and equip them to improve home-based and vocational skills, to promote awareness of health hygiene, nutrition, home management, childcare, and take all measures as to facilitate their marriage after attaining the age of 18 years and even later.

Reproductive and Child Health Programme (RCH)

RCH II has been commenced from 1st April, 2005. The main objective of the programme is to bring about a change in mainly three critical health indicators, i.e. reducing total fertility rate, infant mortality rate and maternal mortality rate with a view to realizing the outcomes envisioned in the Millennium Development Goals, the National Population Policy 2000, and the Tenth Plan Document, the National Health Policy 2002 and Vision 2020 India.

Status of Women's Health and Empowerment in Assam: A Look through Millennium Development Goals

Goals 3 and 5 of MDG highlights the state of health care and women empowerment in Assam.

Goal 3: Promote Gender Equity and Empowerment

Assam ranks 29 out of 32 in the Gender Disparity Index. There is significant disparity in education, employment and health sectors in terms of gender. Further, the tribes in Assam are patriarchal unlike Meghalaya which is matrilineal. The position of women in Assam is not different from that of women in other regions of the country. In fact, in some respects, women in Assam are more disadvantaged. Using the equally distributed indices for income, health and education, the GDI for Assam in 2001 is estimated to be 0.537. N C Hills has the first rank in the GDI, while its rank in the HDI is 11. It is followed by Morigaon, Jorhat, Kamrup and Dibrugarh. Gender inequity is most visible in the health sphere and reflected in adverse sex ratios, higher mortality rates and a higher incidence of morbidity. Being patriarchal women also get lesser share of their patriarchal property. If we look at various development indicators, women face problems of illiteracy, malnutrition, early marriage and child birth. Thus, gender related discrimination is evident through various indicators which are impacting the holistic development of the state. Promoting of women's rights and ensuring equal participation of women would help bridging this gap.

Goal 5: Improve Maternal Mortality

According to the records the Maternal Mortality Rate of the state is 390 in (2007–09) compared to 480 in (2004–06). The major causes of maternal death are septic abortion and eclampsia and this is mainly noticed among referral patients mainly from lower Assam and parts of Meghalaya. Majority of studies indicate that early effects of malnutrition, poverty and neglect contribute to high MMR. Poor nutrition also leads to anemia among pregnant women, ultimately leading to high mortality rates during the reproductive age. Early marriage, cohabitation and childbearing contribute to higher morbidity and mortality rates. Inadequate utilization of available medical infrastructure is an extremely important causal factor, and one of the major challenges that needs to be addressed by the health care system (Sanyal, 2011, unpublished).

Reflections from Cachar District

Cachar district is located in the southernmost part of Assam. It is bounded on the north by Barail and Jayantia hill ranges, on the south by the State of Mizoram and on the east by the districts of Hailakandi and Karimganj. An important indicator of gender parity is the number of females per thousand males. As per the 2001 census data, the sex ratio of Cachar stands at 945 females per thousand males while the child sex ratio for (0-6 years) is 960. Significantly, the sex ratio for rural areas stands lower than the district total. Caste and religious group-wise sex ratio shows that the Hindus and the SC population have low sex ratios in the district. The Muslims are better than the Hindus and the SCs.

The health infrastructure of the district includes 22 PHCs, 288 sub-centres and 9 dispensaries. The number of beds available in the government health institution is 112. Thus, every PHC/Sub-centre in the district covers an average of 4011 persons while number of beds is only 9 per one lakh population in the rural areas of the district. The district has a total of 14 birth and death registration centres.

Studies revealed that the major development deficits in Cachar district includes its poor housing status, low infrastructure-roads, communication and power, social infrastructure-education and health, low farm investment and productivity, increasing landlessness and casualisation of labour. Involvement of women in different spheres like work, livelihood, health care and decision making is fairly restricted and empowerment becomes questionable. The study therefore intended to focus on women's decision in health care in Fakirtilla village of Cachar district. The total population of *Fakirtilla* is 7000 persons approximately as per the 2001 census. There are three wards in the village, Ward No. 7 with 1480 population [approx], Ward No 8 with population of 3040 [approx], and Ward 9 with 2080 population [approx]. The male female ratio of the different wards is 55:45.

Method of the Study

A sample of 1000 married women has been retrieved through simple random sampling method. Questionnaire was designed to assess women's decision-making capabilities and choices in the context of their health care. The results of the study are presented in Figure 4.1.

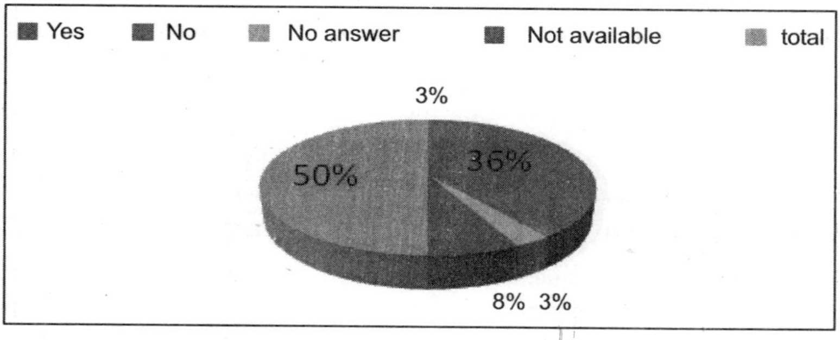

Fig. 4.1: Women's Decision-Making in Health Care.

Decision-Making Capacity for Health Care

The study revealed that 730 out of 1000 women have absolute no decision-making capacity in health care whereas 60 women said that they have exercised their choices to health care. 60 respondents refrained from answering whereas 150 were unavailable.

The community being semi-urban, the nearest health centre is the Silchar Medical College and Hospital. The accessibility to the hospital is easy however without proper supervision and accompany from the male family members so often women seek health services not on priority basis but on the convenience of the male members of the family. 820 women out of 1000 stated that they are not allowed to visit doctor alone, whereas 70 stated that they are allowed. 50 respondents were unavailable whereas 60 did not answer. (Fig. 4.2)

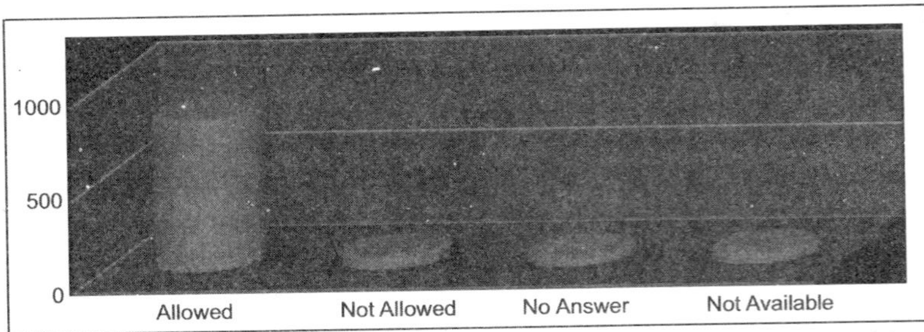

Fig. 4.2: Permission to Access Health Care Services without Family Supervision.

With matters regarding reproductive health, 147 women said that they have been able to exercise their decision-making in terms of child-birth and spacing between children whereas 770 women said that the decision to have children lies with the male member of the family. 30 women did not respond and 53 were unavailable. (Fig. 4.3)

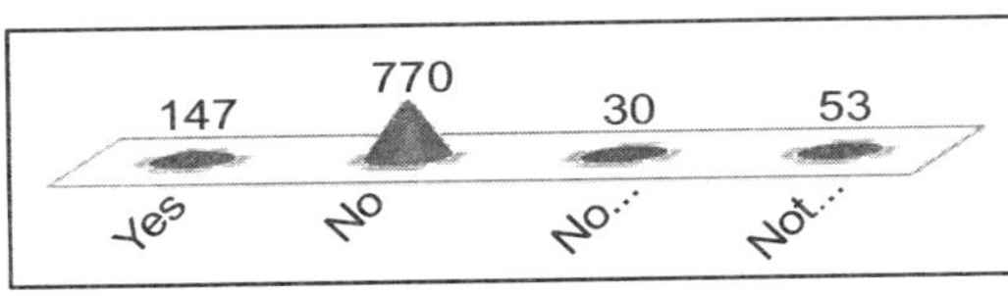

Fig. 4.3: Permission to take decisions regarding child-birth.

630 out of 1000 women said that their marriage was at 18 or less and have had early and successive pregnancies leading to reproductive health difficulties. 60 respondents did not answer and 100 were unavailable for the study. (Fig. 4.4)

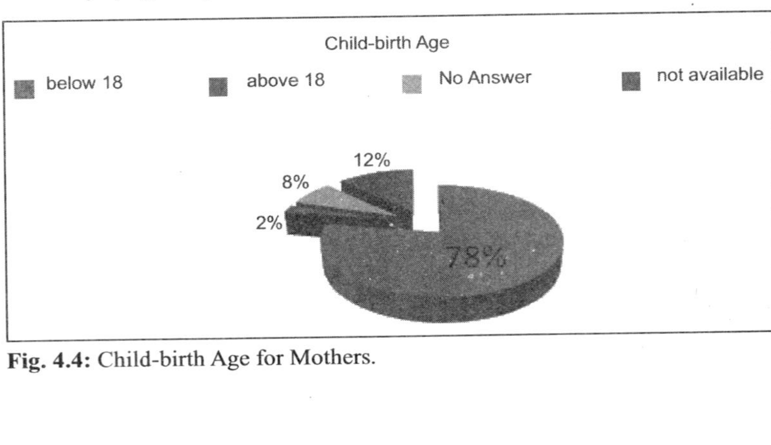

Fig. 4.4: Child-birth Age for Mothers.

The village does not have a health centre. There have been 30 deaths in the last year during child-birth and this is due to non-institutional delivery and tender age of the mother.

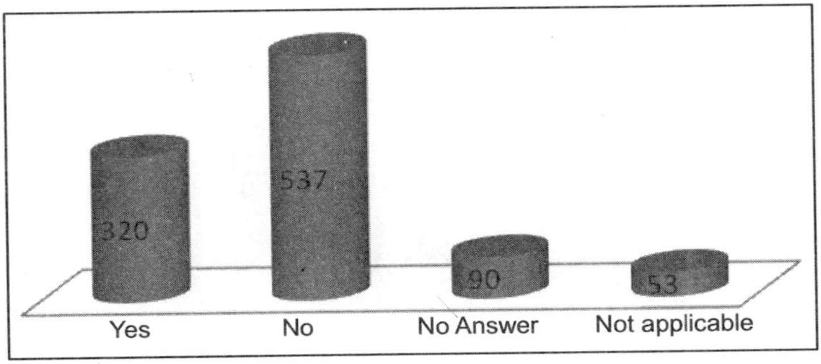

Fig. 4.5: Number of Women undergone Family Planning Methods.

320 women out of 1000 have undergone family planning operations post birth of 3-4 children. 537 did not undergo any kind of operations. 90 did not answer and 53 respondents did not participate in the question. (Fig. 4.5)

150 women out of 1000 spoke about using contraceptives and other safe sex practices with their partners whereas 765 did not know about use of contraceptives. 37 did not participate in the process of interview and 48 did not answer. (Fig. 4.6)

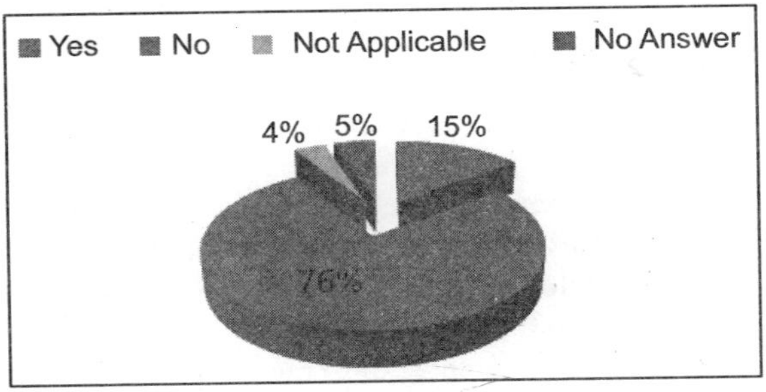

Fig. 4.6: Knowledge of Contraceptive Methods.

320 women knew about the different government schemes for women health and safe institutional delivery practices. 160 women have so far availed different schemes and programmes offered by the government and 8 more have applied for the same, 357 do not know about the schemes and 155 did not answer. (Fig. 4.7)

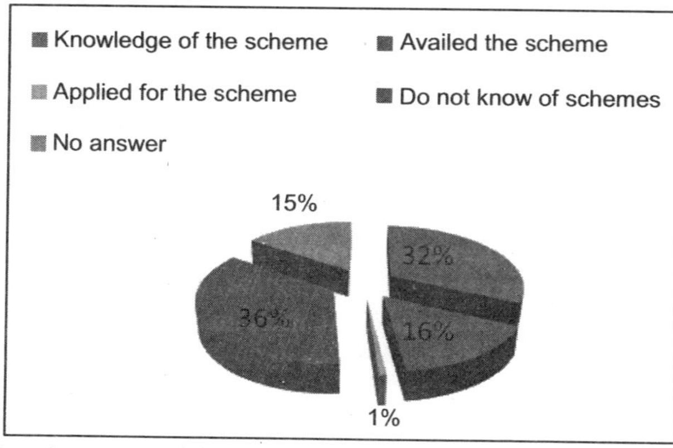

Fig. 4.7: Awareness of Government Schemes and Programmes among women in the village.

Analysis

The study revealed that majority of the women have absolute no decision-making capacity in health care. The community being semi-urban the nearest health centre is the Silchar Medical College and Hospital. The accessibility to the hospital is easy however without proper supervision and accompany from the male family members so often women seek health services not on priority basis but on the convenience of the male members of the family. Only a few women said that they have been able to exercise their decision-making in terms of child-birth and spacing between children. Regarding child-birth majority of women said that the decision to have children lies with the male member of the family. Mostly their marriage was at 18 or less and they had early and successive pregnancies leading to reproductive health difficulties. The village does not have a health centre. There have been few deaths in the last year during child-birth and this is due to non-institutional delivery and tender age of the mother. A handful of couple have undergone family planning operations post birth of 3-4 children. Few women spoke about using contraceptives and other safe sex practices with their partners. Very few women knew about the different government schemes for women health and safe institutional delivery practices. Few women have so far availed different schemes and programmes offered by the government and 8 more have applied for the same. Majority of women have stressed the need for more awareness generation and health camps in their village by the government on a regular basis. Decision-making regarding reproductive health matters is significantly absent.

Commentary

The current very high burden of disease in India is a barrier to its economic growth and poverty reduction efforts. The cost of investing in people's health is much less compared to the cost of paying inadequate attention to it. Following upon the adoption of the Millennium Development Goals at the Millennium Summit of the United Nations in September 2000, the Report of the Commission on Macroeconomics and Health in 2001 argued that poor health was one of the most important determinants of poverty and urged the governments of developing nations to upscale their health systems and commit to the improving and investing in their people's health (Bajpai and Goyal, 2004).

Health being a social phenomenon is impacted heavily by the socio-economic condition of the people. Despite government efforts, women lack complete or holistic health care because of their "positioning" in the society. Systematic patriarchal influence often impacts 'say' of women. Often successive child-birth impacts maternal mortality, women's voice with regards to child-birth is unheard. It is but assumed that a woman should "follow" the sexual privileges demanded by her husband after marriage. There are a few aspects which need to be looked into for this purpose:

- There is an urgent need for quality management and quality assurance in health care delivery system so as to make the same more effective, economical and accountable. No concerted effort has been made so far to prepare comprehensive standards for the sub-centres. The launching of NRHM has provided the opportunity for framing Indian Public Health Standards. Women's access to health care delivery system is needed.
- Health care system should be designed to encourage women to feel free to decide her reproductive health rights. Awareness generation and creating of a socially conscious environment specially which changes the 'male dominated" mindset is required. Most young women have little autonomy to make decisions about health, including contraception, care surrounding pregnancy, and post-natal care. The content and coverage of initiatives for adolescent health should be strengthened. Innovative ways to provide counselling to young people about

sexual and reproductive health services, and supplies are urgently needed.

- Concerted efforts are required towards making health services and facilities accessible and available to the women, especially the underprivileged, through the regionalization of health services, rational transfer policies, incentives and career development opportunities for health professionals so that all facilities are accessible to rural areas.
- Gender sensitive policies are a must and gender budgeting must come with a perspective wherein the patriarchal values and their penetration into programme strategies has to be consciously eliminated.
- There is a need to ensure equitable distribution of health facilities, especially in underserved areas, and promote autonomy in the use of allocated funds for maintaining buildings, equipment and supplies. Cachar district being backward suffers the pains of lack of infrastructure and updated medical equipments and facilities. This will ensure better health care service for rural women.
- Though the Government is primarily responsible for public health it alone cannot deliver public health. Engaging the private sector through public–private partnerships can potentially strengthen human resources required for improving service delivery in underserved areas and thus reducing gaps in the supply, needs and demands for human resources, and achieving national public health goals.
- It is also necessary to review the current human resource policies and organizational structures and the capacity to develop and manage health manpower.
- Health professionals and health workers need strong, integrated health systems at both national and local levels to support the delivery of universal care and services. Proven, affordable interventions, provided within an integrated network of care, from community to referral centres, can prevent millions of needless deaths and disabilities.
- Identify innovative strategies and good practices with regard to development and management of health workforce within the district and making use of them is important and essential.
- Referral services need to be strengthened between different levels of services in Cachar District and this does need good public

transport systems to support patient movement. Innovative schemes could be tested in this sphere.

- Besides strengthening the health care services in Silchar, efforts need to be made to promote social change towards women empowerment. Not only upgraded medical facilities is required there is an urgent need to develop and promote social consciousness towards women's rights and decision-making in terms of health care.
- The ASHA workers and ANMs can play a major role in building awareness in the villages promoting women's say and women's decision regarding reproductive health care.

It is easy to say that providing of appropriate services and implementing people-centred policies will improve the "gendered" health care practices in the district. But often do we realise that our 'social order' plays a major role in our accessibility to any services in the country. Be it health, drinking water, sanitation or employment, women have to invest efforts to break their social barriers and demand for their rights and services. It is very important that awareness is build in this male dominated society that women's say in reproductive health is essentially important. Correct spacing between children, family planning, the aspiration for male child and successive pregnancies–all these mindsets and taboos needs to be looked into so that effective health care is sought and morbidity and mortality indicators are taken care of. Thus, integrating women empowerment with rural health care will help implement better health care initiatives and reach the MDG targets by 2015.

REFERENCES

Bajpai, N. and Goyal, S. (2004). "Primary Health Care in India: Coverage and Quality Issues", CGSD Working Paper 15, June. Retrieved from: http://www.earthinstitute.columbia. edu/cgsd/documents/bajpai_primaryhealth.pdf. (Accessed on September 10, 2010)

Ministry of Minority Affairs and Omeo Kumar Das Institute of Social Development, District Report of Cachar; retrieved on 5th October, 2011 from http://www.icssr.org/Cachar.pdf

Ministry of Women and Child Development (MOWCD) website, retrieved on 15th October, 2011 from http://wcd.nic.in/

Sanyal, S. (2011) "Assam and Millennium Development Goals: The Way So Far", Unpublished.

5

Voice, Gender and Space in Time:

The Idea of Lata Mangeshkar and Lalrindiki Khiangte

Pankaj Roy and *H. Vanlalveni*

Lata Mangeshkar, Femininity and Space of the Nation

This discussion is not concerned with whether Lata's voice is 'good', 'bad', 'authentically' Indian or otherwise, but rather, with the tendencies that come together about her singing style and attribute to it the characteristic of 'authentically' Indian-feminine. Though the discourse of nationalism looms large in what follows, this should not be taken to mean that projects of modernity can simply be reduced to it. Clearly, nationalist ideology is only one of the grids upon which post-colonial modernity is situated. So, while I primarily concentrate on pleasure as a nationalist project, it clearly does not exhaust inquiry into the topic. During the last and the current century, Indian popular music has, in the main, been connected with films and whilst in the early films many of the songs were sung by the actors themselves, during the 1940s this practice gave way to 'playback' singing where the actors' singing voice was provided by someone else. So, as is well-known, in India, singers are not necessarily stars in themselves and, till quite recently, commercial music was sold in the market under the banner of the film with which the songs were associated. Singers cultivated little public presence and rather than the personality of the singer, it was their voice that functioned as a 'sign'. This situation has only recently begun to change and even can't be compared to the situation of western pop music. Lata Mangeshkar was born in 1929 in Indore, and as a child, both she and her sister Asha Bhonsle learnt music from a series of accomplished musicians. Lata recorded her first song in 1942 and since then has, reputedly, sung in 18 Indian languages. One source estimates that by 2011 she had recorded around

16,000 songs, while journalistic accounts speak of a substantially greater corpus. Among female playback singers, then, Lata's voice has dominated the Indian popular music scene. And, along with this dominance, she established a specific vocal style, which in conjunction with the factors I will discuss below, became recognised as an aesthetic marker of 'classical' Indian female identity. If "vocal style (aside from the language) is the single most important marker of aesthetic identity" (Manuel, 1993:52), then it can be argued that Lata's singing voice has instituted a very specific identity for Indian womanhood, one which has almost no precedence in traditional forms of Indian music. In other words, the 'woman' conjured by Lata Mangeshkar's singing voice is the product of certain development that are peculiar to the processes of Indian modernity. One music critic has noted that Lata's style has become "the ultimate measure of sweetness in a woman's voice. [And that] Its chief characteristic was the skilled use of a particular kind of falsetto, which did not exist in quite the same way before her coming" (Raghava Menon quoted in Manuel (1993: 53). Another suggests that singers from musical genres with their own distinct style began to mimic Lata's voice and that it soon "became difficult to imagine a female voice that is not Lata Mangeshkar's" (Chandavarkar quoted in Manuel, 1993: 53). There is, it could be said, almost no precedence for Lata's voice and the kind of femininity it conjures in the wider sphere of female singing styles in India, one marked by an extraordinary diversity of expressive traditions. Given this diversity, it is important to think about how Lata Mangeshkar's shrill adolescent girl falsetto came to be established as the 'ideal' in 'Indian popular music and film culture in general' [Manuel, 1993:53]. The mélange of female singing styles found in the subcontinent ranges from group singing at family ritual occasions (a wedding being the most common), to organised public performances. In some instances, many earlier ritual linked performances have become part of the commercial performance milieu. However, no matter what the context, women's singing styles in India, at least those not connected with the film industry, have been marked by a striking heterogeneity of tonal and other styles. Here comes Daduhi of Mizoram, who sang romantic melodies, oral traditional themes in her time and established herself as a heavy voiced singer. Now, if the 'Dholi' Gayikayen of Jodhpur sing of a wife demanding jewellery from her husband in 'heavy' and nasal tones, then the Hindustani classical music singer Gangubai Hangal's delivery ranges between the low alto and the upper tenor ranges and frequently confuses unacquainted listeners as to the gender of the artiste. And, though the artiste's gender is not really difficult to determine in the case of an early (1911) recording by the Hindustani classical music virtuoso Zohra Bai, her voice is nevertheless imbued with a quality best described as playful aggressiveness. The ghazal singing of Pakistan's Farida Khanum provides another example of the heterogeneity of which I speak. Khanum's voice, alternately sensuous, pleading, and cajoling, manages to reproduce the complexities of a subject position that is a combination of "a desperate lover intoxicated with passion, a rapt visionary absorbed in mystic illumination, (and) an iconoclastic drunkard celebrating the omnipotence of wine" (Rahman, Faruqi and Pritchett, 1994:94]. Again Daduhi, with her heavy voice represents the same sort of gender displacement in a region, where most of the female singers hail from Church-Gospel singing background. These examples could be multiplied manifold, with many regional and other styles vying for a place. One perspective which seeks to account for the dominance and the subsequent stylistic homogeneity ushered in by Lata's style speaks of the "creation of film music as a common-denominator mass-music style, produced in corporate, urban studios and superimposed on a heterogeneous audience; this audience has no active role in the creation of this music, and can exercise only indirect influence by choosing among the songs and styles proffered by the industry" (Manuel, 1993:53). This is, no doubt, an important aspect to consider.

However, this standpoint can be usefully supplemented through an analysis of the wider cultural and historical dynamic which contributes towards constituting the field of the aesthetic, and in turn, influences the representation of identities, including gender identities. Consideration of aspects of the discourse of early Indian nationalism provides a good starting point towards this objective. As feminist scholarship has pointed out 'woman' functioned as an important sign in the masculinist constructions of the idea of the nation-to-be which comes to be represented through the notion of the "mother–who-is-the-nation" (Zutshi, 1993:94). In some versions this was achieved through representing India as a Hindu Goddess. However, this formulation engendered a specific problem, as far as the nationalists were concerned, in that "the image Woman (could) be perceived to contain a charge of sexuality which always threatens to run free" (Zutshil, 1993:102). How, then, to deal with this dilemma? In part, it has been suggested, the resolution of the 'woman question' was achieved through identifying women not just as the carriers of 'tradition' but tradition itself: women's bodies became the site on which tradition was seen to be (Chatterjee, 1993a; Mani, 1993). The suggestion is that this formulation of the issue should be treated with some of caution as it may capture only one of several scenarios; that, the public life of the Indian family and 'its' women also had a role to play in debates about engagements with modernity. The following discussion seeks to explore this very public dimension of the 'woman question' in the career of Indian modernity through the pervasive influence of two singers who has, as if, crafted an entire structure of emotions in the post-colonial era.

With the coming of cinema in India, the tableau of public forms became inextricably attached to the possibilities of cinematic representation and men and women become public figures, attached to the natural and human topographies. This, it might be suggested, was a result of the particular interpretation of the term 'culture' that had come to be established during the modern period. This was an interpretation of film techniques which had almost a natural affinity too. I am referring to the understanding of culture which represented it as linked to geographical places (Clifford, 1988; Gupta and Ferguson, 1992), and to landscape (Gibson, 1993), such that Indian culture becomes attached to specific natural and human-made sites: the Himalayas, hill stations, the Ganges, the Taj Mahal, ruins of past 'civilisations', religious sites, and office buildings which constituted the representational iconography of the fledgling nation state. The relationship between geography and the nation may have received scant attention from scholars of India; however, its importance was explicitly recognized by nationalists of various hues. One of the pithiest examples is to be encountered in the work of Sister Nivedita (Margaret Noble) and occurs in an article on the 'Future Education of Indian Woman'. A fundamental aspect of women's education in India, Sister Nivedita was to say, must lie in making women more 'efficient' (Sister Nivedita, 1923:59). This called for, among other things, the making of 'queen and housewife, saint and citizen'. Such an 'efficiency drive' towards a new society, the Sister noted, required that women be imparted a geographical sensibility. For, geographical knowledge constituted the fundamental building block of the consciousness of national feeling (Sister Nivedita, 1923:59). This might be achieved through resources already at 'our' disposal: "the wandering Bhagabatas or Kathakas, with the magic lantern, may popularise geography, by showing slides illustrative of various pilgrimages"(1923:61):

> Picture, pictures, pictures, these are the first of instruments in trying to concretise ideas, pictures and the mother-tongue. If we would impart a love of country, we must give a country to love. How shall women be enthusiastic about something they cannot imagine?

It can be argued that the above derives from a 'modern' view of culture as a territorialized and fixed concept, rather than as the relationship between human beings. One can contrast this with the absence of the realist convention in representing landscape in, say, certain schools of Indian art such as the Madhubani style (Thakur, 1982) and Mughal miniatures (Beach, 1992) where landscape represents human emotional states or religious beliefs rather than standing for culture itself. A similar point has been made with respect to the absence of a realist tradition in medieval Hindi poetry that provides a contrast with developments in the modem period. Karine Schomer points out that "nature had not been absent from (medieval) Braj poetry, but it was an idealised nature, usually relegated to the role of enhancing human emotions. ...The treatment of nature in the (modern) Dwivedi period was quite different. Not only was it made an independent poetic subject, but it was described in realistic, concrete detail" (Schomer, 1983:11). It is precisely this modern 'realistic' sensibility of landscape and territory that found play in early cinema. However, even during the modern period, a sensibility of culture as a relationship between humans rather than with fixed space could also be found. A Marathi book published towards the end of last century provides a tantalizing glimpse into this alternative worldview. The book *Manjha Prawas*, published in Hindi as *Ankhon Dekha Gadar* is an account of the travels of the Vishnubhatt Godse from Pune to Mathura some time in 1857. For the modern reader, Godse's travelogue has a strangely disorienting effect. For, the familiar and comforting descriptions of scenery and landscape are almost entirely absent in an account that is, instead, teeming with people, procedures, and transactions. We can only begin to comprehend this transactional sensibility if we think of it as part of a very different understanding of culture to that which we have become accustomed. It is, in fact, a different way of organising culture. Now, when Indian culture becomes attached to landscape and territory, the heroes and heroines of Indian films come to meet, and sing and dance in these places which come to constitute Indian cultural and national spaces. And herein lay one of the problems for the 'woman question' in India, and where Lata Mangeshkar has been particularly helpful. For, many of these spaces of Indian culture were public spaces, i.e., defined as 'not–home'. An important aspect of the definition of 'culture' once it becomes attached to territories and landscapes is, indeed, its public nature, an aspect that is crucial for illustrating what 'Indian' culture is. And yet, how was the 'fraternal contract' (Pateman, 1980) which was nationalism to deal with this increasing visibility of the filmic woman 'out of place', i.e., in public spaces? And, most importantly, what was at issue was not just visibility but also given the 'musical' nature of Indian cinema, the audibility of women in public spaces. Here was a great dilemma. Indian films both contributed towards the consolidation of a national imagination on a mass scale-these sites are India, they said but also seemed to threaten one of the fundamental organising principles of the discourses on nationalism, viz., the positioning of women within it. It would appear that the Lata's stylistic innovation offered a viable solution to the above problem of representation in the public sphere: at the same time that women's bodies became visible in public spaces via films, their presence was 'thinned' through the expressive timbre granted to them. The heroines for whom Lata provided the singing voice may well have been prancing around hill sides and streets while performing a song sequence, but this gesture which otherwise threatened male dominance of theses paces, was domesticated through the timbre, tonality and stylistic stricture that marked that presence. The potentially powerful image of the heroine enjoying the freedom of the public space in equal measure to the male hero and singing in a voice that may express an ambiguous femininity was, through Lata's voice, undermined. However, it is not enough to say that Lata provides the bridge between colonial-nationalist history and modern cinematic problematic of representations. Her 'art' is almost fundamental to another process of modernity: the recasting of the relationship between the performer and the audience. Writing at the turn of the century, Ananda Coomaraswamy, an interesting and problematic scholar of Indian (or rather, Hindu) aesthetics made what is a particularly profound observation in this regard. He suggested that in Indian music the relationship between the performer and the audience is one where the audience also brings artistry to listening: "the listener (responds) with an art of his own" (Coomaraswamy, 1974:103). And further, that "the musician in India finds a model audience technically critical, but somewhat indifferent of voice production"(1974:103). The artistry of the performer, in other words is not (or was not) hegemonic, since it faced the skill of the audience in receiving the performance. It is not therefore "the voice that makes the singer, as so often happens in Europe" Coomaraswamy (1974:104) was to note. Lata Mangeshkar manages to break this dynamic relationship between the performer and the audience and impose a code of interpretation through the dramatic emphasis on the singing rather than the song, through the "sensuous perfection of the voice" (Coomaraswamy, 1974:103) where now the feminine can only be articulated through a constricted timbre and style. The audience is now instructed on what femininity is. One of the ways in which this dominance may have been achieved might be illustrated through reference to the relationship between orality and literariness. It would appear that the wider context in which the audience exists as an active entity with its own artistry is the context where 'orality' continues to be a valued mode of interaction; the performative contexts of orality can be thought of as the situation where the listener may talk back, interrupt, and reinterpret. The dynamics of the oral context are one where the artistry of the performer is not reduced to any singular characteristic, and certainly not the voice. This view finds strong support in contemporary scholarship through the absence of any discussion that seeks to define a norm for voice quality in Indian performative traditions. Susan Wadley's discussion of the 'performance strategies' of the artistes of the north Indian epic of *Dhola* is a case in point. Wadley suggests that the great popularity of the most highly regarded of these, Swarup Singh, is due to "his magnificently expressive voice covering a range of performance styles" (Wadley, 1989:81). There is no suggestion here that anyone particular type of tonality is considered to be the mark of 'good' singing. Effective performances of *Dhola*, Wadley suggests, depend on two things: "telling the story in a clear fashion and providing variety". Since 'traditional' Indian music was not written music, it belonged to this milieu. Lata's music, on the other hand, derives from a 'compositional' context: for "the elaborate arrangements (of Indian film music) reflect a pre-composed and notated (i.e., written) approach to music composition and performance" (Manuel, 1993:50) The compositional or literary mode of performance can be linked to a wider sensibility about the relationship between performers and audiences, and between readers and texts: it is a sensibility which has the potential to privilege the 'expert' and disenfranchises the 'layperson'. It is in this sense that Lata's voice becomes the unquestionable authority on the feminine idea and, inasmuch as that ideal becomes entrenched; the artistry of the audience in receiving the performance is of a far more limited kind. So, here, the consolidation of 'literariness' as an aspect of Indian modernity served to codify representations of femininity. Lata's adolescent girl voice for the adult woman comes, then, to establish the authority of the written word over the recalcitrant possibilities of orality, overriding the "substantial amount of melodic, rhythmic, and textually expressive play" (Hansen, 1992:243) that marks the later's expressive universe. Further, through the historical association of writing with men, this also legitimized the authority of male notions of the sign 'woman'. The other aspect to this is that it simultaneously established the dominance of bourgeois notions of gender, communication and being in the world, 'marginalising' other existing worldviews. In this sense as well, it was expressive of certain contexts of Indian nationalist discourse. So, Lata's voice is the simultaneous site of both gender and class. It is interesting to note that when Lata did give public performances it was, as Manuel (1993) points out, just as likely that she would stand rigidly on stage, and sing with her head buried in a notebook. Here, at least two contexts are at play. First, what matters is the voice and the way it has been defined by the 'notebook', by the authority of the writing. And second is Lata's own public persona (on record, cassette and CD cover sleeves, and in magazines) is of the respectable housewife, perhaps even a mother, a mother of the nation who has given that nation a voice: "For the very heart of India throbs in your voice", as the lyricist Naushad Ali was to write in a ghazal in praise of Lata (quoted in Bhimani, 1995:16). Lata's motherhood falls, in this context, within the realms of the 'virgin mother'. It is important to note that Lata has almost never been dogged by relationship linked gossip that surrounds many other women in the entertainment industry. In addition to the virgin mother thematic, there is (to resort to culturally mixed metaphors) also an aura of the cult of Meera, the medieval princess-poetess and an iconic figure in the Bhakti movement, about her. Like the Bhakti poets, Lata too has forsaken her sexuality and domesticity for devotion to a greater cause, namely, the endowment of national-pleasure through a redefinition of modern Indian feminine identity. And, in the process, she has become iconcised as virgin mother (sister?) of the nation. So, Lata, the mother who has breathed life into the 'national' woman (the most famous of them all is the character of Radha in Mehboob Khan's 1957 epic *Mother India*, comes immediately to mind) articulates a gendered intertextual space where the seemingly disreputable public role of the woman as entertainer is contained by the representational strategies of motherliness and sisterliness. The most obvious contrast is with the ghazal singer Begum Akhtar who both drank and smoked and made no effort, even in old age, to project the image of either an asexual mother figure or a generically 'respectable' grandmother. But in case of Daduhi, such complicacy of 'sign' is absent; she is more an ethnic 'icon', an icon of 'voice-de-locale' representing an ethnic identity: of religious and romantic feelings alike, which rouses emotions of the Mizos. She sings in Mizo as well as English, both of which are the language of Christianity and ethnicity. It is so because all the inhabitants of Mizoram, particularly all the tribal population, who are westernised and habitual to western hard music, understand her, feels at home with her songs. The habitual listening of the heavy voice of the female chorus singers in the Church also has made most of the Mizos align with Daduhi as a female icon singer, where Lata's adolescent female voice is a distant child's one.

But the processes through which Lata's voice became established as aesthetic epitome of Indian feminine identity can also be seen as part of the cultural politics of the making of the 'modern' Indian women within the matrices of upper-caste, Hindu milieus. In other words, Lata's singing voice was part of the broader processes of nationalist thought where the figure of the women-citizen, inasmuch as she was the object of debate and discussion, emerged out of the skin of colonial and post-colonised caste and communal politics. In a discussion of radio broadcasting in India, David Lelyveld has suggested that the Hindu-Muslim context is an important one for understanding the formulation of 'national programming' (Lelyveld, 1995:55) and the attempts to inculcate a 'national' culture through All-India Radio (AIR). And though Lelyveld's attention is mainly directed towards exploring the strategies and manoeuvres through which Indian classical music was sought to be Hinduised in the immediate post-independence period, I think there is an important link between his discussion and the case of Indian film music. In what follows, I do not mean to imply that there existed at all levels of Indian society a fundamental hostility between Hindus and Muslims. There is sufficient historical, anthropological and literary material to indicate otherwise. Rather, that specific historical circumstance coalesced during the second half of the 19th century to produce a milieu within which an anti-Muslim rhetoric was prevalent in many aspects of Indian life. In the post-independence period, the Hindu-Muslim angle in the context of producing a 'national' music culture came to the fore in several ways. And, inasmuch as the post-colonised nation state's cultural capital (Bourdieu, 1986)—its 'ancient heritage', its various architectural landmarks, its philosophical and cultural achievements, etc.—received as much attention as the debates around creating more economic capital, the task of producing a 'national' musical culture was taken up in a particularly prominent manner. Some of these debates were intrinsically linked to the supposed fate of Indian music during colonial rule. So, B.V. Keskar, Minister of Information and Broadcasting from 1950 to 1962 was to suggest that "only with national independence, and indeed, primarily through radio broadcasting... could the musical heritage of India be saved" (Lelyveld, 1995:55). However, Keskar did not believe that the blame for the lamentable state of Indian music could be traced exclusively to accidental disdain for Oriental cultural forms and to 'imperial neglect' of native traditions; he was of the unequivocal opinion that the deleterious effects to which it had been subject also derived from the actions of north Indian Muslims. This community, he suggested, "had appropriated and distorted the ancient art, turning it into the secret craft of exclusive lineages, the *gharanas*, and ignorant of Sanskrit, divorced it from the religious context of Hindu civilization" (Lelyveld, 1995:55). The wider context of Keskar's remarks is, by now, a familiar one: that the post-colonised nation state must reinvigorate the ancient Sanskrit culture which had been neglected by the British and, more fundamentally, corrupted by the Muslims. So, in another context, the 'reformist' Arya Samaj sought, through the Gurukul education movement, to re-vivify a 'fallen' society through the task of forming "a sound, active and decisive character in... students". Hence within the Gurukul of 'Ancient' and 'Vedic' origin "the students were called Brahmacharis on the pattern of the Ancient Gurukulas". Keskar's thinking on Indian music was, then, heir to the history of what might be termed 'Hindu contextualism' (Srivastava, 1998) of the late 19th and early 20th century nationalist discourse in India. And, as is well-known, Keskar was not alone in his elaboration of this theme. Vishnu Narayan Bhatkhande (1860–1936) was another extremely influential figure in the movement that sought to construct a 'national' music culture through returning Indian music to its putative ancient Hindu roots (Lelyveld, 1995). These ideas formed an important sub-text in debates regarding the development of a 'civil' post-colonised identity, and constituted the backdrop to the attempted Hinduisation and gentrification of Indian culture. Lelyveld points out, for instance, that under Vallabhbhai Patel's reign as Minister for Information and Broadcasting (1946), the effort towards producing a purified national culture was manifested in the prohibition of "singers and musicians from the courtesan culture", anyone (as one source put it) "whose public life was a scandal" (Lelyveld, 1995:57). As well, during Keskar's tenure as Minister, there came to be instituted a bureaucratic selection procedure for All-India Radio musicians whose most explicit aim appears to have been the undermining of the Gharana system. An important outcome of this process of linking employment possibility within AIR with "certification from recognised music academies" (Lelyveld, 1995:58) was the entry into the profession of many who were described as being from 'respectable' backgrounds; those, in other words, who had skirted the illicit influence of the Muslim, dominated Gharana and allied systems of performance. All this is to say that within early 20th century nationalist discourse there existed a strong theme which linked the emergence of the modern Indian self to a 'pure' and 'ancient' Hindu genealogy (Sunder Rajan, 1993; Chatterjee, 1993) and to a 'respectable' bourgeois milieu. An additional way of thinking about this issue is to suggest, as Lelyveld does, that "the great enemy in this effort to construct a new music by administrative decree was the increasingly popular new style of film songs" (Chakravarty, 1993; Barnouw and Krishnaswamy, 1963, pp. 200–205). However, it is possible to suggest that the ideology of a 'pure' and 'respectable' national culture found voice in the realms of popular (that is film) music itself. And, that Lata Mangeshkar's singing style was the most obvious manifestation of this process. Hence, I suggest that the gradual development of Lata's singing voice into what it became at the peak of her popularity for her very early singing style, carries a strong resonance of the Pakistani singer Noorjehan's nasality, was part of the process of purifying, Hinduising and gentrifying the figure of the 'ideal' Indian woman of post-coloniality. This was to be the woman fit to carry the mantle of 'bearer of our traditions'.

In an essay on the actress Nasim Bano, Sadat Hasan Manto recalls the making of the 1942 film *Ujala*. Due to a weak story line, ordinary music, and poor direction, the film flopped and the owner of the production company 'Ahsan Sahib' had to suffer great financial loss. However,

> During the process (of completing the film) he fell in love with (the heroine) Nasim Bano. Nasim, however, was no stranger to Ahsan Sahib. For, his father, Khanbahadur Muhammad Sulaiman, Chief Engineer, had been an acquaintance of Naseem's mother, Chamia. In fact, for all intents and purposes, she was his second wife. So, Ahsan Sahib must have had ample opportunity of meeting Nasim on various occasions.
>
> (1984, pp. 19-20).

It is this context, where 'Muslimness' and 'debauchery' became conjoined through an emerging discourse of middle class Hindu respectability, which became the object of the project of post-colonial purification; and Lata's voice was one of the several sites upon which this project unfolded, though the purge, it could be suggested, was only partially successful. It is no doubt true that the classical music milieu was an explicit target for the 'reform' project discussed above, however, the mass appeal of the film industry and its by-products, also made it a target of the reformers, zeal. For, the 'good' name of the nation is most often at risk from the retrograde tendencies of its masses, and it is always the responsibility of enlightened citizenry to shepherd the former towards the portals of citizenship and civilized action. Through Lata's artistry, the 'disreputableness' of ambiguous tonalities and the threat of uncertain femininity–the mizzen scene of Krishna Sobti's great novel *Mitro Marjani* [(1958) 1991], for example—was brought into alignment with the discourses of the 'pure' and controllable Hindu womanhood. The most obvious counterpoint to Lata's style was what could be referred to as the 'Kotha' (brothel/courtesan) style of singing, echoes of which can be discerned in, say, singer Shamshad Begum's voice. It is difficult to convey the qualities of a voice—the social and emotional contexts it may conjure for the listener—in a discussion such as this. However, it is possible to say that, through certain historical processes of which the nationalist discourse was perhaps the most important, public singing by women, unless connected to religious and ritual purposes (such as weddings), came to carry the taint of disrepute; it became the preserve of the *tawaif* (the courtesan), the lower caste women. And, the tonalities of such public singing which itself remained unfettered by the definitional constraints of a 'good' voice became associated with 'disreputable' undomesticated conduct. At a later point, when the 'Muslim problem', and the search for a 'proper' controllable femininity (and hence a 'proper' masculinity) became part of the nationalist project of cultural redemption, certain kinds of voices came to be marked as an unacceptable aspect of 'proper' post-coloniality. There emerged an inventory of 'impurities' with respect to 'proper' post-colonial femininity: included in this inventory, it is possible to say, was nasality and a 'heavy' (i.e., masculine) voice. And, whilst it is true that quite a number of feminine identities came to be seen as not possessing a 'proper' voice, most commonly, however, it is the Muslim tawaif who became inextricably connected to that kind of voice. For it was she who, in the redemptive projects of turn-of-the-century nationalism posed the greatest threat to middle class Hindu masculinity: for, she was dexterous not merely in matters of physical allure, but could also, at least as far as popular mythology would have it, match wits with her male clientele. So, it is at this juncture where a variety of modem processes of culture came together—that Lata's skill as a forever adolescent voice, singing out, but through the controllable timbre of a child-woman, is situated. She provided another resolution of the 'woman question' in the post-colonial context: how to have women in public, but also within the firm grip of a watchful, adult, masculinity, such that the public woman became forever infantilised. The process of 'purifying' Indian public culture took the form, then, of purging it of its Muslim associations and its connections of various realms of (non-middle class) disreputability. Lata Mangeshkar's voice, it can be argued, became the site for the unfolding of this project: a place at the cross-roads of a public culture where the adolescent girl's voice-persona appeared to provide the opportunity of both expressing an appropriately modern femininity and a suitably Hinduised nationality. This point is nicely encapsulated in some stray comments in Harish Bhimani's hagiographic *In Search of Lata Mangeshkar* (1995). Lata sometimes cancelled her recording schedules, Bhimani says, if she felt that her voice was "not at its best" (1995:21). And, that it may have been a lapse in her judgment (as Bhimani portrays it) that led her to record the song 'Paaon chhoo lene do…' for Roshan's [sic] in *Tajmahal*. [For,] It has a perceptible nasal twang to it" (1995, p. 21). A few pages later, speaking of a pre-recorded introduction by Lata to "an orchestral version of ten of her favourite tunes", Bhimani notes that "Her voice was clear and soft. Like that of a girl on the threshold of adolescence" (1995, p. 34). It is this heterosexual male fantasy of a Hindu adolescent girl both controllable ever ready to please that is an overwhelming aspect of the desire that congregates around Lata's voice. And, in keeping with the unbridled possibilities of fantasies, the voice that conjures the pliable adolescent girl also concurrently facilitates the invocatory gesture that imagines the 'mother'. I do not, however, mean to present Lata herself as a passive figure, merely singing to the tunes ministered by her professional mentors. For, there is no reason to assume that she herself has not been an active participant in the project of 'fine-tuning' her voice to the point of its classic recognisability. Finally, in this context, the project of purification tended, as mentioned above, to remain incomplete: so whilst the 'ideal' feminine voice of Indian popular culture did, in fact, became derivative of Lata's style, the Muslimness of Indian filmic culture also remained an inescapable fact. Throughout the post-independence period, film titles and song lyrics continued to borrow heavily from Persian and Urdu and many of the most prominent lyricists and actors. Now, we might also consider reading the filmic romance of the 1950s and 1960s era as narratives for the 'future development' of the individual.

Conclusion

If we keep in mind the asymmetry between Indian metropolitan and cultural spheres, then it is not difficult to speak of the provincial male (and female) as the subject of the movie romance and the complex role of the latter as the site of a narrative of the 'future development' denied by the economic process. To be 'in love', could then, in some but not all contexts, act as a metonym for 'freedom': the freedom to 'achieve', to individual choice, and, finally, to 'fulfilment'. So here, my suggestion is that the Hindi film of the above era was really a compact between those who made the film and those watched it. The (provincial male) audience found itself fully represented on the screen, and, most of the song writers, script writers were, in fact, provincial men for whom the film industry was a means of employment which did not require any formal qualifications. And, the 'check' which was sought to be imposed on filmic women through Lata's voice was expressed in another way which brings to the fore the provincial-metropolitan angle of my discussion. The heroine singing in a public place not only sang in an adolescent girl voice, but also mouthed lyrics which, in addition to Urdu, also drew heavily from the various dialects of Hindi. In other words, from the various provincial versions of Hindi in its national incarnation, has been Sanskritised in order to give it a classical genealogy. It could be suggested, then, that Lata's voice, her artistry was also a part of the process where men from strong patriarchal backgrounds—the film industry people—sought to exercise control over the representation of women through both an expressive timbre and a vocabulary which resonated with more 'controllable' environment: the village and the province. The city can, potentially, be a threat to male hegemony, and the presence of the screen woman in its public places compounded this threat. So, if the heroine figure was infantilised through Lata's voice, she was also produced as familiar and speaking or, rather, singing in the language of 'home' and the controllable domestic space rather than a recently produced public sphere, the nation. However, it would be naive to posit a simple relationship between a 'modern' metropolitan milieu and the lack of patriarchal strictures; writers and thinkers such as Krishna Sobti, Fanishwarnath Renu, Rajendra Yadav also tell us something about other sites of 'progressive' thinking. It may be more fruitful, then, to suggest that if on the one hand, the Lata complex emerged from the patriarchal concerns of provincial male culture, it was no less connected to the modernisation of patriarchal forms prevalent in Indian metropolitan culture. In addition to the 'scientific' persona of the hero in films, it is also worth noting that his 'task' was usually positioned *vis-a-vis* the countryside: he acted to bring enlightenment to India's villages, a theme borrowed from, among others, Orientalist and development theory orientated discourses about the 'irrational' peasants and their recalcitrance to the logic of modernity. Now, in asmuch as the heroine sang in her adolescent girl voice and the songs were sprinkled liberally with words from village dialects, 'woman' as sign also came to represent the village (or province; e.g., '*Anuradha*', 1960); that which needed to be 'improved', to be made more 'rational' through the efforts of men who embodied the new knowledge which had made the west 'progressive', and India backward. The metropolitan theme has an important history in Indian nationalist discourse (Srivastava, 1998) and it is this which also finds play in the case of Lata and her music: men became the progressive 'metropolis' and women, the backward 'countryside'. Further the 'imbrications of sexuality, sex, gender, and nature' happens in Lata's case through the voice itself: the 'natural' identity of the woman is aligned to that of the girl child, and hence adult femaleness is naturalized through associating the adult woman as forever closer to childhood, inasmuch as in popular discourse the child is seen to be closer to nature. Hence, either way through 'traditional' provincial masculine politics or 'modern' metropolitan nationalist discourse the sign of 'woman' continued to be inscribed through masculine ideologies. 'Lata Mangeshkar' is the conjunctional site, then, of the prolix technologies and ideologies of masculinity and patriarchy, colonialism, Indian nationalism, the relationship between the metropolis and the province, and that of modern 'territorialised' understanding of 'culture' whereas Daduhi, in contrast, is the meeting site of fantasy of sound, orality, religious traditions along with identity and ethnicity.

REFERENCES

Beach, M.C. *Mughal and Rajput Painting*, Cambridge University Press, Cambridge, 1992.

Bhabha, H.K., *The Location of Culture*, Routledge, London, 1994.

Bhimani, H., *In Search of Lata Mangeshkar*, Indus, New Delhi, 1995.

Chakravarty, S., *National Identity in Indian Popular Cinema. 1947–1987*, University of Texas Press, Austin, 1993.

Chatterjee, Partha, "The Nationalist Resolution of the Women's Question", in K. Sangari and S. Vaid (eds.), *Recasting Women*. Essays in Colonial History, Kali for Women, New Delhi, 1993a.

——, *The Nation and its Fragments: Colonial and Post-colonial Histories*, Princeton University Press, Princeton, 1993b.

Coomaraswamy, A.K., *The Dance of Shiva*: *Fourteen Indian Essays*, Munshiram Manoharlal, New Delhi, 1974.

Derrida, Jacques, *Of Grammatology*, Johns Hopkins Press, Baltimore, 1976.

Foucault, M., *The History of Sexuality, Volume 1: An Introduction*, Penguin, London, 1990.

Godse, V. *Ankhon Dekha Gadar* (translated into Hindi with an introduction by Amritlal Nagar), Rajpal and Sons, Delhi, 1986.

Gupta, A. and J. Ferguson, "Beyond 'Culture': Space, Identity and the Politics of Difference", *Cultural Anthropology* 7(1): 6–23, 1992.

Kakar, Sudhir, *Intimate Relations: Exploring Indian Sexuality*, University of Chicago Press, Chicago, 1990.

Kesavan, Mukul "Urdu, Awadh and the Tawaif: The Islamicate Roots of Indian Cinema" in Zoya Hasan (ed), *Forging Identities: Gender, Communities and the State in India*, Westview Press, Boulder, 1994.

Lelyveld, David, "Upon the Subdominant: Administering Music on All India Radio" in Carol A. Breckenridge (ed), *Consuming Modernity: Public Culture in a South Asian World*, University of Minnesota Press, Minneapolis, 1995.

Manto, S.H. *Meenabazar* (memoirs, in Hindi), Rajkamal Paperbacks, Delhi, 1984 (first published 1962).

Manuel, Peter, *Cassette Culture: Popular Music and Technology in Northern India*, University of Chicago Press, Chicago, 1993.

Pateman, C., *The Disorder of Women: Democracy, Feminism and Political Discourse*, Polity Press, Cambridge, 1989.

Rahman, S.R. Faruqi, "Lyric Poerty in Urdu: The Ghazal" in Barbara Stoler Miller and F.W. Pritchett (ed.), *Masterworks of Asian Literature in Contemporary Perspective: A Guide for Teaching*, M.E. Sharpe, New York, 1994.

Renu, Fanishwarnath, *Kalank Mukti* (novel, in Hindi), Rajkamal Paperbacks, Delhi, 1992.

Sankrityayan, Rahul, *Ghummakkad Shashtra* (Hindi), Kitab Mahal, Delhi, 1994 (first published 1948).

Sister Nivedita, *Hints on National Education in India*, Ubodhan, Calcutta, 1923.

Sobti, Krishna, *Mitro Marjani* (novel, in Hindi), Rajkamal Paperbacks, New Delhi, 1994, (first published 1967).

Srivastava, S., "The Garden of Rational Delights: The Nation as Experiment, Science, as Masculinity", *Social Analysis*, No. 39:119–148, 1996.

——, *Constructing Post-Colonial India: National Character and the Doon School*, Routledge, London, 1998.

——, "Non-Gandhian Sexuality, Commodity Cultures and a 'Happy Married Life' Masculine and Sexual Cultures in the Metropolis" in S. Srivastava (ed.), *Sexual Sites, Seminal Attitudes*, Sage, New Delhi, 2004.

Sunder Rajan, R., *Real and Imagined Women*, Routledge, London, 1993.

Zutshi, S., "Women, Nation and the Outsider in Contemporary Hindi Cinema" in T. Niranjana, P. Sudhir and V. Dhareshwar (eds), *Interrogating Modernity: Culture and Colonialism in India*, Seagull, Calcutta, 1993.

SECTION II

Women's Empowerment: North East India Perspective

6

Women Empowerment through MNREGS:

A North East India Perspective

Elangbam Nixon Singh and *Zonunsanga Zote*

> *"Priority" should be given to women in the allocation of work "in such a way that at least one-third of the beneficiaries shall be women*". [Schedule II, Para 6, NREGA]

Introduction

Empowerment is a multi-acted, multi-dimensional and multi-layered concept. Women's Empowerment is a process in which women gain greater share of control over resources-material, human and intellectual like knowledge, information, ideas and financial resources like money and access to money and control over decision-making in the community, society and nation and to gain 'power'. According to Country Report of Government of India, "Empowerment means moving form a position of unforced powerlessness to one of power". The concept of empowerment is defined as the process by which women take control and ownership of their choices. The core elements of empowerment have been defined as agency (the ability to define one's goals and act upon them), awareness of gendered power structures, self-esteem and self-confidence (Kabeer, 2001). Empowerment can take place at a hierarchy of different levels—individual, household, community and society—and is facilitated by providing encouraging factors (e.g. exposure to new activities, which can build capacities) and removing inhibiting factors (e.g. lack of resources and skills).

The concept of empowerment gained prominence with the feminist movement in the 1980s. There are various views and perceptions on empowerment (Luttrell *et al.*, 2009). To some, it is a process and to others, it is an outcome. Many consider it to be both a process and an outcome. The process approach emphasises organisational capacity building that enhances the access of disadvantaged groups to the process of development, while the outcome approach emphasises increased access to economic resources. To Kabeer, "empowerment refers to the expansion in people's ability to make strategic life choices in a context where this ability was previously denied to them" (2001a: 19). She elaborates three dimensions of empowerment: (1) resources (conditions); (2) agency (process); and (3) achievement (outcomes).

The present study takes a broader view of empowerment and defines it "both as a process and as an outcome that alters the position of women inside and outside their households; with this altered position, women are able to realise better individual and social life".

NREGS as a Source of Women Empowerment

The National Rural Employment Guarantee Act, 2005 (NREGA) is one of the most progressive legislations enacted since independence. Its significance is evident from a variety of perspectives. First, it is a bold and unique experiment in the provision of rural employment—in India and indeed in the world at large. Second, it is the first expression of the right to work as an enforceable legal entitlement. In a country where labour is the only economic asset for millions of people, gainful employment is a prerequisite for the fulfilment of other basic rights—the right to life, the right to food, and the right to education.

There is much that the NREGA promises from the perspective of women's empowerment as well. Most boldly, in a rural milieu marked by stark inequalities between men and women—in the opportunities for gainful employment afforded as well as wage rates—NREGA represents action on both these counts. The Act stipulates that wages will be equal for men and women. It is also committed to ensuring that at least 33 per cent of the workers shall be women. By generating employment for women at fair wages in the village, NREGA can play a substantial role in economically empowering women and laying the basis for greater independence and self-esteem.

Ever since the NREGA which was later renamed as MNREGS (Mahatma Gandhi National Rural Employment Guarantee Scheme) on 2nd October, 2009[1] schemes have been implemented in every locality of rural areas in North East India, women have been able to augment their family incomes. The male folk of the village move to nearby towns in search of jobs, where they can earn between Rs. 120 to Rs. 150 per day on an average. Lack of job opportunities for women in the area has made them remain at home. Be it for an increase in the family income or a crucial tool for living, North East India Region engages a substantial number of women in NREGA projects as compared to other regions in India. In some pockets like Jirania and Dukli blocks in Tripura, participation of women in NREGA works is amazing[2].

NREGS is a highly gender-sensitive scheme. It is mandatory that at least one-third of workers should be women. A North East India states' progress report of the MNREGS activities shows (Table 6.1) that women's participation which is as high as more than 50 per cent. One of the most important observations is the emergence of women's identity and their empowerment with the coming of NREGA as an economic opportunity provider. Except in Arunachal Pradesh and Assam, percentage of women participation in MNREGS was found to be more than 30 per cent. As such, it is self-evident that in all the states women have been found to be very optimistic about the importance of NREGs in their lives. The state of Sikkim stands out distinctively in this regard as 51.24 per cent of NREGS work were undertaken by women folk as compared to that of Manipur (47.98%), Meghalaya (47.20%) etc.

Table 6.1: Participation of Marginalised Groups (FY 2009–2010)

Sl. No.	*States*	*% of SC participation*	*% of ST participation*	*% of women participation*	*Rank of women participation*
1.	A. Pradesh	0.00	97.76	17.20	8
2.	Assam	12.15	31.02	27.70	7
3.	Manipur	27.53	42.85	47.98	2
4.	Meghalaya	0.52	94.09	47.20	3
5.	Mizoram	0.01	99.86	34.99	6
6.	Nagaland	0.00	100.00	43.53	4
7.	Sikkim	9.66	42.55	51.24	1
8.	Tripura	18.03	40.98	41.09	5

Source: *Complied from data available from* www.nrega.nic.in

Review of Literature

The NREGA programme has immense potential to improve the gap between urban and rural India and lead to rural development in terms of basic infrastructure like roads, in terms of agricultural productivity from irrigation works, and it provides a stable income for the workers, their income graph would be much smoother with the NREGA bolstering their earnings in the 100 days between agricultural seasons. The efforts made by the Villupuram authorities, though there still might be some irregularities in the implementation, should be used as a model in other regions to help realize the potential of this Act (Jacob, Naomi: 2008). Even though NREGA was not envisioned as a women's empowerment programme, the opportunity taken by a large number of women indicates a preference for "government work" which provides dignity and higher wages than available in the market. Its implementation in the ongoing phase could be strengthened by provisioning of what is already available in the Act, such as worksite facilities, e.g. work shed and safe drinking water and to some extent child care facilities. Some "gender-neutral measures" such as increase in participation of women in planning and social audits of NREGA implementation, in turn, will create an opportunity for women's role in asset management. These were seen as possible measures with forthcoming provision of 50 per cent reservation of women in Gram Panchayat (IHD-UNIFEM Workshop: 2009).

As successive social audits of the NREGA have revealed, there are standout success stories. In Rajasthan, where public awareness of the programme is high, 77 days of employment per rural household were provided in 2006-07. In Tamil Nadu, the participation of women was as high as 81 per cent. In both States, social audits in different districts have shown that embezzlement of funds, irregularities in the muster rolls, and other types of corruption have declined substantially. In Uttar Pradesh and Jharkhand, the NREGA has created positive changes in the implementation of public works programmes. A recent delegation of the Central Employment Guarantee Council to Sonebhadra district in U.P. found a number of major improvements since the days of the National Food For Work Programme: the scale of employment has increased, minimum wages are being paid, delays in wage payments have been sharply reduced, and the exploitative practices of private contractors are a thing of the past. In some States, notably in Orissa, corruption is very much in evidence but this only reinforces the urgent need to implement the transparency safeguards (*The Hindu*: 2008). Similar assessments have been made of the NREGS by several other observers and activists. Dreze and Khera noted that, where employment under NREGA is provided, "wages are rising, migration is slowing down, productive assets are being created and the power equations are changing too" (*Frontline*: 2009). The implementation of NREGS is gaining momentum and the programme was extended to all rural districts (615) in the country in 2008. Evidence of positive outcomes of the programme is emerging from some districts.

However, challenges remain. To address these challenges, UNDP will continue the MoRD to build on the work that has already been done, by improving awareness and demand for the work including functional literacy of workers; commissioning documentation of NREGS case studies and assessment studies on various aspects of the design and implementation of NREGS; and developing quality material to train communities and officials to better implementation (*UNDP*:2009). The statistics reveal that about 10.62 per cent of the total 3,38,89,122 registered rural households in 2007-08 were provided 100-days of employment (*Business Standard*: 2009). The NREGA was renamed as Mahatma Gandhi National Rural Employment Guarantee Act (MNREGA) after the Father of Nation Mahatma Gandhi and observing the year 2009-10 as the "Year of Gram Sabha" by the Prime Minister, Dr. Manmohan Singh in presence of the UPA Chairperson Sonia Gandhi, Panchayati Raj and Rural Development Minister, Dr. C.P. Joshi and a large number of Gram Pradhans, Sarpanchs and village representatives from all-over the country (*PTI*: 2009).

The economic fabric of rural India is changing with households consciously trying to reduce risk by diversifying their job profiles. Though farming continues to be the main profession, most male members of a typical rural family are taking up non-agricultural jobs while the womenfolk continued to focus on agriculture. The shift will ensure that income in rural households is not choked with a failed monsoon, Pronab Sen, Secretary, Ministry of Statistics and Programme Implementation, told Financial Express. "Job opportunities are no more as scarce as it is used to be, thanks to the National Rural Employment Guarantee Scheme (NREGS)," he said, adding that India being an agrarian society a major shift from agriculture may not be feasible (Venkatesh, Mahua: 2008).

The extension of the NREGA to the whole country is an unprecedented opportunity to build the foundations of a social security system in rural India, revive village economies, promote social equity, and empower rural labour. Ever since its enactment in mid-2005, the National Rural Employment Guarantee Act (NREGA) has been a target of relentless attacks in the corporate-sponsored media. Numerous business columnists most of whom have never seen an NREGA worksite (except perhaps from an airplane), have gone out of their way to rubbish this programme. "Expensive gravy train", "money guzzler", "costly joke" and "wonky idea" are the colourful terms they have used to describe it (Drèze, Jean: 2007).

It is also interesting to note that an 'impact assessment study of the National Rural Employment Generation Scheme (NREGS)' has found that the scheme "provided economic independence to women" in the district. Women were in the forefront of the scheme execution as out of the 11.57 lakh person-days generated, 8.9 lakh went to women. The scheme also enabled many women to come out of social barriers and traditional and religious inhibitions. It provided "equal wage for equal work" to both women and men for the first time in the history of Kerala, the study said. The study commissioned by the Union Ministry of Rural Development and conducted by the Centre for Rural Management (CRM), Kottayam, found that more women got employment under the scheme as men went out for other works as the market wage rates for men were higher (*The Hindu*: 2007).

The Union Finance Minister has allocated a sum of Rs. 39,100 crore in the 2009-10 budget for the NREGS. The importance and success of the flagship scheme could be gauged from the fact that the budgetary allocation for 2009-10 marked a 144 per cent increase over the last fiscal's budget of Rs. 16,000 crore. With this, the government also announced a commitment to provide Rs. 100 a day as a entitlement under NREGA (*India Today*: 2009).

In a contribution to the *International Herald Tribune*, the Chief Economist at the World Bank argued that to overcome poverty 'we must not confine ourselves to following sound economic policies and focusing on measures which are directly oriented to the poor'. The poor have to be empowered by strengthening their participation in local decision-making and 'removing social barriers that result from distinctions of gender, race, ethnicity and social status'.[3]

Nair *et al.* (2009) studied the impact of the National Rural Employment Guarantee Programme in three Grama Panchayats of Kasaragod District of Kerala, namely Madikai, Ajanoor and Trikarpur. While the worker registration is appreciably good in all the three Grama Panchayats including registration of SC and ST categories, however, there is a sharp drop in the number of people who demanded jobs in 2007-08 which was below one-fourth in two Panchayats and just above one-third in the third Panchayat. There was further drop in the number in the following year.

Data show that 71.9 per cent of India's population still resides in rural areas (2002), and given that the majority of India's poor also resides in rural areas, the NREGA can be thought of as a policy to boost rural income, stabilize agricultural production and reduce the population pressure in urban areas through migration (Mukherjee, Diganta *et al.*, 2011).

Dreze and Khera (2009) find that 98 per cent of the sample workers stated that they were ready to work for 100 days in the year--the "upper limit" under the Act. NREGA as of now meets only a fraction of this demand: in their survey only 13 per cent of the respondents had actually secured 100 days of NREGA work in the preceding 12 months.

Since the government has given a direction for account payment of NREGS wages, it is likely to be universalised in other places as well. Account payment of wages also creates some other effects. Apart from increasing the chances for greater control over earnings, it leads to the development of a saving habit. Initially, most of these workers used to withdraw their entire wages at one go. Gradually, they have started withdrawing as per their needs. This has an added advantage as women are able to save money from wasteful expenditure, if husbands or other male members tend to spend on items like liquor. Women were also found to invest in fixed deposit schemes in the same bank. Greater linkage of women with financial institutions may trigger many individual and community-level social and economic effects (Kabeer, 2001b).

Access to finance for those belonging to poor and vulnerable groups is a prerequisite for poverty reduction and social cohesion. This has to become an integral part of our efforts to promote inclusive growth.[4] In fact, providing access to finance is a form of empowerment of the vulnerable groups. Financial inclusion denotes delivery of financial services at an affordable cost to the vast sections of the disadvantaged and low-income groups. The various financial services include credit, savings, insurance and payments and remittance facilities. At present 96 million accounts opened in banks and post offices for Mahatma Gandhi NREGA workers makes this the largest financial inclusion scheme of the rural poor. Wages are disbursed through these accounts. These accounts have also encouraged thrift and saving among some of the poorest families.

Objective of the Article

In the context of North East India, the number of poor is found to be very high in rural areas as compared with that of urban. Majority of the rural people depend on agricultural activities. Many schemes, particularly centrally sponsored, are being formulated and implemented in India. NREGS is also one of such, which is meant to eradicate rural poverty and at present being implemented in full swing in this part of the country.

At the same time, MNREGS has increased the choice set for women by reducing economic dependence on their family members. Further, paid employment under scheme has enhanced both freedom and the choice to use earnings.

Working together gives women an opportunity to share grievances and personal problems, and helps in the development of women solidarity. Women were observed to be exchanging help, for example, borrowing money and battering goods among themselves for which they were earlier dependent on other people.

The objectives of the present paper are as follows:

- To have an overview of MNREGS in North East India,
- To ascertain various problems and prospects of women participation in MNREGS in North East India,
- To offer suggestions for the empowerment of women in North East India through NREGS.

Research Design

The present study is purely based on various secondary data/reports published by each state government of North East India and the Ministry of Rural Development, Government of India, from time to time. Periodicity of the present study is based on the data available from 2006-07 to 2009-10. Personal interviews were conducted with the officials of District Programme Coordinator (DPC) of each of the state. For the present study, only variables viz., women's participation in MNREGS along with their literacy rate and sex ratio, wage rate, asset creation and employment generated are taken for the present women empowerment analysis.

Findings of the Study

(a) Female Literacy and their Participation Rates in MNREGA

From the available data, an effort is made here to analyse the female literacy and their participation in MNREGS activities in all the eight (8) states of the North East India (Table 6.2). As can be seen, the female literacy rate was found to be the highest in the state of Mizoram (86%) as compared to other states of the region. The minimum is in Arunachal Pradesh (44%). Quite interestingly, Arunachal Pradesh which had the least female literacy rate had also the least women participation rate in MNREGS, both in 2008-09 (26%) and 2009-10 (17%), decreasing at the rate of 9 per cent. In case of Mizoram, it also had a decreasing women participation rate of 2 per cent from 2008-09 (37%) to 2009-10 (35%) in MNREGS jobs. The maximum rate of decrease in women participation was found in the state of Tripura (10%). On the other hand, Nagaland is found to be state from amongst the states of North East India where the women's participation in MNREGS had the highest rate of increase (7%) for the period under analysis.

Table 6.2: Female Literacy and their Participation Rates in MNREGA

Sl. No.	*States*	*Female Sex Ratio*	*Female Literacy Ratio*	*Women Participation Rate in*		*Increase/ Decrease in Women Participation*
				2008-09	*2009-10*	
1.	Arunachal Pradesh	91	44	26	17	(–) 9
2.	Assam	94	56	27	28	(+) 1
3.	Meghalaya	97	60	41	47	(+) 6
4.	Mizoram	92	86	37	35	(–) 2
5.	Manipur	97	60	46	48	(+) 2
6.	Nagaland	92	62	37	44	(+) 7
7.	Sikkim	88	61	38	51	(+) 3
8.	Tripura	95	65	51	41	(–) 10

Source: Compiled from data available from www.nrega.nic.in

(b) Wage Rate

Another variable taken for analysis here is the wage rate prevailing for agricultural labourers in these North Eastern states. Two periods i.e., pre-MGNREGA and post-MGNREGA is considered for the present analysis. As can be seen from Table 6.3, with the implementation of MNREGS, the wage rates for agricultural labourers in these states are found to be almost doubled. This can be verified from the fact that the wage rate prior to MNREGA was only Rs. 62 in Assam which was revised and increased to Rs. 130 after the implementation of MNREGA. It was only Rs. 79.6 as on 1st December, 2008. It is also the same in case of Tripura, Manipur, Nagaland etc. As we all know how the increase in wage rates for agricultural labourers in these states can affect other parameters of life, we can conclude that MNREGA has actually improved the socio-economic conditions of the rural people of these states which also includes the empowerment of its women-folk.

(c) Performance of the MGNREGA

The overall performance of MNREGS for the country as a whole is shown in Table 6.4. As can be seen, there has been an increasing trend, not only in the total number of job cards issued so far but also in the number of districts covered under MNREGS. As regards to the number of districts

Table 6.3: Wage Rate (from Pre-MGNREGA to Post-MGNREGA)

Sl. No.	*States*	*Minimum Wages for Agricultural Labourers*		
		(2005–06) Pre–MGNREGA	*as on 1st Dec, 2008*	*Under Section 6.1 for MGNREGA*
1.	Arunachal Pradesh	55–57	65–67	118
2.	Assam	62	79.6	130
3.	Meghalaya	70	70	117
4.	Mizoram	91	91	129
5.	Manipur	66	81.4	126
6.	Nagaland	66	100	118
7.	Sikkim	85	100	118
8.	Tripura	60	85	118

Source: *Compiled from data available from* www.nrega.nic.in

Table 6.4: Performance of the MGNREGS (National Overview)

	(FY 2006-07) 200 Districts	*(FY 2007-08) 330 Districts*	*(FY 2008-09) 600 Districts*	*(FY 2009-10) 619 Districts (Up to March, 2010)*
Total Job Cards issued	3.78 crores	6.48 crores	10.1 crores	11.25 crores
Employment provided to households	2.10 crores	3.39 crores	4.51 crores	5.26 crores
Person days [in crores]:				
Total:	90.5	143.59	216.32	283.59
SCs:	22.95 [25%]	39.36 [27%]	63.36 [29%]	86.45 [30%]
STs:	32.98 [36%]	42.07[29%]	55.02 [25%]	58.74 [21%]
Women:	36.40 [40%]	61.15 [43%]	103.57 [48%]	136.40 [48%]
Others:	34.56 [38%]	62.16 [43%]	97.95 [45%]	138.40 [49%]
Person days Per HH	43 days	42 days	48 days	54 days
Budget Outlays (in Rupees crores)	11,300	12,000	30,000	39,100

Source: *Compiled from data available from* www.nrega.nic.in

covered by the scheme, it was only 200 in the FY 2006–07 whereas it has increased to 619 districts in the FY 2009-10 (up to March 2010). It is an interesting and equally important task being achieved. At the same time, job cards issued till March 2010 had already reached 11.25 crores as against 3.78 crores only in the FY 2006-07.

Further, employment under the Act had been given to 5.26 crore rural households up to March 2010. Persondays in crores was found to be 283.59 as compared to only 90.5 in the FY 2006-07. Out of which, women's share in the persondays is 48 per cent (FY 2009-10) as compared to only 40 per cent in the FY 2006-07.

Another interesting point to be found is that persondays per household has also been increased from 43 days in the FY 2006-07 to 54 days in FY 2009-10. And accordingly the budget outlays had also been increased.

Difficulties and Obstacles for Women Workers

- The MGNREGS is yet to yield desired results. Not only the scheme could not provide employment to all the eligible people, in many cases the labourer did not get the stipulated rate of wages too. According to survey in 2006-07, only 6 per cent of households registered in the scheme in the country got 100 days of employment (Singh, Rajmani: 2008).
- NREGS benefits for women have not come easily—working hours for women have increased; their leisure time has vanished; and they have to bear with physical and emotional strains. Even during the official lunch break, some of them return home to take care of the children and other family members. Wage payment is linked to a task-based SOR, and since the SOR is prepared based on the average output of a healthy, invariably male worker, women have to work very hard to earn minimum wages. This is much more difficult for old, physically weak, and lactating women.
- In the absence of (proper) crèche facilities, lactating women and women with young children leave their children at home while working at the worksite. Only 28 per cent of the women with children under the age of five brought them to the worksite; 62 per cent left their children in the care of siblings/elders; and another 10 per cent of women left their children without proper care. Since, they have to remain away from home for a minimum of eight hours at the NREGS worksite, they remain anxious about the well-being of their children. Eighty-one per cent confessed that they remain emotionally strained while they are working at the worksite and their children are left at home, either unattended

or in another's care. There are also some reports of the continued presence of contractors and harassment of women workers. Khera and Nayak in their 2009 study found that at worksites where contractors were present, 35 per cent of women reported various types of harassment. Also, worksite facilities were negligible on these worksites (Khera and Nayak, 2009: 54).

Pitfalls of MNREGS in North East India

Lack of Social Audit

Till date, there is no social audit in the works so far done under the scheme. Even though it is mandatory under the MNREGA, no ombudsman has been appointed by many of the state governments of this region. Of course, the process has been recently taken up for its appointment in October, this year. The success and effectiveness of MNREGS largely depends on voluntary and compulsory social audit, which seems to be lacking in many of the states concerned.

Insurgency

It is also another burning problem in many of the states of North East India. Not a single day passed off without shootouts, kidnappings, bomb blasts in state like Manipur. The recent killing of Dr. Kishan Singh, SDO of Ukhrul district of Manipur[5] was also one way or another related to MNREGS. Extortions or percentage cuts from government funds meant for developmental works by unlawful outfits is prevalent in many cases.

Delay in Release of Funds

After personal interviews with officials of DPC, it has come to light that funds released by centre for MNREGS in these states is, many a times, late. And it is quite obvious that the state share is also late correspondingly, resulting into delays in payment of wages to job-card holders working under MNREGS. At present, there is a deficit of Rs. 31 crores from the central share for the running financial year (DPC, Imphal West district).

Shortage of Staff, Over-burdening and Multiplicity of Programmes

All the staffs being employed for the implementation of MNREGS in these states are deputed or contracted from DRDA or RD, government of the respective states. At any moment of time, they are so engaged in other rural development schemes that there is always a problem of staff shortage for MNREGS. Due to multiplicity of programmes, they are over-burdened and sometimes it leads to problems in proper implementation of MNREGS in the state thereby leading to misunderstanding between job-card holders and DPC officials in many cases.

Delay in Wage Payment

Payment of wages for MNREGS is always a problem in these states. Underpayment or non-payment is so common. Just recently, for instance, the Sub-Divisional Officer (SDO) of Saikul Sub-Division in Senapati district of Manipur has allegedly stalled payment of due wages to the job holders under Mahatma Gandhi National Rural Employment Guarantee Scheme (MNREGS) in the sub-division on the insistence that each of them should first join the Micro Insurance Policy of LIC.

Lack of Bank Accounts for Several Households

It has also come to light after the study that many a registered households under the scheme are lacking bank accounts leading to chances of manipulation or underpayment of wages of job-card holders. Being rural areas, lack of enough bank branches is also another reason for not opening necessary accounts. The advantage of receiving wages in accounts is missing in such a case.

Too Many Records to Maintain

It is another problem confronting officials dealing with MNREGS. They have to maintain many a records. Sometimes, it leads to overburdening of works which was already so due to shortage of staffs.

Lack of Co-ordination and Control on Works Carried Out by Line Departments

Proper implementation of MNREGS is possible only with the cooperation of other line departments of the state like electricity, water supply, public health, family welfare, flood control, etc. This cooperation is very much missing in these states. Proper coordination is lacking which may otherwise be required at the most.

Rampant Corruption Issues

Many instances of corruption/wastage etc. have been identified in so many field studies. However, these tend to be disproportionately blown up by media and critics of the programme, especially in the context of much more extensive corruption in other government activities (such as infrastructure) and in society generally. CAG report identified lack of capacity as main implementation concern, rather than corruption. MNREGA contains many safeguards in terms of transparency and accountability; however, these are likely to be resisted by elites at different levels and must be continuously fought for through local mobilisation. Therefore, while corruption is an important concern, it cannot be seen as a reason to condemn the programme, but rather to make it work better. Inadequate preparedness of local authorities and Panchayats should also be given due consideration for its timely correction.

Conclusion and Suggestions

Empowerment of women has emerged as unintended consequences of MNREGS. Women have benefited more as workers than as a community. Women as individuals have gained because of their ability to earn independently, made possible due to the paid employment opportunity under MNREGS. Independent and monetized earnings have increased consumption choices and reduced economic dependence. This has helped women in registering their tangible contribution to the household's income. The overall effects of these have translated into an increased say for women in household affairs.

A minimum representation of women among the MNREGS functionaries like programme officers, members of vigilance and monitoring committees, etc. would be useful.

The MNREGA can never meet its objectives without the active participation of people in its implementation. And it is here, that the Right to Information Act, 2005 is an indispensable tool in the hands of the poor—to fight leakages, claim entitlements and make the MNREGA meaningful for themselves. The gap between progressive laws and their implementation lays some possibilities of containing the fear, genuine or otherwise, of the MNREGA becoming a victim of systematic corruption, thereby defeating the very purpose for which it was implemented.

The MNREGA can become a major instrument for galvanising Panchayati Raj Institution in India. But how far this actually happens will depend a great deal on the mobilisation of disadvantaged groups like women, SCs, STs and the poor. Without their mobilization and empowerment, the full socio-political potential of the Act will not be realized.

The following suggestions may be given due consideration for inclusion of more number of women in MNREGS so that it can empower them in the long run:

- As far as possible, women should be kept in the forefront for planning, implementing and evaluation of the programme.
- Apart from manual work, MNREGS should also include soft skilled as well as semi-skilled jobs. By such inclusion, the services of women could be utilised in social service and rural health schemes.
- Women who are employed in various skilled and semi-skilled ventures possess good technical skills but they require financial help to support their activities. For success of the programme, it is important that local resources are utilised to the fullest and capacity of local communities and institutions are built. Government should conduct a National survey to identify the entrepreneurs, tiny and micro enterprises, to provide financial assistance through MNREGA. This will call for involvement of various other Ministries like HRD, Commerce and Industry.
- Besides one person from one family, a special provision should be made for individual entitlements in case of widows, persons with disabilities, single and deserted women in each household, so that it becomes compulsory for the authority to include them in the list of employment. Measures ought to be taken to ensure women's participation so they are not pushed disproportionately out of the scheme. The Gram Panchayat or village council can regularly update the list of beneficiaries in the villages by conducting routine surveys in their area.
- Grass roots organizations of the poor should be involved in the process of implementation. This will include anganwadi workers, health workers, village development committees; self-help groups, cooperatives and mandals etc. Capacity of such individuals, groups and institutions should be built by providing training so that they learn the administrative procedures to avail various schemes including MNREGS.
- Empowerment of workers and their holistic development depends, in terms of their strategies to a great extent on the linkages of MNREGA and other development programmes. Linkages with social welfare programmes such as rural health mission, literacy programme and anganwadi scheme is needed to ensure basic human entitlements to the workers that, in turn will enhance their capacity to negotiate their right under the act.[6]
- It is essential to provide mobile health care facilities and Sarva Shiksha Abhiyan classes to the workers so that the educational

and health needs of the children, women and others can be met on the worksites. Mobile crèches for infants and growing children should be provided. Since the anganwadi services are available in every village their working time can be extended for the period of time till the work is in progress on NREGS' worksite. In such situation additional salary or stipend to anganwadi workers and helpers can be adjusted from the budget provided for NREGS. Since women and particularly poor women are malnourished and weak, it is necessary to allow them to work on less strenuous activities. Food for work scheme or anganwadi services can be introduced in such situations at the worksite.

- Special facilities for disabled women and men such as, accessible toilets and barrier free environment should be ensured. Based on the various provisions made by The Disability Act, 1995, work to the disabled persons should be provided near their residence. Appropriate transport facilities should be provided to them. Each person with disability should be considered as a separate household regardless of whether he/she has family or not. Their wages should be time based and not work based. Social audit, vigilance committee, State and Central data should include the information about the person with disability.
- It is important to seek women's participation in the social audit of MNREGS to make it more effective. Monitoring should be an integral part of the scheme. Mahila mandals, self-help groups, and anganwadi workers could play an important role in making it successful by reaching out to women in the community. Safety of women workers on worksite is must. The Gram Panchayats can arrange a place for their night stay in nearby villages.

NOTES

1. http://www.ptinews.com/news/310479_Union-cabinet-gives-NREGA-the-Mahatma-Gandhi-tag
2. Roy, Sanjoy (2010), 'Implementation of NREGS in Tripura: An Evaluation', *The NEHU Journal,* Vol. VIII, No. 1, January, p. 64.
3. Nicholas Stern, 'Opportunity, empowerment and security—the key to attacking poverty', www.worldbank.org/knowledge/chiefecon
4. Report of the Committee on Financial Inclusion, Reserve Bank of India, 2008.

5. Singh, Nixon (2009), 'NREGS as Tool for Rural Empowerment: A Case Study of Manipur", Paper presented at the National Seminar on "Rural Empowerment in North East India" held at Tura, Meghalaya, 26-27 November.
6. Panot, Anita (2009), 'Inclusion of Women in NREGA: The Challenges Ahead', *Catalyst*, Vol. VII, Issue 2, Newsletter of Cyriac Elias Voluntary Association (CEVA), Kochi.

REFERENCES

Business Standard, November 23, 2009: "Few people get 100 day employment under NREGA".

Dreze Jean and Khera, Reetika, 2009, "The battle for employment guarantee", *Frontline*, 26 (01), Jan. 03–16. *Frontline*, January 16, 2009.

Drèze, Jean (2007): "Employment Guarantee: Beyond Propaganda", *The Hindu*, December 11.

India Today, 23rd November, 2009.

Jacob, Naomi (2008): "The Impact of NREGA on Rural-Urban Migration: Field Survey of Villupuram District, Tamil Nadu", *CCS Working Paper No. 202*, Summer Research Internship Programme, Centre for Civil Society.

Kabeer, Naila (2001a): "Reflections on the Measurement of Women's Empowerment" in *Discussing Women's Empowerment: Theory and Practice*, Sida Studies 3, Stockholm.

——, (2001b): "Conflict Over Credit: Re-evaluating the Empowerment Potential of Loans to Women in Rural Bangladesh", *World Development*, 29 (1): 63–84.

Khera, Reetika and Nandini Nayak (2009): "Women Workers and Perceptions of the National Rural Employment Guarantee Act", *Economic and Political Weekly*, 44(43): 49–57.

Luttrell, Cecilia, Sitna Quiroz, with Claire Scrutton and Kate Bird (2009): "Understanding and Operationalising Empowerment", *Working Paper 308*, Overseas Development Institute, London.

Mukherjee, Diganta and Uday Bhanu Sinha (2011), "Understanding NREGA: A Simple Theory and Some Facts", Centre for Development Economics, Department of Economics, Delhi School of Economics, *Working Paper No. 196*.

Nair, K.N., T.P. Sreedharan and M. Anoopkumar, 2009, "A Study of National Rural Employment Guarantee Programme in Three Grama Panchayats of Kasaragod District", *Working Paper 413*, Centre for Development Studies, Trivandrum, India.

Press Trust of India, 2nd October, 2009.

Singh, Rajmani (2008): "Centrally Sponsored Schemes for Upliftment of Rural Economy of North East India: An Analysis", Ray, A.K. *et al.* (Ed.) "Society

Politics and Development in North East India", Concept Publishing Co., New Delhi, pp. 316–328.

Summing up Points of the Institute for Human Development–UNIFEM Workshop "Engendering NREGA: Women's Empowerment through Guaranteed Employment", 31st August, 2009, at India International Centre, New Delhi.

The Hindu (January 23, 2008).

The Hindu, September 29, 2007: "NREGS Helps to Empower Women".

UNDP, March 2009.

Venkatesh, Mahua (2008): "Rural India learns to cut job risk", *The Financial Express*, 31, January.

7

Women in Panchayat

A Tripura Perspective

Chandrika Basu Majumder

> "*As long as women of India do not take part in public life there can be no salvation for the country*". –Mahatma Gandhi

Changing Role of Panchayats in the New Millennium

Panchayats have been institutions of village administration since times immemorial. Article 40 of the Constitution also left the issue of reservation for women to state legislatures. During late 1950s, the Central Council of Local Government, 1957 argued for co-opting two women who are interested in work among women and children as members of panchayats. The report of the Balvant Ray Mehta study team also endorsed this. In 1978, the Ashoka Mehta Committee reviewed the Panchayati Raj System and recommended that if no women were elected on their own, two women who get the highest number of votes in Zilla Parishad (ZP) elections should become members and if no women came forward they might be enabled through co-option. The Committee on the Status of Women in India (CSWI), 1971, in view of the ineffectiveness of token representation of women in panchayats, recommended constituting separate women's statutory panchayats at the village level. But the idea could not be fructified as none of the states were in favour. The interesting turning point on the debate took place when the Government of Andhra Pradesh in 1979 recommended 5 per cent reservation for women for the post of Sarpanchs in each block for women where the percentage of women electors is comparatively higher.

The major breakthrough took place in 1988 after the emergence of the National Perspective Plan for Women (NPPW) which recommended:

Reservation should be made of 30 per cent seats at Panchayat to Zilla Parishad level and local municipal bodies for women. Wherever possible, higher representation of dalits, *tribals*, women of weaker sections should be ensured. 30 per cent of executive heads of all bodies from village Panchayat to district level and a certain percentage of chief executives of Panchayati Raj bodies at lower, middle and higher levels must be reserved for women. A more effective step would be to declare a certain percentage of constituencies in the lower tier of Panchayati Raj as exclusively women constituencies and all executive positions in certain number of territorial jurisdictions reserved for women candidates. (National Perspective Plan, 1988: 164-65). [1]

This was probably the basis for giving positive discrimination for women in Panchayats by legislating the 73rd Amendment Act. The Constitution (73rd Amendment) Act, 1993 might be regarded as heralding a new beginning in the life of the Panchayati Raj. The Act inserts Part IX into the Constitution, entitled 'The Panchayats' and gives constitutional sanction and structural legitimacy to the Panchayats for the first time. Every state shall have a three-tier structure with elected Panchayat bodies at the village and district levels and at the Block level. The Act was considered a gigantic step towards empowerment of women and ensured women's representation in PRI. An important feature of the 73rd Amendment Act is that to guarantee financial autonomy of the Panchayats it provides that every five years the State Government shall constitute a Finance Commission to review financial position of the Panchayats and make appropriate recommendations to the Governor. However, the success of the Panchayat Raj depends not simply on structural change but on the rising democratic consciousness of the rural masses to use Panchayats as instruments of social change and social justice.

The provision for participation of women was further strengthened by another significant decision. On 4th June, 2009, the President in her speech in the joint session of Parliament wished to have more seats reserved for women in the Panchayats to lessen gender deprivation. Accordingly, on 27th August, 2009, the Indian Cabinet approved a proposal for enhancing the reservation of directly elected seats for women from one-third to fifty per cent in all the three tiers through an amendment of Article 243(D) (3) of the Constitution. The proposed amendment seeks to provide for reservation of seats for women 'not less than half'.

Tripura went a step further. It not only amended its Panchayat Act of 1993 to this effect but also brought its urban local bodies within the ambit through Tripura Municipal (Fourth Amendment) Bill.

Tripura at a Glance

Tripura, one of the North-Eastern States of India, is surrounded by Bangladesh on the north, west, and south. On the east it is bounded by Mizoram and on the north-east by Assam, both states of India. Tripura was an independent Hindu kingdom for more than 1,300 years before it acceded to India on 15th October, 1949 and was designated a Union Territory in 1956. It acquired full status as a state on 21st January 1972. The population of Tripura as per 2011, stood at 36,71,032 comprising 18,71,867 male and 17,99,165 female.

Head	2001 Tripura	2001 India	2011Tripura	2011India
Sex ratio	946	933	961	940
Literacy Rate	73.2	65.38	87.8	74
Female Literacy			83.2	65.46

Source: Tripura at a glance, 2010-11, Directorate of Economics and Statistics, Government of Tripura.[2]

Action Plan for the Empowerment of Women

The principle of gender equality is enshrined in the Indian Constitution in its preamble, Fundamental Rights, Fundamental Duties and Directive Principles. There still exist a wide gap between the goals enunciated in the Constitution, legislation, policies, plans, programmes and related mechanisms on the one hand, and the situational reality of the status of women in India on the other. The Government of Tripura has taken an Action Plan in 2003 for empowerment of women. The goal of this Action Plan is to bring about further advancement, development and empowerment of women. The objectives of this policy include:

Creating an environment through positive economic and social policies for development of women to enable them to realize their full potential and to ensure equal rights and opportunity to women in social, economic and political life of a nation. Access to participation and decision making of women in social, political and economic life of the nation.[3]

Evolution of Panchayati Raj in Tripura

During the long princely period also the North East Frontier had indigenous institution of local self-government at the grass roots level. During the rule of Maharaja also each Tripuri village was self-governing. Prior to the introduction of statutory panchayat in 1962, there were informal panchayats in hills and plains in Tripura. The King ruled in the Capital and the Village

Chief in every village and the Maharajas of Tripura hardly intervened in the local self-administration of the village. While describing the social organization of the Tribes of Tripura Prof. N. Ranjan Roy Chowdhury observed: The tribal society was dominated by the chiefs. Each tribe had its own chief under whom there were others with status in descending order down to the choudhuri for each village. In the village, the authority of the chief was absolute. For any decision of social, economic and political nature they had to depend upon the advice and decision of their chiefs. Village disputes, which were rare, were settled in community trials where the chief of the village presided. The general punishment was the imposition of fine and the money realized from it were spent in community feast and functions. The Chiefs by dint of their specially privileged position made various exactions from the ordinary tribals... [4] After the merger of Tripura with the Indian Union in 1959, the task of forming Gram Panchayat started in Tripura keeping in mind the guidelines of the U.P. Panchayat Act, 1947. In 1961, the Code of Conduct of the Panchayat Act was framed. But until 1978, no step was taken to hold election to the Panchayats on the basis of secret ballot. Following the 73rd Amendment to the Constitution of India in 1992 a new Act "The Tripura Panchayats Act, 1993'was enacted in the State. The Act aimed at reorganizing Panchayats in the rural areas of Tripura in conformity with the purpose, substance and directions of the amended provisions of the Constitution.

The main characteristics of 'The Tripura Panchayat Act', 1993 are as follows:

1. Gram Panchayats will be the foundation of democratic decentralized administration at grass roots level.
2. The three-tier Panchayat system will establish a coordinating link between the villages, block and district level.
3. The Act provides for reservation of seats for Scheduled Castes and Scheduled Tribes in proportion to their population in respective level.
4. The Act also makes provisions for reservation of seats of not less than one-third of total seats for women.
5. In order to ensure rural empowerment, 29 matters relating to development were transferred in the hands of the Panchayats.[5]
6. As per "The Tripura Panchayat Act,1993', three tier Panchayat elections were held four times i.e., in 1994,1999, 2004 and 2009. In all these four elections of Panchayati Raj Institutions, the members were elected directly by the adults who were 18 years old and the reservation of women as per the Act was fully ensured.

Elected Members in 3-tier Panchayats during Panchayat Elections, 1994, in Tripura

1.	Total No. of Elected Members of Gram Panchayat	5427
2.	Total No. of Elected Women Member of Gram Panchayat	1809 (33.24%)
3.	Total No. of Elected Members of Panchayat Samiti	196
4.	Total No. of Elected Women Members of Panchayat Samiti	67 (34.18%)
5.	Total Number of Elected Members of Zilla Parishad	70

Elected Members in 3-tier Panchayats during Panchayat Election, 1999 in Tripura

1.	Total Number of Elected Members of Gram Panchayat	5685
2.	Total Number of Elected Women Members of Gram Panchayat	1895 (33.33%)
3.	Total Number of Elected Members of Panchayat Samiti	299
4.	Total Number of Elected Women Members of Panchayat Samiti	106 (35.45%)
5.	Total Number of Elected Members of Zilla Parishad	82
6.	Total Number of Elected Women Members of Zilla Parishad	28 (34.14%)

Elected Members in 3-tier Panchayats during Panchayat Election, 2004 in Tripura

1.	Total Number of Elected Members of Gram Panchayat	5352
2.	Total Number of Elected Women Members of Gram Panchayat	1785 (33.35%)
3.	Total Number of Elected Members of Panchayat Samiti	29

4.	Total No of Elected Women Members of Panchayat Samiti	106 (35.45%)
5.	Total Number of Elected Members of Zilla Parishad	82
6.	Total Number of Elected Women Members of Zilla Parishad	28 (34.15%)

Elected Members in 3-tier Panchayats during Panchayat Election, 2009 in Tripura

1.	Zilla Parishads	4
2.	Elected Members of Zilla Parishads	82
3.	Women Elected Members of Zilla Parishads	28 (34%)
4.	Panchayat Samitis	23
5.	Elected Members of Panchayat Samitis	299
6.	Women Elected Members of Panchayat Samitis	107 (35%)
7.	Grams (Outside–ADC)	511
8.	Elected Members of Gram Panchayat	5,295
9.	Women Elected Members of Gram Panchayat	1,909 (36%)
10.	Gram Panchayat run by Women	01

Source: Tripura at a glance, 2010-11, Directorate of Economics and Statistics, Government of Tripura.

It has been observed that the power structure in the rural areas of Tripura has a mix of all castes, communities and class. Gender disparity has been reduced with the participation of women being more than the requisite numbers provided by the constitutional means. While studying occupational pattern of the Panchayat members it has been observed by the scholar that out of 38 Gram Panchayat leaders, 30 members belong to farmer and worker class, which indicates that micro level Gram Panchayat leadership is often in the hands of peasants and working classes. On the other hand, in regards to Panchayat Samitis, the main leadership goes to the hands of middle class. The leadership in Zilla Parishad comes from heterogeneous occupation and a sizeable portion is whole-time party workers getting some honorarium from the respective party and interestingly all whole-time party workers belong to the CPI(M).[6] While sharing the working experience of some Panchayat Officers as well as Chairperson of Panchayat Samiti who are working in the field years together, the author has been informed that although there are many obstacles in the field of participation by women, gradually they are playing an active and positive role in local administration. The following observations were made:

- Despite several stumbling blocks women PRI members have generally performed well throughout the State.
- In maximum cases women members of Panchayats are over-burdened with domestic and household responsibilities.
- No doubt, some exception is there where members get full family support to do her task but this is not the general picture.
- Various training programmes are being pertained by the Block Authorities for proper performance of the functionaries but it has been noticed that women member lack interest as well as capabilities to deal with the complex issues.
- The system of positive distribution and affirmative action work best when they are accompanied by capacity building and training programme.
- Communication problem hinders performance as most of the correspondences, rules and regulation of various schemes and projects are framed in English.
- A supportive family, preferably one with a political background has been found congenial for the political empowerment of women at the grass roots level.
- Women are less mobile and dynamic than men are and domestic responsibilities puts limits on the time they can spend in such processes. There are historical as well as sociological prejudices. Consistent efforts will have to be made over a period of time to engender the political process and institutions.
- Another significant development has been noticed in relation to the formation of Self-Help Groups for economic upliftment of marginalized section which increases a sense of self-confidence among its members. Still there is room for improvement as SHGs are being breaking down in the middle way because of lack of co-ordination and absence of proper leadership.

Recommendations

A study of the issues related to the participation of women in Panchayati Raj Institution in Tripura it has been revealed that after the implementation of 73rd Amendment at least one-third reservation for women has been ensured in Tripura. Now, a cabinet decision has been taken to increase the reservation of women in local self-government up to fifty per cent.

- While giving nomination to a women candidate, the party should take into account the physical as well as domestic background of the nominee and this is a pre-condition of proper functioning of the responsibilities of the member.(e.g. a pregnant women or mother of a new born baby should not be entrusted with serious responsibilities).
- Education plays a vital role and the women candidate is likely to have educational qualification and good experiences as well as leadership qualities so that they can perform their assigned responsibilities in a proper way.
- As there is communication problem correspondence may be done in their known language.
- There should be increased emphasis on ensuring the participation of women in the meetings of Panchayats at all levels. 'This is needed' as has been observed by Dr. Paridha, 'to promote and enhance their leadership qualities and self-confidence. It will help them to perform better in the Panchayats to ensure their participation in the meetings. Attendance of all women must be made compulsory from Gram Panchayat to Zilla Parishad'.[7]
- For sustainable economic and social development to take place in the country, it is necessary that women should participate in the political process but at the same time they should be properly empowered economically. The honorarium of the Pradhan should be increased immediately and T.A. & D.A. should be given to make the entire process effective and fruitful.
- Satisfactory devolution of powers and functions to Panchayats are the most significant challenges that lie ahead for PRIs. To Mr. Aureliano Fernandes, 'poor finances, poor support to Panchayats in terms of public participation at the Gram Sabha, and administrative shortcomings coupled with epistemic and operational constraints are the three most important challenges faced by Panchayat'. The observation seems to be applicable to Tripura also.
- Since motherhood is still considered as the main role of women, women need the following conducive conditions in order to participate effectively in the public realm:
  (a) a supportive family preferably one with a political background,

(b) someone from within the extended family willing to take-over a large part of the family responsibilities, specially caring and raring of the children,
(c) economic stability of the family,
(d) healthy political environment in the working place.

To conclude, more women have come in Tripura as leaders in panchayats than mandated in the Constitution and they have been instrumental in creating ripples in the existing system of governance which was dominated by their counterparts. The effective participation of women can be ensured through capacity building process and taking up action-oriented training programmes and guaranteeing adequate representation to women in local administration. 'Moreover as we have a federal system' as has been observed by George Mathew, 'the governments and political parties must show the political will to give power to the people at the centre and state levels.'[9]

NOTES

1. National Perspective Plan, 1988, 164-65.
2. *Government of Tripura (2010-11): Tripura at a Glance*, Directorate of Economics & Statistics, Agartala.
3. *Government of Tripura* (2003): *Action Plan for the Empowerment of Women*, Social Welfare and Social Education Department, Agartala.
4. *Tripura through the Ages*, Nalini Ranjan Roy Choudhury, Sterling Publishers Private Limited, New Delhi, 1983.
5. The Tripura Panchayats Act, 1993.
6. Unpublishid thesis entitled "Grass Roots Democracy and Panchayati Raj in Tripura" by Nityananda Das, submitted to Tripura University, December 2007.
7. *Women and Panchayati Raj—A Study* by Dr. Dayanidhi Parida, *Orissa Review*, February, March-2010.
8. *Changing Role of Panchayats in the New Millennium*, Aureliano Fernandes, Kurukshetra, November, 2001.
9. *Needed a New Deal for Panchayati Raj*, George Mathew, *Yojana*, A Development Monthly, February, 2011.

8
Status of Women Empowerment and Health:
An Analytical Study of Tripura

Sanjay Sinha and *Sumanash Datta*

Introduction

Women are at the centre stage of all programmes that aim at improving maternal and child health. The successful achievements of other desired demographic goals also depend on the role that women play in the society and in child-bearing and rearing. An understanding of the status and empowerment of women in society and within their households is thus critical for promoting change in reproductive attitudes and behaviour, especially in patriarchal societies (Dyson and Moore, 1983; Jejeebhoy, 1995; Jeffery and Basu, 1996; Kabeer, 2001). The National Population Policy 2000, specifically identified the low status of women in India as an important barrier to the achievement of population and maternal and child welfare goals (Ministry of Health and Family Welfare, 2000).

Results of several studies have shown that for a long time, women's health has been viewed within a narrow perspective of their child-bearing and reproductive role. The studies done so far on women's health have a tendency to equate women's health with maternal health (Begum, 1986; Khan, 1988; Chen *et al.*, 1974; Chaudhury, 1984; BARC, 1990; GOB, 1975, 1980, 1985, 1990). But, the issue of women's health takes on a new dimension following the phenomenal increase in recent years of women's participation in the labour force.

Women's empowerment and health are now the issues that are viewed from a much broader perspective. The decades of the 1980s and the 1990s have been characterised by a variety of pressures on the Government of India and State Governments, especially from international bodies and from groups within for affirmative action in favour of women. The Millennium Development Goals (2000) specially targeted elimination of gender discrimination, reducing child mortality and improving maternal health substantially within a time-frame of latest by 2015. A concerted effort is now noticeable in incorporating gender issues in policy planning. One of the primary objectives of the Ninth Five-Year Plan (1997–2002) is also to create an enabling environment 'where women can freely exercise their rights both within and outside home as equal partners along with men. The Ninth Plan document further states that this will be realised through early finalisation and adoption of the 'National Policy for Empowerment of Women'.

In all societies economic policies, such as those that enslave women in low-wage jobs under dangerous conditions, and development strategies, like those that take land out of subsistence farming and put it into cash crops, have a profound effect on the health status of women and their families. Mothers, many of whom are single head of households, are burdened not only with economic problems but also with the consequences of civil conflict and environmental degradation. They are often ignored by male-dominated health and social services delivery systems or denied equal access to services. Even within the family disparities exist because of social and cultural bias. For example, preference for the son can lead to the daughters being given less food. The girl child is also expected to do more work and has less access to education and medical care than the boy. Consequently, girls are often ill-prepared to marry and bear children, which they do before they are physically, psychologically and financially equipped to take on the responsibility. Often premature marriage generates a vicious cycle of malnutrition, where underweight mothers have underweight babies who are at risk of suffering from nutritional and educational deprivations. The problems facing women and girl children are, then, to be tackled at all levels: in the family, in the community, and in society at large. The problem of empowering women and improving their health has social, cultural and economic dimensions. The present paper, however, attempts to portray the status of women empowerment and health in Tripura from a much narrower perspective in view of limitations such as availability of adequate data, printed materials etc.

State Profile

The State of Tripura has an area of 10,491.69 sq km having 856 kms of international border with Bangladesh, 109 kms long border with

Mizoram and 53 kms border with Assam. Around two-third of the State of Tripura is hilly with six major hills running in the North-South direction. The hilly terrain makes a large area of the State difficult to access and this has implications on the accessibility of the people to formal health care.

Demography

Tripura is the second most populous state in North-East India, after Assam. According to the Census, 2011, Tripura has a total population of 3,671,032 with 1,871,867 males and 1,77,165 females, the sex ratio of the state is 961 females per thousand males. The density of population is 350 persons per km. Tripura constitutes only 0.3 per cent of India's total population. In the 2001 Census of India, Bengalis represent almost 70 per cent of Tripura's population and the native tribal populations represent the rest 30 per cent. The tribal population comprises of several different tribes and ethnic groups with diverse languages and cultures, the largest tribal group being the Kokborok-speaking tribe, the Tripuri (They alone constitute 16 per cent of the state population). Tripura ranks 22nd in the human resource development index and 24th in the poverty index in India according to 1991 data sources. The literacy rate of Tripura in 2011 was 87.75 per cent which is higher than the national average of 74.04 per cent.

Status of Women's Empowerment

"Status of Women Empowerment" refers to both the aspects accorded to individuals and the personal power available to them (Mason, 1993). While women value prestige, it is the level of personal autonomy that appears to influence demographic behaviour and resulting outcomes (Basu, 1992; Jejeebhoy, 1991). Empowerment has been defined as the capacity to manipulate one's personal environment through control over resources and information in order to make decisions about one's own concerns or about close family members (Basu, 1992; Dyson and Moore, 1983; Miles-Done and Bisharat, 1990). Women's empowerment thus can be conceptualized as their ability to determine events in their lives, even though men and other women may be opposed to their wishes (Mason, 1984; Safilios-Rothschild, 1982). In this paper the indicator 'Women participation in the household decision-making' has been taken to highlight [illegible] empowerment status of Tripura.

Women's participation in decision-making in Tripura

The data in respect of Tripura is taken from NFHS-3 where the aspects 'percentage of currently married women who usually make decision on four specific kinds of decisions either by themselves or jointly with their husband', and 'percentage of men who say that wives should have an equal or greater say than their husband in specific kinds of decisions' are taken to assess the level of empowerment of women. Table 8.1 shows the picture of empowerment of women in these aspects.

Table 8.1 provides information by state on currently married women's participation in the four decisions women were asked about and currently married men's opinion with regard to a wife having an equal or greater say in the four decisions men were asked about. The proportion of currently married women who participated in all four decisions varies from a high of 77 per cent in Meghalaya and 30.2 per cent in Tripura to a low of 25 per cent in Jammu and Kashmir compared to 36.7 per cent in all-India. In fact, in Tripura less than half of currently married women say that they participate in all four decisions. The proportion of participation in decision-making in selected dimensions range from lowest 43.4 per cent in Jammu and Kashmir to highest 87.5 per cent in Meghalaya. In case of Tripura, women's participation in all four decisions is very low at 30.2 per cent only.

In the country as a whole, 52.9 per cent of currently married women participate in decisions about making major household purchases and 60–62 per cent participate in each of the remaining three decisions. However, among 4 states selected for comparison, women's pattern of participation by decision varies greatly by state. The percentage of currently married men who say that a wife should have at least equal say as her husband in all five decisions is lowest in Tripura (22.8%). The overall picture shows women's level of empowerment in terms of decision-making in poor light in Tripura.

Women's Health

The social structure of Indian society and the secondary position women occupy significantly influence every aspect of health. Very often the goals of many programmes for women are a rehash of internationally set goals, some of which are not achievable. The second-class status of women in Indian society continues despite efforts by the government and non-governmental organisations. Women's perspectives continue to be missing, marginalised or ignored. Many community health programmes in the

Table 8.1: Women's Participation in Decision-Making in the State

State	Percentage of women who usually make specific decisions alone or jointly with their husbands						Percentage of men who say that wives should have the final say alone or jointly with their husband in:	
	Own health care	Making major household purchases	Making purchases for daily household needs	Visits to her family or relatives	Participate in all four decisions	Participate in none of the four decisions	All of the four decisions	None of the four decisions
Tripura	59.7	48.1	56.9	60.4	30.2	18.9	22.8	1.0
Meghalaya	87.5	82.5	84.1	87.3	77.3	9.3	69.8	10.5
Jammu & Kashmir	43.5	44.7	46.9	43.4	25.2	37.3	55.6	5.2
India	62.2	52.9	60.1	60.5	36.7	20.5	49.7	3.6

Source: NFHS-3.

developing world seek to address the issues of gender bias and the unequal status of women, with an emphasis on women's health, education and employment. In spite of such efforts, women face discrimination and continued adversity. Out of the various indicators of women health, only Mean Ages at Marriage and a few maternal care indicators are taken into consideration to health status of women in Tripura.

Table 8.2: Mean Ages at Marriage

Year	*1971*	*1981*	*1991*	*1993*	*1998–99*
Mean age at marriage	18.5	20.3	21	21.2	22

Source: HDR Tripura 2007.

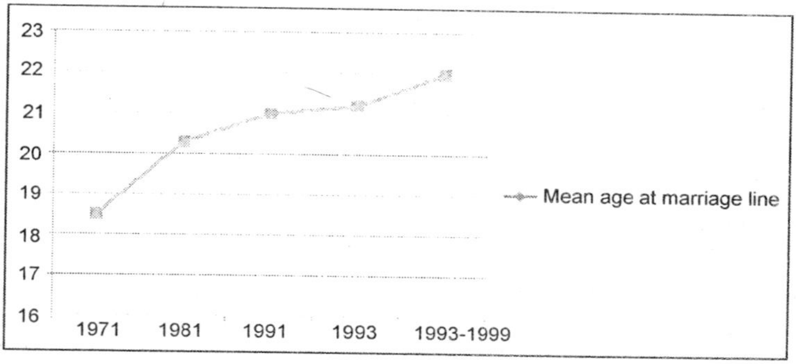

Fig. 8.1: Mean age at marriage line.

Mean age at marriage is an important factor in determining women's health, particularly since it is an important factor in determining the age of first pregnancy. The mean age at marriage of women in Tripura (22 years in 1998-99) is higher than the national figure (19.7 years). The data suggest that the mean age at marriage of females has been rising significantly since 1971. This improvement is related to enhancement in literacy rates both in urban as well as rural areas.

Maternal Care Indicators in Tripura

Table 8.3 shows percentage of women covered under five maternal care indicators for births. These indicators together summarize the extent to which the state has progressed towards achieving safe motherhood goals at all three stages of the birth process: ante-natal, delivery, and post-natal. The first indicator is a summary of ante-natal care indicator which shows the percentage of last live births whose mothers had all of the following: three or more ante-natal care visits (with the first visit within the first trimester of pregnancy), two or more tetanus toxic injections, and iron and folic acid tablets or syrup for three or more months. The next two indicators pertain to care during delivery and show the percentage of births delivered in medical institutions and deliveries assisted by health personnel. The last two indicators pertain to post-natal care for mothers and show the percentage of deliveries with a postpartum check-up within 42 days of the birth and within two days of birth.

Table 8.3: Maternal Care Indicators in Tripura

Maternal care indicators for births during the five years preceding the survey by state, India, 2005-06

State	*Percentage who received all recommended types of ante-natal care*	*Percentage of births delivered in a health facility*	*Percentage of deliveries assisted by health personnel*	*Percentage of deliveries with a post-natal check-up*	*Percentage of deliveries with a post-natal check-up within two days of birth*
Tripura	10.6	46.9	48.8	33.7	30.3
India	15.0	38.7	46.6	41.2	37.3

Source: NFHS-3, 2005-06.

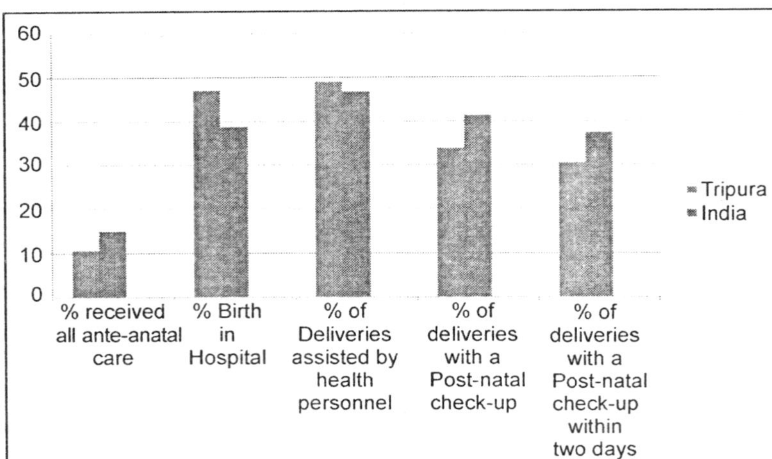

Fig.: 8.2: Maternal care indicators.

The achievement of the State Tripura is lower than the national average in areas of 'percentage of women who received all recommended types of ante-natal care', 'percentage of deliveries with a post-natal check-up', and 'percentage of deliveries with a post-natal check-up within two days of birth'. The point that only 10.6 per cent mothers received all types of ante-natal care in Tripura alone is a testimony of the fact that women in Tripura are still an endangered community so far their health and life is concerned.

Conclusion

The study reveals the fact that large number of married women in Tripura do not participate in decision-making alone or jointly with their husbands pertaining to their own health care, household matters and outdoor activities. The observation substantiates the low status of women in the society of Tripura which is tantamount to a severe wastage of human resources of the State. The overall picture of women health that emerges is also not very encouraging. The mean age at marriage in the State is still very low indicating the existence of a pre-capitalist agrarian set-up of the economy in the State. The success of the State in providing basic maternal care facilities to the mothers is also found to be wanting. All these areas need special care and action for improving the level of women empowerment and health in Tripura.

REFERENCES

1. Elizabeth Jacob, Mini *et al.* (2006): "A Community Health Programme in Rural Tamil Nadu, India: The Need for Gender Justice for Women", Reproductive Health Matters.
2. Govt of India: NFHS-2, 1998-1999.
3. ——: HDR Tripura 2007.
4. ——: NFHS-3, 2005-6.
5. Kishor, Sunita and Kamla Gupta (2004): "Women's Empowerment in India and Its States: Evidence from the NFHS-2", *Economic and Political Weekly*, Vol. 39, No. 7, Feb. 14–20.
6. Paul-Majumder, Pratima (1996): "Health Impact of Women's Wage Employment: A Case Study of the Garment Industry of Bangladesh", *The Bangladesh Development Studies*, Vol. XXIV, March–June.
7. Rajagopal, Shobhita and Kanchan Mathur *(2000):* "Women's Empowerment through State", *Economic and Political Weekly*, Vol. 35, No. 33, Aug. 12–18.

8. S. Bloom. Shelah, David Wypij, Monica Das Gupta (2010): "Dimensions of Women's Autonomy and the Influence on Maternal Health Care Utilization in a North Indian City", *Demography*, Vol. 38, No. 1, Feb., 2001.

SECTION III

Political Empowerment and Women of Mizoram

9

Religion and Political Empowerment:

A Study on the Impact of Christianity on the Empowerment of the Tribal Women of Mizoram

Debasish Paul

> "*We must agree that most women want freedom and most women want equality as well. This is what makes us similarly human. That we may define these constructs differently also makes us uniquely human.*"
>
> –Zillah Eisenstein

At the outset I would like to share my discomfort with the word 'Empowerment' in the sense in which it is used. 'Empowerment' literally means the act of conferring legality or sanction. Thus, when we talk about women empowerment it infers to confer legality or sanction to women with the objective to attain equality. To be more precise, it means to make women at par with men. But the question is if it is conferred by men to women then how can the later be at par with the former. One cannot give the other. Likewise, one cannot take from the other. Nature has given everyone its due. Equality is a myth. Hence, the act of conferment to women for their development is no solution but is only creating confusion and we scholars and politicians have a mouth-watering topic for discussion.

However, it is a fact that women in the past, and even today, were not given enough freedom to act according to their choice and capacity. Their participation was primarily confined within the private sphere of the home and the family. History, on the other hand, has largely remained a record of public events and personae to the exclusion of the private sphere of the home and the family. It is often argued that History is 'HIS STORY'; without 'HER STORY'. (Bhasin, 2000). In an emancipated society, the worst form of discrimination is to see differently a man from a woman. From time immemorial, people across countries have nurtured and sustained this ridiculous thought of looking down upon women.

In India, where social customs and practices have been deeply rooted, the common man brings about discrimination between a man and a woman, though there are no religious sanctions about it. Women in India, on the contrary, is adored and worshipped in various forms; Goddess Saraswati, Laksmi and Durga are considered to be the custodian of Knowledge, Wealth and Power respectively. The perennial rivers are considered holy and they are all given feminine names: Ganga, Yamuna, Saraswati, Kaveri, Narmada, Godavari, Krishna and others. In spite of such special recognition for women, there is a strong tendency to discriminate against women in every sphere of life.

The situation is no different for the tribals of North East in general and the Mizos in particular as even Mizo the history is no exception in this regard. The role of women in the history of Mizo society remained relatively unexplored, though their potential contribution to the understanding of social change appears quite obvious. Also, the role of women in history has largely been ignored and seldom recorded even by the Mizo historians. For instance, the role of Mizo women in the Mizo National Front (MNF) unrest during the period 1966–1987 is hardly sung anywhere.

Like women in general and of most other tribes, Mizo women too had life without due political rights and opportunities before the arrival of Christianity in Mizoram. Their traditional political organization shows that village political institutions like Village Council and its different political offices were exclusively occupied by male members. From "*Tlangao*" (village messenger) to village Chief; men dominated women in every sphere of life. Practically, there was no scope for a Mizo woman to participate in village administration. They, therefore, did not have political status and their role was confined to domestic activities only.

While there were contributive factors for change in man-woman relationship, the most revolutionary thing which the Mizos learnt from Christianity was the equality of man before God. This equality led to the abolition of the traditional chieftainship. Moreover, Christianity was also productive in developing political consciousness among them and this consciousness culminated into the demand for separate administrative unit. It was headed by Mizo Union which was formed in 1947 in Mizoram.

The union paved the way for Mizo women's participation in political activities by forming a women's wing. The wing worked with men's wing. The ultimate object of the wing was to lend themselves to the struggle for the integration of all Mizo-inhabited areas to Lushai hill or Mizoram. Towards this end and for effective assertion of their rights and opportunities, Mizo women formed Mizo Women Association. The Association vows to work for gender equality by eradicating gender-based harmful practices such as commercialization of bride-price, dowry system, sexual exploitation of any kind and form, fight against inequality between men and women etc.

The aforesaid developments gave a new momentum to the issue of women's identity in the Mizo society. It has been felt that male predominance tends to ignore the role of women in the pre-colonial Mizo society. There is a general assumption that many aspects of life of the Mizo society is influenced by modernization/westernization and this began particularly after the early part of 20th century i.e. since when the Mizos came in contact with the British and the Christian Missionaries. Of course, traditional cultures were re-defined; while sensitization towards women based issues also continues to be guided within the frame of western patriarchal paradigm. This not only re-established but also consolidated men's dominance in the society and patriarchy lineal society gained a stronger hold then the pre-colonial period. (Lalrinchhani, 1998). Although the influence of modernization in terms of material culture is very much evident among the Mizos, 'traditionalism' still continues to influence the Mizo society at the level of consciousness and ideas. Mizo customary laws in relation to women practically have not changed. (Hmar, 2002) Initially, women consciousness stated within the framework of the Church was mostly based on protestant ethics. Unfortunately, many Churches not often give equal rights to women since the ideology of the Church is also based on a patriarchal model. Ordination of women pastors/reverends is unknown despite the development of the Baptist Church's broad–mindedness towards the appointment of women as Church elders/officials or Kohhran Upa/Rawngbawltu. (Chhakchhuak, 2002).

Political consciousness during the post-independent era initiated a succession of changes in the Mizo society. But despite the rise of a new educated class who created a consciousness within the society, political parties and social organisations fail to address the importance of gender issues. Dissatisfaction followed by deprivation gave rise to the formation of women's organizations like the Hmeichhe Tangrual Pawl (HTP) in 1946 followed by the Mizo women's organisation called Mizo Hmeichhe Insuihkhawm Pawl, popularly known as MHIP, in 1964. Initially, the new women organisation raised the need to reform traditional and cultural practices of the Mizos. They raised their voice against discrimination and injustice in the society. Today their activities range from the set-up of orphanage, drug de-addiction camp, movement of protests against rape, domestic violence, reform of customary laws, reform of bride price and many others. But unfortunately these issues usually end up in nothing beyond mere discussions.

Women (mostly women theologians) who speak publicly about gender discrimination are regarded as fanatic or Hmeichhe Nasa. Of course, there are some women activists, researchers and the likes that prefer to keep quiet and show nothing but compliance to the existing order of the society due to fear of insult and further marginalisation.

Recent works on women studies, for instance, Lalruatfela Nu's "Engvangin nge Hmeichhiate hi tihchak an tul?" (*The Aizawl Post*, Feb. 25, 2005) talks about empowerment of Mizo women. The article starts with gender division based on the genetic postulation in which the author mentions *'men are stronger than women'*. Taking this into consideration, one can hastily presume that physical strength has been an important criterion of gender division in society. Most women intellectuals would argue that 'difference between men and women's achievements and participations are result of socially constructed gender roles rather than of biological difference. (2000, p. 62) Moreover, there is no point of questioning the biological factor which will not change at all. Physical strength might have played a role in the caveman days…but not since. And further, had women not been able to "gather" and thereby watch the camp for possible intruders (multi-tasking) we may have not survived either.

Most of the Mizo women activists have claimed–and disowned–the label "feminist". This is not surprising as who would want to be a feminist in a society where gender issues are strongly opposed. For instance, Rualfela Nu declares "I'm not a feminist to the extent that I would fight for 'gender equality' in the Mizo society". (*The Aizawl Post*, 25 Feb, 2005) One must wonder what 'equality' and 'gender' means to her? Her paradigm in her previous book "Nawhchizawrna leh a kaihnawihna" was very much a part of a significant issue in feminist thought and activism. (Lalruatfela Nu, 2004) What makes her is not always *herself*, but something that comes from her. It is likely that she outwardly rejected the term 'feminism' but not the feminist's gender issues. Ruatfela Nu does not directly contest male-centred ways of knowing even as she questions the gender discrimination in Mizo society.

Marginality of women could be seen in the trend of women's participation in the political process of the state. In pre-British society women played significant role in the village administration as there were many female rulers among the Mizos. Ropuiliani Chieftainess gave her life for defending her territory where most Mizo chiefs gave up. Now, the role of women in pre-British Mizo politics becomes a history as current politics is virtually dominated by men. There are no women members in State Legislative Assembly. Even at the district level, there are very few women in the village council.

Political parties usually make promises to women for a better and sustainable future, but mostly such promises end up in discussion and gaining consensus. Very few women find a place in the decision-making committees of political parties. However, mere entry into the political system does not guarantee transparency, accountability and commitment for women's progress. Instead of being inundated in the vastness of events and procedures, the progress must reach its destination of equality and empowerment. The task is, of course, mounting, but is not impossible. Women's entry into politics is necessary to help them in their struggle against injustice and to strengthen democracy. (Thakkar) If mainstream Indian women like Mamta Banerjee, Sonia Gandhi, Uma Bharti, Jaya Lalitha and the likes may play such an important role at both the regional and national level politics, why not Mizo women? (Remsangpuii Nu, 2001).

The realm of politics has been and still is considered a man's arena. However, in recent times, women have come out of their homes to prove their worth as much more than caretakers of the house. Highlighting this phenomenon is the landmark decision of the Mizoram Government allotting 33 per cent reservation for women in the upcoming Municipal Council Elections. Besides, the Panchayat Mahila Shakti Abhiyan (PMSA) scheme is a means for the Elected Women Representatives (EWRs) to build their confidence and capacity to get over the institutional, societal and political constraints that prevent them from active participation in rural local self-government.

For the first time in the history of Mizoram the 33 per cent reservation for women is complied with. Fulfilling Constitutional mandate, 6 wards out of 19 were allotted to women. But it is very interesting and question arises over the manner in which these 6 reserve wards were selected. The presence of male chauvinism also may not be ruled out. It is for information that these 6 wards were selected by a draw of lot. The question is why such a method adopted? Why not these 6 wards selected on the basis of the number of women voters? Normally, in other states, the number of women voters present in a ward plays the determining role for the first election.

It is a fact that women candidates who contest these elections are mostly public figures, well-known to the people and are accepted and appreciated by the voters for their work in other fields. There are very few women candidates who have political affiliations prior to the elections. Candidates include women who are mostly representatives of civil society organizations. This is again another kind of discrimination in which a group of women who are relatively less free due to economic dependence faces discrimination against those who are relatively more free and enjoy greater freedom due to their economic independence. Thus, the very purpose of empowering women is defeated as the group representing the former is larger than the later group.

Despite the point made above, we may still appreciate the step taken in positive note and be hopeful that this will certainly bring a change in the established mindset of the society. This is of course a beginning towards greater participation of women in politics, administration and also in religious institutions relating to ordinations in various denominations of the Churches.

Gender bias has been and still continues to be one of the major social evils of our society at large. However, in due course and as they say, with time comes change. This is very true as in today's world we witness the presence of the so-called socially branded weaker gender rising to positions of high status and power in almost every sphere of life. But one must not forget that gender equality is a myth, whereas gender discrimination can be checked. To put it precisely, gender equality means socio-economic and political 'participation' of persons based on one's ability to possess and perform, without any discrimination based on sex, caste, creed and colour. And of all the factors, religion is the supreme factor that cannot only free women from the dominance of their complementary counterpart (man) but can also ensure the creation of a mindset wherein people are not discriminated on the basis of sex, caste, creed or colour but on the basis of one's ability and performance. It is hoped that the Mizo intellectuals, scholars, activists and Church leaders will come forward and take up the challenge in addressing these chronic issues of 'gender discrimination' or 'gender biasness' or 'empowerment' of the tribal women of Mizoram and create an indiscriminate society: when and how only remains to be seen.

To conclude, it reminds me of a statement made in 1906 by Sarojini Naidu, the Nightingale of India, on the issue of women. Rightly she said, "Restore to your women their ancient rights, for as I have said, it is we, and not you, who are the real nation builders, and without our active cooperation at all points of progress, all your congresses and conferences are in vain. Educate your women and the nation will take care of itself, for it is as true today as it was yesterday and will be to the end of human life that the hand that rocks the cradle rules the world."

REFERENCES

Bhasin, Kamla (2000); "Understanding Gender", Delhi.

Chhakchhuak; Linda "Patriarchy in Religion", http://www.indiatogether. org/ women/worklife/churchpatriarch.htm, accessed on 10th July, 2011.

Eisenstein, Zillah (2004); "What's In A Name? Seeing Feminism, Universalism, and Modernity", Wagadu Volume 1: Spring.

Hmar, Laldena (2002); "Status of Mizo Women", *The Sangai Express*, 2002.

Hmingthanzuali and H. Vanlalhruaia (2007), "Women Issues in Mizo Society."

Lalrinchhani, B. (1998); "Christianity and Women in Mizoram, unpublished M.Phil. Dissertation, North Eastern Hill University.

Poonacha, Veena (2004); "Recovering Women's Histories: An Enquiry into Methodological Questions and Challenges", *Indian Journal of Gender Studies*, Vol. 11. No. 3, Sage Publications, New Delhi.

Ruatfela Nu (2005); "Engvangin nge Hmeichhiate hi tihchak an tul?" in *The Aizawl Post*, (Daily Newspaper, Mizoram) 25. Feb.

Singh, Amar Kumar and C. Rajyalakshmi (1993): "Status of Tribal Women in India." *Social Change*. Dec. 23(4). Location: SNDT Churchgate.

Thakkar, Usha, "Endengering Politics for Good Governance: Advocacy by Women for Social and Political Change."

www.manipuronline.com, accessed on 12th July, 2011.

10

Political Empowerment and Women of Mizoram: An Overview

M. Pathak and *R.K. Vanlalsiammawia*

Introduction

Empowerment is related to the word power. In English, the concept leans on its original meaning of investment with legal power—permission to act for some specific goal or purpose (Rappaport, 1987). The development of skills, based on insights and abilities, the essential features of which are a critical political consciousness, an ability to participate with others, a capacity to cope with frustrations and to struggle for influence over the environment is the real meaning of the term. Empowerment of any section of a society will prove to be a myth until there is a complete recognition of the inherent dignity, freedom and of equal rights to all the members of the society. Gender inequality has always been an issue of great concern for the people with a holistic approach. Gender based discrimination has been a deep rooted social menace in India and this 'social menace' has dampened women's march towards progress not only socially but politically, economically and legally also. To cope up with the malice of gender inequality, there is a need to fight against the aberrated psyche of the society which oppose women empowerment and, that would be possible only if political system serves as an efficient tool.

Since ancient period, women were not given much weightage in political processes. They were not considered worth to share the state secrets even. We find references in ancient texts which ratifies the status of women during that period. The presence of women was restricted at the place where the king used to hold consultations. Our society had been basically patriarchal in nature since beginning and hence it has been male dominated all along. Thus, giving equal space to the female counterpart was and is perhaps against the male chauvinism. Thus, the women remained suppressed, exploited and neglected through the ages. For a long time women faced problems of violence, property rights, legal status, political participation etc. However, some women like Razia Sultana, Durgavati, Jijabai, Nur Jahan and Chand Bibi managed to showcase their political skills at national level. So far as the State of Mizoram is concerned, during pre-British period, there were few female rulers among the Mizos. Ropuiliani is one of them who gave her life for defending her territory where most Mizo chiefs gave up. Mizo woman, as in other patriarchal societies, seldom participated directly in public life.

The women in Mizoram constitute about 49.37 per cent of the population and majority of them are involved in informal sector. A small faction of women is in Govt. jobs, of which some are occupying high positions too. Most of them are indulged in running small shops like 'Kuva Dawr' (pan shop), vegetable shops, as sales girls and vendors as they don't have much working capital. The employment statistics of four major districts of the state is highlighted in Table 10.1. The data reflected in this table may also not be perfect as many persons are not getting themselves registered in the employment exchanges.

The literacy rate of the State of Mizoram is quite high as compared to the National data. Even for females, it is higher by 23.94 per cent. The female here are not only literate but also well qualified. A sizeble number of women are having higher degrees too. Table 10.2 elaborate the status of literacy in the State with a comparison with national literacy percentage.

These statistics suggest that the State is not at all backward educationally, but at the same time it is not being translated into political empowerment. Thus, it may be inferred that other factors such as cultural, socio-economic, political reasons are more responsible. Woman representation in any political decision-making processes is abysmally low. The data shows the women in the local self–government (i.e. in the Village Council) since its inception (Table 10.3).

The women's representation to the post of VCPs in the state since 1954 to 2009 was a meagre 4.77 per cent only. This clearly indicates that something is wrong somewhere. The realm of politics has been and still is considered a man's arena. Highlighting this phenomenon is the landmark decision of the Mizoram Government which allotted 33 per cent reservation for women in the Municipal Council Elections of 2011 as per the 74th Constitutional Amendment. Out of 19 wards, 6 wards go to women

Table 10.1: Comprehensive Employment Statistics of four Major Districts of Mizoram (Namely Aizawl, Lunglei, Saiha and Champhai) Employment Exchange as on March 2010 from Live Register

Sl. No.	*Category*	*Male*	*Female*	*Total*
	Population (provisional)	**5,52,339**	**5,38,675**	**10,91,014**
1.	Unskilled	235	179	414
2.	Class VI to IX	12,563	4,790	17,353
3.	Matric/HSLC	5,942	4,567	10,509
4.	PUC/HSSLC	3,688	3,102	6,790
5.	Graduate			
	(i) General	1,708	1,398	3,106
	(ii) Honours	1,064	857	1,921
	(iii) Medical	81	56	137
	(iv) Science (Gen.)	33	18	51
	(v) Science (Hons.)	180	284	464
	(vi) Engineering	191	45	236
	(vii) Commerce	174	100	274
	(viii) Others	181	135	316
6.	Post graduate			
	(i) Arts/Humanities	669	769	1,438
	(ii) Science	118	102	220
	(iii) Commerce	49	49	98
	(iv) Engineering	nil	nil	nil
	(v) Others	31	31	62
7.	Hindi (Matric & above)	1,132	2,821	3,953
8.	Typist	19	53	72
9.	Driver	367	nil	367
10.	Conductor	23	nil	23
11.	Technical Grade	573	876	1,449
12.	Physically Handicapped	87	24	111
13.	Non-Mizo	461	119	580
	Total	**29,450**	**20,375**	**49,825**

Source: (i) 2011 Census; Provisional Population Totals and Socio Economics Map of Lunglei District; RD Block-wise, Published by District Research Officer, Economics and Statistics, Lunglei, (ii) Statistical Handbook, Mizoram 2010; Published by Directorate of Economics and Statistics; Govt. of Mizoram.

Table 10.2: Literacy rate by Sex: A National Comparison with the State of Mizoram 2010-11

Sl. No.	*India /State*	*Literacy Rate in percentage*		
		Male	*Female*	*Overall*
1.	India	82.14	65.46	74.04
2.	Mizoram	93.72	89.40	91.58

Source: 2011 Census; Provisional Population Totals and Socio Economics Map of Lunglei District; RD Block-wise Published by District Research Officer, Economics and Statistics, Lunglei.

to fulfil the Constitutional mandate for the first time in Mizoram. But, the manners in which these 6 reserve wards are selected revealed the presence of male chauvinism. These 6 wards are selected by a draw of lot. Why didn't they select these 6 wards on the basis of the number of women voters present in the ward? Normally, in other states, the number of women voters present in that ward is used as criteria for the first election. The more the number of women voters, the ward shall go to reservation and *vice versa.*

Causes of Marginalization

1. Cultural Background and Customary Law

Mizo society is basically patriarchal in nature which is mainly responsible for the development of hyper-masculine biasness thereby tending to push the woman to traditional domestic roles. As a result, patriarchal elites in Mizo society continue to dominate the society and politics till today. This is also true in the case of East Asian and South East Asian societies. In a Mizo family in the past, a woman had no right either in a family or society. As a matter of fact, she belonged in body and mind, from her birth till her death, to her father and to her husband after her marriage. The woman possessed nothing even though she did most of the work within and outside the house. The following sayings, among many others, clearly testify the inferior status of Mizo woman in the past: (1) the wisdom of woman does not extend beyond the bank of a river; (2) woman (wife) and old fencing can be replaced any time; (3) let a woman and a dog bark as they like; (4) woman and crab have no religion; etc. Unlike the male child, by custom and convention, a Mizo woman had no inheritance right or share in the property of her father. The Mizo customary laws were also male-biased and did not at all protect woman's interests.

Table 10.3: Women's in Village Council Elections since 1954 to 2009

Year	*No. of villages participating in VC election*	*No. of Women Candidates winning*	*Name of the Constituency from which winning*	*District of the Constituency*	*Remarks*
1954	338	02	Sawleng	Aizawl	1. Ms. Kairumi 2. Ms.Thliahthangpuii
1957	381	Nil			
1960	381	Nil			
1963	422	01	Rahsi Veng	Lunglei	Ms. Kapchhingi
1975	422	01	Saron/Chhinga Veng	Aizawl	Ms.Zathuami
1982		02	Vaivakawn & Saron	Aizawl	1. Ms.Thangliani 2. Ms.Zathuami
1984	412	06	05 01	Aizawl Lunglei	
1987	468	04		Aizawl	
1988	16 (Bye-election)	03			
1990		18			
1994		23	18 05	Aizawl Lunglei	
1997		15			

(Contd.)

1999		20	16 04	Aizawl Lunglei	
2002	532	54	42,08,02,01 & 01	Aizawl, Lunglei, Mamit, Champhai & Kolasib respectively	
2006	556	34	25,06,01,01 & 01	Aizawl, Lunglei, Mamit, Serchhip & Kolasib respectively	
2007	02(Bye –election)	Nil			
2009	555* (554)	31	22,06,01,01 & 01	Aizawl, Lunglei, Mamit, Serchhip & Kolasib respectively	*Election was not held for Serchhip IV
Grand Total	4484	214			#Percentage of women candidates winning since 1954 = 4.77

The percentage calculation is done by the authors.

Source: Mizoram Village Council Golden Jubilee 1954–2004 Souvenir.

2. Lack of Exposure, Opportunities and Confidence

Since women were not free from the domestic responsibilities assigned to them culturally, they are hardly getting any chance to participate in the activities of public life. This practice prolonged from ancient period till pre-independence era. Lack of opportunities for such a long span of time has shaken the very morale of women in the State and at the present stage also they lack confidence. They don't find themselves confident of taking charge of most of the assignments and feel that they may not be competent enough to discharge their responsibilities. Of course, there are exceptions too. The development of this psyche is detrimental to them as well to the society. Although, scenario is changing fast with the fact more and more women are getting educated. Many of the barriers to women empowerment and equity lie ingrained into the cultures of certain nations and societies. Many women feel these pressures, while others have become accustomed to being treated inferior to men.

3. Demographic Situation of the State of Mizoram

The State is bestowed with lush green forest and natural beauty but the terrain is hilly. Its location is far from mainland and thus there had been less positive interaction with outer world. Till recently, the transport and communication facilities were poor which prevented people from linking with other parts of the country and the world. This aspect also reduced the chance of women to learn and develop the facets of personality which their counterparts were doing elsewhere. However, the arrival of Christian Missionaries in the State changed the atmosphere to some extent.

4. Socio-economic Factors

For generations, women are subjected to social and familial conditioning, to make their families the sole focus of their lives. It is a well-known fact that women are left unappreciated and unpaid for the time and energy they spend in domestic activities, from childcare to housework. As such, her time and energies are severely limited when it comes to actively participating in public life. For political empowerment of women to happen, this scenario has to change, perhaps with better support from her family or better understanding from society. Most of the women work in agricultural sector either as workers and in household farms or as wageworkers. State government's policies for alleviating poverty have failed to produce any desirable results.

There are many successful women organizations working for the overall upliftment of the rural women like Shri Mahila Griha Udyog Lijjat Papad (1959), Self-Employed Women Association (SEWA) established in 1972, The Working Women's Forum (WWF) in 1978, Rashtriya Mahila Kosh (RMK), for women established in 1993, Mann Deshi Mahila Sahakari Bank Ltd. (MDMSB) in 1997 etc. Though there can be no magic bullet, which can bring about radical structural transformation that the empowerment of women needs, the success of micro financing organizations in building up the organizational capacity of the poor women provides the basis for their social mobilization that many other class interventions have not been able to achieve. Social and economic changes combined with modernization should help a woman overcome many of the social barriers which are ingrained in the patriarchal culture of Mizo society. In the final analysis, overall democratization of Mizos in the socio-economic and political structures can be expected to promote women's empowerment and emancipation. This will mean clear-cut reservation of electoral seats right from the grass roots level as it has been implemented in the Panchayati Raj Institutions where even a fixed quota of Pradhan (Chairperson) in Gram Panchayats and Adhyakshas (Chairpersons) in Zilla Parishads are reserved for elected women. The enhanced political representation will again enable them to enhance their political power so that they can have more equitable share in decision-making for their society. Given this political power, women even within the patriarchal cultural domination, will be able to exercise their political rights for more fulfilling and rewarding roles in the society.

Concluding Remarks

Women's empowerment has become a global issue and the question of the Mizo women's political empowerment need to be considered in the context of what is being done and implemented in East Asia and South-East Asian regions. Democratization and empowerment can provide a Mizo woman an avenue through which she can continue her long journey towards her total emancipation. To be more specific, two political mechanisms may be considered in this regard: increased proportional representation of women in all elected bodies and organizing workshops/ seminars to enlighten the women-folk, verbal persuasion and economic freedom. However, the real empowerment will come only when the women themselves are mentally ready to take up the challenge with positive support of the society.

REFERENCES

Desai, Neera and Usha Thakkar (2005): "Women in Indian Society", National Book Trust, New Delhi.

Fadia, L. (2005): "Indian Government and Politics", Sahitya Bhawan Publications, Agra.

Joseph, Neena (2001): "Gender Related Problems of Women: Women's Empowerment and Panchayati Raj". Himalayan Publishing House, New Delhi.

Krook, Mona Lena (2009): "Quotas for Women in Politics: Gender and Candidate Selection Reform Worldwide". New York: Oxford University Press.

Lal Dena (2011): Status of Mizo Women/ Lal Dena, http://www.Zogamonline.com/articles/atangpi/246– accessed on 13th August.

Mizoram Village Council Golden Jubilee 1954–2004, Souvenir.

Ralhan, O.P. (1995) "Indian Women Through Ages" (ed.), Anmol Publications Pvt. Ltd., New Delhi.

(Rappaport, 1987): "Empowerment: Definitions and Meanings", Chapter 2.

Sharma, Bharti: "Political Empowerment of Women: A Literary Reflection", Assistant Professor, Department of English, Rajdhani College, University of Delhi.

"Statistical Handbook of Mizoram" (2010): Published by Directorate of Economics and Statistics, Govt. of Mizoram.

"The North East Today 2009": The 21st Century Mizo Women; Nangkyntiew Kimi Wason, http://www.Zogamonline.com, accessed on 12th August 2011.

"The Provisional Population Totals and Socio-Economics Map of Lunglei District, Block-wise", Published by District Research Officer, Economics and Statistics, Lunglei 13. The Sentinel (Shillong), 19th May, 2009.

11

Political Empowerment in Patriarchal Society: A Study in Mizoram

B. Lalrinchhani

The principle of gender equality is enshrined in the Indian Constitution in its Preamble, Fundamental Rights, Fundamental Duties and Directive Principles. The Constitution not only grants equality to women, but also empowers the State to adopt measures of positive discrimination in favour of women. The National Commission for Women was set-up by an Act of Parliament in 1990 to safeguard the rights and legal entitlements of women. The 73rd and 74th Amendments (1993) to the Constitution of India have provided for reservation of seats in the local bodies of Panchayats and Municipalities for women, thereby laying a strong foundation for their participation in decision-making at the local levels.[1] The National Policy also affirmed that "women's equality in power sharing and active participation in decision-making, including decision-making in political process at all levels will be ensured for the achievement of the goals of empowerment. All measures will be taken to guarantee women equal access to and full participation in decision-making bodies at every level, including the legislative, executive, judicial, corporate, statutory bodies…."[2] The policies adopted by the government clearly indicate that women have been discriminated in all spheres of life. The decision-making in all levels especially in the political decision-making has been the domain of men. Women hardly had any place in the decision-making processes. In the international level also the UN had taken up the issue of empowering women in the political arena and this is seen in The Millennium Development Goals Report (UN, 2005) which noted that the most important factor for achieving gender equality and empowerment of women is providing opportunities for equal participation of women as that of men in the decision-making be it at home or/to the highest level of government.

This paper will focus on the participation of women in the political scenario of Mizoram and try to look into the various problems which hindered women to take an active role in the decision-making level particularly in the public elected offices. The role played by women in the political arena in the traditional period will also be briefly looked into so as to know the developments made by women.

In the traditional period, women were hardly seen in the public sphere. They did not take any part in the political system of the village. All the administrative system was carried out by the Chief and his Council of Elders or *Upas*.[3] In this system women were totally excluded. The position of women in the traditional society was reflected in the sayings such as "Women's wisdom does not cross the village spring" and "Women's words are not words as a crab's meat is not meat". Thus, women were excluded in the important decision-makings such as migration, change of village site, choosing of village jhum and in the war strategies. This led to the women being dominated and subservient to the men.

However, there were instances of women chiefs such as Mangchini Nu, Pi Dari, Darbilhi, Ropuiliani and others. But it should be noted that these women chiefs could hold this position because their husbands had died and their sons had already set-up their own villages or were minors, so their relations to a man enabled them to become chiefs.[4] They nevertheless have played a very important role in the administration of the villages and some of them have been regarded as brave and wise chiefs.

However, things began to change after the introduction of education by the Christian missionaries and the traditional cultures have been re-defined. Girls slowly began to receive education and this opened up many avenues for them in the field of salaried jobs and market economy. The independence of India brought many changes in the country. In Mizoram, there were many radical changes and it witnessed a total abolition of traditional institutions replaced by new institutions like the abolition of the Chief's rule by a democratic system. The new institution which provides a totally different structure also professed different values to be achieved by the people.[5] But it should be noted that traditional values are not necessarily wiped out by new institutions. As noted earlier, women began to emerge out of their private sphere and are employed in various offices, work in business sector and thus their position also appears to have been better than in the traditional period. In the new democratic set up, few women have also emerged in the public elected offices especially in the village levels. Tables 11.1, 11.2 and 11.3 reveal the level of women's participation in the public elected office.

Table 11.1: Number of Male and Female Members of the District Council

Year	Elected members		Nominated members		Total
	Male	Female	Male	Female	
1952	18 (75%)	Nil	5 (20.83%)	1 (4.17%)	24 (100%)
1957	22 (91.67%)	Nil	1 (4.17%)	1 (4.17%)	24 (100%)
1962	22 (91.67%)	Nil	2 (8.33%)	Nil	24 (100%)
1970	22 (91.67%)	Nil	2 (8.33%)	Nil	24 (100%)

Source: C. Hermana. *Zoram Politics Thli TLeh Dan.* Vol I.

Table 11.2: Number of Male and Female Members of the Legislative Assembly of the Union Territory of Mizoram

Year	Elected members		Nominated members		Total
	Male	Female	Male	Female	
1972	30 (90.91%)	Nil	2 (6.06%)	1 (3.03%)	33 (100%)
1978	29 (96.67%)	1 (3.33%)	–	–	30 (100%)
1979	28 (87.5%)	1 (3.13%)	2 (6.25%)	1 (3.13%)	32 (100%)
1984	27 (87.1%)	1 (3.23%)	2 (6.45%)	1 (3.23%)	31 (100%)

Source: C. Hermana, *Zoram Politics Thli TLeh Dan.* Vol II.

Note: The 1978 Assembly was dissolved before nominated members were appointed.

Table 11.3: Male and Female Members of the Legislative Assembly of Mizoram State

Year	Male	Female	Total
1987	39 (97.5%)	1 (2.5%)	40 (100%)
1989	40 (100%)	Nil	40 (100%)
1993	40 (100%)	Nil	40 (100%)
1998	40 (100%)	Nil	40 (100%)
2003	40 (100%)	Nil	40 (100%)
2008	40 (100%)	Nil	40 (100%)

Source: Statistical Handbook, Mizoram, 1987, 1989, 1994, 1998, 2004 and 2008.

Tables 11.1–11.3 thus indicate that women's participation in the elected offices is insignificant. In the Village Council Election of 2009, out of 2102 elected members, 31 members constituted of women whereas 2071 members were male.[6] In the recent elections of the Aizawl Municipal Council, 33 per cent of the seats which were reserved for women were filled up by them. Of the 19 wards, 6 wards were reserved and in these wards women were elected as Councillors. It would be interesting to see in the other wards whether women would be elected if they had contested.

However, if one studies the role of the women in the various political parties, their contribution is remarkable. There are many women party workers who are truly dedicated to their cause. All the parties have their own women's wings and these wings are the only place where women could be the leaders. Women are not seen as leaders in the different political parties as the leaders are the choice of the majority. Hence, women are not seen in the forefront of the various political parties.

In the light of the above statements, it would be interesting to see the reasons as to why women's participation in the public elected offices is very low. Audrey who had done research on the participation of women in politics interviewed people from two villages had asked questions as to why women were not involved in politically involved decision-making process. From the interviews she conducted in two localities so as to know why women are not seen in politics, 50 per cent of male and 36.36 per cent of female regarded that politics is the domain of men while 21.88 per cent of male and 15.15 per cent of female thought that women are not competent enough to take part in politics.[7] When asked if women should participate in politics, 32 per cent of male and 36 per cent of female replied positively while 68 per cent of male and 64 per cent of female replied in the negative.[8] Many people also believed that women should involve themselves in household chores and if a woman is employed outside, she does not have the time to involve herself in other things including politics.[9] Interestingly, these views as seen above are not held by men alone. There are many women who believe that women should not be leaders as they are not capable of it. They also have the idea that politics is a secluded space for men and women should not create a space for themselves in politics.

The belief that women should not take part in decision-making especially in the public elected offices is due to the society being patriarchal in nature. Patriarchy is a system of social structures and practices in which men dominate and exploit women to their satisfaction. It can also be said to be an ideology in which men are seen as superior to women, that women are and should be controlled by men and that they are part of men's properties.[10] This patriarchal thought had dominated the men so much that Aristotle even reasoned that males are superior and female inferior so men rule over women.[11] Many women are also made to internalize the belief that she should be under the authority of the husband. Hence, it is from this unit of family that the first lesson of patriarchy is taught and where a hierarchal system is created. The family not only mirrors the order in the state and educates its children to follow what is being taught; it also creates and constantly reinforces that order. When the children follow this order, the next generation is socialized into those patriarchal ideas through the family.

Patriarchy can be seen in almost all societies in the world. But it should be noted that its nature is different in different societies, in different classes in the same society and also in different periods of time. So, as almost all the societies the worldover are patriarchal, the economic, political, religious, social and cultural institutions are by and large controlled by men. Hence, the structures and institutions of the state have been made by men and embody their interest rather than those of women. There are of course, many women leaders all-over the world, but majority of them are connected to some famous male personalities. They were active in politics but the structure and pattern of gender relationship was not disrupted. So it can be said that women's involvement in politics showed the spirit of cooperation and not of competition with men. Moreover, it can be asked whether they had really challenged patriarchal system. If they had questioned or tried to undermine patriarchy it can be wondered whether they would have been welcomed by other members of the party. Thus, it becomes clear that women hardly have any place in the political institutions and hence "in no country do women have political status, access, or influence equal to men's."[12] The Mizo society is no exception to this. Patriarchal system was the norms in the family and in the society and it was responsible for "the development of hyper-masculine biasness"[13] in which women are often relegated to the background. McCall had opined that "it was a country for men before it is one for women."[14] This holds true till today.

Many of the Mizo population also had the belief that women should not be decision-makers because of the teachings of St. Paul in the Bible who wrote that women should cover their heads and be silent. Hence, they consider that a good Christian woman should be docile and be subservient in the family and society and should not decision-makers.[15] So they assigned different tasks and responsibilities to men and women in the Church and this led to the continuation of the same belief and principle in the state affairs. So it can be said that the teachings of Christianity did not undermine patriarchy but rather reinforce it. Even when women were enrolled in the schools, the various syllabus which was made for them were different from the boy's school. They were taught weaving, knitting, gardening, childcare and other things which would make them "better wives and better mothers".[16] So the primary aim of the girls' education was to ensure the continuity of the institutional structures through the training of women to assist and replace the women missionaries and also be leaders in the women's organizations. The women missionaries who came to Mizoram tried to uplift the women but "one does not find the absolute egalitarianism of the late century feminists".[17] So there was no serious effort to remove women from a position subordinate to males in the society.[18] So it can be known that from the beginning of women's education, Mizo women were not encouraged to be leaders in the society and hence the men continue to stick to the old traditional patriarchal nature.

From the above statements, it can be fairly said that the various provisions and laws which were enacted in favour of women did not really help in empowering the Mizo women. The development in various fields and modernization has failed to undermine the so-called traditional cultural values that emphasize pre-assigned roles based on sex and the traditional values still influence the public at the level of consciousness. Mizo women, therefore, due to the patriarchal norms are not encouraged to carve a space for themselves in the political scene. Women themselves are also very reluctant to take part in it as they regard the political field as a male domain. Though many women are now economically independent and have carved a name for themselves in other spheres, they still need to create a space in the public elected offices. This is mainly because the general public is hesitant to accept a woman as their leader. There are now many women activists who tried to bring about a change in the society but their works sometimes have limitations. This is because many of these women are reluctant to be called feminists as "majority of them have stereotypical views on feminism as 'anti-men' rather than 'emancipation of women'".[19] They have a wrong notion to the term feminists or feminism and the public opinion is also quite negative in what they perceive feminism. The women activists are generally regarded as women extremists and they are often labelled as someone who would henpeck their husbands. Many women are hesitant to work publicly for the emancipation or empowerment of women simply because they are afraid of being insulted and hence remain silent on what they believe. Hence, women activists and intellectuals need to create awareness among the women and the public in general so that the people are more conscious and sensitive to gender issues.

Concluding Remarks: For Mizo women to be politically empowered, nomination and representation or reservation of seats is a very important step but it should be noted that as long as the traditional patriarchal concept is still very strong and it would not really empower the women. Hence, the concept of patriarchy has to be questioned because as long as these norms exist, women would always be marginalised. Thus, to have gender biased free society and women to be politically empowered, the social value system needs to undergo a change. The society also needs men or women in positions of influence who are conscious of gender relations and dare bring about a change in the political system.

NOTES

1. National Policy for the Empowerment of Women (2001) accessed through www.wcd.nic.in/empowerwomen.htm on 27th July, 2011
2. *Ibid.*
3. N.E. Parry, *A Monograph on Lushai Customs and Ceremonies* (Aizawl, reprint, 1988), p. 1.
4. B. Lalrinchhani, "Mizo Migration and Gender Relations: A Historical Analysis" Unpublished Ph.D. Thesis, Deptt of History, NEHU, 2008.
5. Audrey Laldinpuii, "Women's representation in decision-making bodies—A study of two villages in Mizoram" paper presented at NEIHA Conference, Goalpara, 1st–3rd November, 2007, p. 1.
6. Office of the Local Administration Department, Aizawl.
7. Audrey Laldinpuii, *op.cit.* p. 9.
8. *Ibid.*
9. B. Lalrinchhani, "Christianity and Women in Mizoram: A Study of the Impact of Christianity on Women in Lunglei District", Unpublished M.Phil. dissertation, Deptt. of History, NEHU, 1998.
10. Gerda Lerner, *The Creation of Feminist Consciousness* (New York, 1993) pp. 3,4.
11. *Ibid.*, p. 6.
12. Barbara Nelson and Najma Chowdhury(ed.), *Women and Politics Worldwide* (Delhi, 1997), p. 3.
13. Laldena Hmar, "Status of Mizo Women". Accessed through www.zogamonline.com/articles/atangpi/246–status–of–mizo–women–lal–dena.html on 17th August, 2011.
14. A.G. McCall, *Lushai Chrysalis* (Aizawl, reprint, 1977), p. 26.
15. B. Lalrinchhani, *op. cit*, M.Phil. dissertation, p. 98.
16. Chapman and Clark, *Mizo Miracle* (Madras, 1968), p .47.
17. Frederick S. Downs, *The Christian Impact on the Status of Women in North East India* (Shillong, 1996), p. 59.
18. *Ibid.*, p. 60.
19. Hmingthanzuali and H. Vanlalhruaia, "Women Issues in Mizo Society". accessed through www.thangtharculture.blogspot.com/2007/07women–issues–in–mizo–society.html on 19th July, 2010.

12
Women's Participation in Contemporary Mizo Politics: An Analysis

Lalzahawma

Introduction

Looking into the composition of women in the whole State, sex ratio as per 2011 Census is 975 for each 1000 male. This is in fact above the national average of 940:1000. According to the 2011 Census, there are a total of 5,38,675 female citizens in Mizoram as compared to 5,52,339 male. Besides, 89.40 per cent of female (4,08,643 persons) are literate in Mizoram in 2011. To one's surprise, the rate of increase in female population is higher than that of increase in male population during the last decade. Female-population increased by 1,09,211 during 2001 to 2011 while male population witnessed an increase by 93,230 only during the said period.[1]

Moreover, women voters in Mizoram have surpassed men in the updated electoral roll released in January 2011. The State of Mizoram now holds the record of being one of the seven states and Union territories, where women voters outnumber men. The updated rolls had registered a total of 6,40,752 voters in the entire State of which 3,25,079 were women and 3,15,673 men, a lead of 9,406. Again, the revised voters' rolls in Mizoram published in July 2010 also had registered a total of 6,33,455 voters in Mizoram, of which the women voters stood at 3,20,207 and men voters at 3,13,248, giving the women a lead of 6,959.

Despite the figures as cited above, no female member has ever occupied even a single seat in the 40-member Mizoram Legislative Assembly since 1988 till date. Women have always holed-up behind in contesting the Parliamentary and Assembly Elections in the State. In the last Assembly Election held in December 2008, no woman candidate could win though five of them were in the fray. During the last almost four decades that is, since 1972, there had been only five women legislators in Mizoram. They are–Saptawni (1972–1977: nominated), L. Thanmawii (elected two times in 1978 and during 1979–1984), K. Thansiami (1979–1984: nominated; and elected during 1984–1987), Rokungi (1984–1987: nominated) and Lalhlimpuii (1987–1988: elected).[2]

After statehood, only one women namely, Lalhlimpuii, had won from Aizawl North Constituency on Mizo National Front (MNF) ticket in the First Mizoram State Legislative Assembly that too lasted for a short span of time, that is, during 20.2.1987 to 6.9.1988 due to change of government. Since then, no woman has ever got elected in the State Legislative Assembly. It should be mentioned here that, Lalhlimpuii, in 1987, was the only legislator to become a Cabinet Minister among the Mizo women. In fact, women in Mizoram have been hardly fielded by political parties in the State Assembly Elections. In the last State Assembly Elections in 2008, the then ruling Mizo National Front (MNF) party nominated Lalhlimpuii in the Hrangturzo Assembly Constituency while Congress had fielded its women wing supremo Zothankimi in Aizawl West Constituency. The United Democratic Alliance (UDA), a union of two regional political parties, namely–Mizoram People's Conference and Zoram Nationalist Party, fielded H. Lalhmingthangi in Champhai South Constituency against MNF President and the then Chief Minister, Zoramthanga. The Bharatiya Janata Party (BJP) also fielded two women candidates, while other smaller and unrecognised parties too nominated two women candidates in 2008 elections. However, no woman candidate could win even a single seat in the 2008 State Assembly Elections too. Implementation of 33 per cent reservation of seats (actually 6, out of the 19 wards) for women in the Aizawl Municipal Council has unlocked Mizo women's backlog in public administration. Following the State Legislature's passage of the Act in this regard, Aizawl city administration now has six numbers of woman Councillors, namely–Hmingthanzami (ZNP, Ward No. II), Lalmalsawmi (MNF, Ward No. IV), Zamanthangi (MNF, Ward No. VI), Lalchhuanmawii (ZNP, Ward No. XI), Laldinsangi (INC, Ward No. XII) and F. Lalhuthangi (INC, Ward No. XVII).[3] In the meantime, no woman candidate was found from unreserved categories in the municipality election held for the first time in November 3, 2010.

There were 82 women candidates contesting in the 2009 general elections to Village Councils of 6 districts in Mizoram. Among them 31 candidates got elected such as–21 in Aizawl district, 6 in Lunglei district, 1 each in

Serchhip, Champhai, Mamit and Kolasib districts. Representation of women in Village Councils at the grass roots too is not satisfactory in Mizoram.

The following statistics in Table 12.1 shows Mizo women's representation in general election to Village Councils held in 2009 in 6 districts of Mizoram, namely–Aizawl, Lunglei, Serchhip, Champhai, Mamit and Kolasib districts.

From the light of these, we can conclude by saying that Mizo women are not well represented in the politics of Mizoram–state and local level. It is also true that women will never participate well in Mizoram politics as compared to their male counterparts without certain reservation of seats for them. The present proportion of women's representation in politics does not conform to the number of women population in Mizoram. In other words, the members so elected to the State Legislature, Municipality and Local Village Councils do not represent the whole stratum of Mizo women.

Centre—the Role Model for Mizoram towards Women Reservation

The issue of women's representation was first raised in the year 1974 in a report submitted to the Ministry of Education and Social Welfare by a Committee on Status of Women in India. Highlighting the low number of women in political bodies, the report recommended that seats be reserved for women in Panchayats and municipal bodies. Laying a strong foundation for their participation in decision-making at the local levels, the 73rd and 74th Amendments of the Indian Constitution, effective in 1993, have provided for reservation of seats in the Local Bodies of Panchayats and Municipalities for women. As a result, the Indian Constitution under Article 243-D provides for 33 per cent reservation for women in Panchayats.[4] This idea of making legal provisions for reserving seats for women in the Parliament and State Assemblies came into being during Rajiv Gandhi's tenure as the Prime Minister of India.

Women's Reservation Bill in Parliament and State Legislatures was first introduced on 12th September, 1996 in the Parliament by H.D. Deve Gowda's Government as 81st Constitution Amendment Bill. However, the Bill lapsed as Gowda's government became a minority which resulted in dissolution of 11th Lok Sabha. The Bill was reintroduced by the National Democratic Alliance (NDA) Government in the 12th Lok Sabha as the 84th Constitution Amendment Bill in June 26, 1998. This time too, the Bill flopped as 12th Lok Sabha was dissolved prematurely with the Vajpayee Government being reduced to a minority. The NDA Government

Table 12.1: Women in Village Councils

Sl. No.	*VC Statistics*	*Aizawl*	*Lunglei*	*Serchhip*	*Champhai*	*Mamit*	*Kolasib*	*Total*
1.	No. of Village Council (VC)	167	132	41	100	71	44	555
2.	No. of VC seats	689	457	150	358	242	175	2071
3.	No. of voters	2,37,306	88,578	39,906	76,268	43,025	48,051	5,33,134
4.	No. of women candidates	40	20	8	1	7	6	82
5.	No. of successful women	21	6	1	1	1	1	31
6.	% of seats won by women	3.04 %	1.31 %	0.66 %	0.27 %	0.41 %	0.57 %	1.49 %

Source: State Election Commission, Mizoram–2009.

in the 13th Lok Sabha again failed to gather consensus on the issue when the Bill was introduced again on 22nd November, 1999. The NDA Government had brought the Bill to the Lok Sabha twice in 2002 and 2003 but could never get it passed even though the Congress and the Left, constituting a majority, had assured NDA of their support.[5]

After coming to power at the Centre, Congress-led United Progressive Alliance introduced the said Bill in Rajya Sabha on 6th May, 2008 and again tabled in both Houses of Parliament amid protests by Samajwadi Party, Janata Dal(U) and Rastriya Janata Dal (RJD) in December 17, 2009. In what signifies the government's resolve to realise the commitments in the Common Minimum Programme, the Union Cabinet approved Women's Reservation Bill on 25th February, 2010. On 8th March, 2010, the Bill was moved to Rajya Sabha, but voting on it deferred after unruly scenes and threats of withdrawal support to the UPA Government by allies like Samajwadi Party and RJD. Finally, the much-hyped 108th Constitutional Amendment Bill, popularly known as the Women's Reservation Bill which seeks to reserve one-third of seats for women in the Lok Sabha and the State Legislative Assemblies was passed in the Rajya Sabha on 9th March, 2010. The Bill, to become an Act—needless to mention the President of India's mandatory assent which is certain, still has to pass through the Lok Sabha.

Furthermore, the Union Cabinet on 27th August, 2009 approved the proposal for moving amendment to article 243D of the Constitution of India for enhancing reservation for women in Panchayats at all tiers 'from one-third to at least 50 per cent (vide Union Cabinet's press release dated 27th August, 2009; Release ID: 52175).[6] This provision will apply to the total number of seats filled by direct election, offices of chairpersons and seats and offices of chairpersons reserved for Scheduled Castes and Scheduled Tribes. In India, out of the total elected representatives of Panchayats numbering approximately 28.18 lakhs, 36.87 per cent are women.[7] With the proposed Constitutional Amendment, the number of elected women representatives is expected to rise to more than 14 lakhs. This proposal however, will not apply to the Scheduled Areas referred to in clause (1), and the tribal areas referred to in clause (2), of Article 244 of the Indian Constitution like the State of Mizoram etc., as contained in Article 243M.[8]

Moving back to Mizoram, the state administration by an Act of the Mizoram State Legislative Assembly made provision for reservation of one-third of the total seats for women in the recently established Aizawl Municipal Council.[9] As per the said Act, six seats/wards being the nearest to one-third of the total 19 seats in Aizawl Municipal Council have been reserved for women. This in fact was in pursuance of the Constitution of India's provision for reservation of seats to women under Part IX-A, Article 243T (3) and (4). The reserved seats shall be carried out on rotation basis to different wards (constituencies) in every five years and at least six months prior announcement by the Election Commission.

Conclusion

Women's Reservation Bill or the 108th Constitutional Amendment Bill in its current form envisages reserving 181 seats out of 545 in the House of People for women. It means 181 male members of Parliament would not be able to contest elections if the Bill is passed. Also, as there is to be a rotation of seats, a male Member of Parliament cannot represent the same constituency for more than two consecutive terms. To those who oppose women reservation, 181 seats in Parliament is too great a number to be sacrificed just for the sake of women's empowerment or adequate political representation.

Likewise, reservation of 6 seats out of the total 19 wards/seats for women in the Aizawl Municipal Council suggests necessary participation of Mizo women in urban local body. This reservation regime in other words, proves to be a compelling force that drags Mizo women too into the political affairs. In the meantime, it is a matter of concern whether or not to implement 50 per cent reservation of seats for women at the village/grass roots level (referring to the Constitution (One Hundred and Tenth Amendment) Bill, 2009) in the State of Mizoram. Women's empowerment through legislation and reservation is necessary in case of Mizoram in particular.

NOTES

1. The Mizoram Municipalities (Amendment) Act, 2009.
2. PUCL Bulletin, August 2004.
3. PUCL Bulletin, July 2003.
4. Annual Report 2009-2010, Ministry of Rural Development, Govt. of India, March, 2010.
5. Report of the 'National Policy for the Empowerment of Women', 2001.
6. Census of India, 2011–Provisional Totals, Mizoram Series-16, 2011.
7. The Constitution of India.
8. *30 Years of Mizoram Legislative Assembly*, published by Mizoram Legislative Assembly Secretariat, 2003.
9. http://indiacurrentaffairs.org, accessed on 13th August, 2011.

SECTION IV

Social and Economic Empowerment: Perspectives on Mizoram

13

Socio-economic Empowerment of Women:

A Study with Special Reference to Mizoram

A. Sundaram

Introduction

Empowering of women is a prerequisite for creating a good nation. When women are empowered, society with stability is assured. Empowerment of women is essential as their value systems lead to the development of a good family, good society and ultimately good nation (Dr. A.P.J. Abdul Kalam).

The reality is that no country in the world, no matter how advanced, has achieved true gender equality. Gender inequalities and disparities exist, even in countries without glaring male-domination. Understanding these disparities and inequalities is a necessary step towards implementing corrective policies. This study is an attempt to evaluate the strengths and weaknesses of women and their status and the size of the gender gap in Mizoram. This is perhaps the right time to discuss this topic because the Mizo Hmeichhe Insuihkhawm Pawl (MHIP) or Mizo Women's Federation has declared 2010-11 as the Year of Women Empowerment.

The present paper mainly focuses on what is women empowerment? Why is empowerment of women very important in Mizoram? What is the current status of women in Mizoram? What hinders the empowerment of women in Mizoram? How empowerment of women can be achieved in Mizoram?

Let us discuss one by one as follows:

What is Empowerment of Women?

The empowerment of women refers to providing the necessary rights and responsibilities to women in order to make them self–reliant. Empowerment is the process of building capacities of women, creating an atmosphere which will enable people to fully utilize their creative potentials. Empowerment gives women the capacity to influence decision-making process, planning, implementation and evaluation.

Women's empowerment allover the world have been challenging and changing gender inequalities since the beginnings of history. Four important dimensions of female empowerment and opportunity have been chosen for examination, based mainly on the findings of UNIFEM (United Nations Fund for Empowerment of Women) and World Economic Forum (WEF), concerning global patterns of inequality between men and women:

These components are as follows:

1. Economic participation
2. Political empowerment
3. Educational attainment
4. Health and Well-being.

Economic Participation is concerned with:

- Female unemployment (in female labour force) as percentage of male unemployment (in male labour force),
- Equality between women and men for private and public sector employment,
- Ratio of estimated female to male earned income,
- Female economic activity rate as percentage of male economic activity rate,
- Wage equality between women and men for similar work,
- Female professional and technical workers (as percentage of total).

Educational Attainment is Concerned with:

- Female to male ratio, gross primary level enrolment,
- Female to male ratio, gross secondary level enrolment,
- Female to male ratio, gross tertiary level enrolment,
- Adult literacy, female rate as percentage of male rate.

Health and Well-being is Concerned with:

- Adolescent fertility rate (births per woman, age 15–19),
- Maternal mortality ratio per 1,00,000 live births,
- Infant mortality rate, per 1,000 live births,
- Effectiveness of government efforts to reduce poverty and inequality.

Political Empowerment is Concerned with:

- Number of years of a female President or Prime Minister in the last 50 years,
- Women in government at ministerial level (as percentage of total),
- Seats in Parliament held by women (as percentage of total),
- Female Legislators, senior officials and managers (as of total).

Why is Empowerment of Women very Important in Mizoram?

Empowering women to ensure their full participation in all spheres of life and at all levels of activity is necessary:

- To create a strong economy.
- To build a more stable and just society.
- To improve the quality of life for women, men, families and communities, and the activities of private businesses and promote their goals.
- To not only for lowering the disproportionate levels of poverty among women, but also as an important step towards raising household income and encouraging economic development in State and the Country as a whole.
- To gain visibility and voice at home, workplace and the community.
- To save half of our population from the clutches of poverty and reduce the deep-rooted gender gaps in the society.
- To increase the women's self-confidence, self-image, prevent women from becoming a doormat, gain courage, self-discovery, better health and also their basic needs of survival and to generate new ideas among women and help them to develop new consciousness and willpower.
- To improve women's access to credit and finance—this forms the basis of overall development.
- To bring women into mainstream economic activities so as to ensure their equality and empowerment.
- To remove blocks towards the overall empowerment of women and to participate in formal economic activities on terms and conditions which reflect the productive capacity of women, and their control over their own incomes, are some of the important dimensions of economic empowerment.

- To remove economic dependence of women and make them free from emotional and psychological violence.
- To reduce economic exploitation of women from various types of violence that women face and to allow them to live a dignified life. They find their very survival easy.
- To act as a panacea for most ills in society and it can lead women to have choices on their health. They can take a good care of themselves as well as their families.
- To help in eradicating of many social evils like prostitution, immoral trafficking of women, HIV/AIDS etc. It will change the lives of poor women and help them to gain a good status at their homes as well as in their community.
- By identifying and quantifying the gender gap helps policy-makers with a tool offering direction and focus for the work of significantly improving the economic, political and social potential of all their citizens.
- To provide the impetus for policy-makers to strengthen their commitment to the idea of women's empowerment, and to concentrate the political will, energy and resources, in concert with aid agencies and civil society organizations, to make gender equality a reality.

What is the Current Status of Women in Mizoram?

By analysing women participation in different sectors of Mizoram, we may understand the current status of economic empowerment of women in Mizoram.

Tables 13.1 and 13.2 reveals that the female work participation rate is less than male work participation for total workers, main workers, rural and urban area in Mizoram. The female marginal and non-workers, participation rate is higher than male participation rate for the same. Of course, the female work participation rate has increased for total workers, total rural workers, marginal workers, rural marginal workers, non-workers, and rural non-workers except for main workers from 1991 to 2001. Female work participation rate of 47.63 per cent for Mizoram was higher than the national average of 25.68 per cent.

The female work participation has increased from male workers participation for cultivators, agricultural labourers and household industry except for other workers in 2001.

Table 13.1: Percentage of Total Workers, Main Workers, Marginal Workers and Non-Workers to Total Population by Residence and Sex

State	Total/ Rural/ Urban	Persons/ Males/ Females	Percentage of Population							
			Workers							
			Total Workers		Main Workers		Marginal Workers		Non-Workers	
			1991	2001	1991	2001	1991	2001	1991	2001
Mizoram	T	P	49.46	52.70	42.64	40.83	6.82	11.87	50.54	47.30
		M	53.87	57.45	49.59	49.29	4.28	8.16	46.13	42.55
		F	44.68	47.63	35.11	31.82	9.57	15.82	55.32	52.37
	R	P	52.22	57.22	46.57	44.94	5.65	12.27	47.78	42.78
		M	54.92	59.52	51.29	51.74	3.63	7.79	45.08	40.48
		F	49.27	54.73	41.40	37.61	7.87	17.12	50.73	45.27
	U	P	46.23	47.87	38.05	36.64	8.18	11.45	53.77	51.91
		M	52.63	52.32	47.57	46.76	5.06	8.55	47.37	44.68
		F	39.37	40.50	27.83	25.99	11.54	14.50	60.63	59.50

Source: Census of Mizoram-2001.

Table 13.2: Percentage of Total Workers (Main and Marginal) 2001

State	P/M/F	T.W (Main+ Marginal)	Cultivators	Ag. Labourers	H. industry	Other Workers
	P	469597	53.91	5.85	1.40	38.83
Mizoram	M	264162	48.77	4.93	1.20	45.11
	F	205435	60.52	7.05	1.66	30.77

Source: Census of Mizoram, 2001.

There exist 6332 registered small scale industrial units in the state in the year 2007. The gender-wise distribution of workers in SSI sector shows that 17.08 per cent of the total SSI workers were female and 82.92 per cent were male.

According to the 2001 Census report that the employment of women in the organized sector (both Public 10.6 per cent and Private Sectors 0.6 per cent) was about 11 per cent. Organised sector of female employment constitutes a small share of total employment in Mizoram. Even within the organised sector most women are located in the lower rungs of the hierarchy. Very few are managers or decision-makers.

The average female distribution of employees in Group A, Group B, Group C and Group D in statutory, State Government, Central Government, Semi-Government, Banking and Insurance and District Councils was less than 20 per cent in Mizoram between 2001–2003. This report also reveals that the female employment given in Groups A, B, C, D, is far lagging behind male employment in both State Government and Central Government sector.

Mizoram accounts for only 0.04 per cent of workers in unorganised sector. Number of enterprises in select service sectors in unorganised sector is 5132. Even though unorganised sector is growing quickly in Mizoram, female work participation is less than 12 per cent. Unemployment rate in Mizoram was 7.1, out of which male 6.27 and female 8.05 in 2001and it was in 1991 the female rate was less than one per cent.

Table 13.3 explains the EI = Index of 'Economic Participation and Decision-making Power'; POERI = Index of 'Power Over Economic Resources'; PI =Index of 'Political Participation and Decision-making Power'; and GEM = Gender Empowerment Measure for Mizoram and India.

A research study was conducted to find out the overall improvement in performance on GEM over the decade for all the States/UTs for 1996 and 2006. In this study, Mizoram was categorised as best 3rd category parameters in 2006 (0.316 to 0.415–Orissa, Tripura, Bihar, Mizoram, Jammu and Kashmir and Meghalaya) and in 1996 it was categorised as worst 4th category parameters (0.165 to 0.315= Assam, Mizoram, Arunachal Pradesh, Sikkim, Jharkhand, Bihar, Meghalaya, Nagaland).

Table 13.3: Dimension-wise GEM Scores, 2006

	EI	*POERI*	*PI*	*GEM*
Mizoram	0.418	0.455	0.250	0.374
India	0.546	0.319	0.625	0.497

Source: Ministry of Human Resource Development Report.

The indicators used to estimate each of these dimensions are listed below:

Indicators for the Dimension 'Power Over Economic Resources'

(i) Per cent Female/Male operational landholdings (due to data gaps in assets)
(ii) Per cent Females/Males with Bank Accounts in Scheduled Commercial Banks (with credit limit above Rs. 2 lakh)
(iii) Female/Male Estimated Earned Income Share per capita per annum.

Indicators for the Dimension 'Political Participation and Decision-making Power'

(i) Per cent Share of Parliamentary Seats (elected)
(ii) Per cent Share of Seats in Legislature (elected)
(iii) Per cent Share of Seats in *Zilla Parishads* (elected)
(iv) Per cent Share of Seats in *Gram Panchayats* (elected)
(v) Per cent Candidates in Electoral Process in National Parties
(vi) Per cent Electors exercising the right to vote.

Indicators for the Dimension 'Economic Participation and Decision-making Power'

(i) Per cent Share of officials in service in Indian Administrative Service, Indian Police Service and Forest Service.
(ii) Per cent Share of enrolment in medical and engineering colleges.

Gender Empowerment Measure (GEM) measures women's and men's ability to participate actively in economic and political life and their command over economic resources. It focuses on opportunities and captures gender equality and inequality in three key areas, 'Political

Participation and Decision-making Power', 'Economic Participation and Decision-making Power' and 'Power Over Economic Resources'.

The values attained reflect the existence of equalities and sharp disparities in gender empowerment. The low scores attained on any of these aspects draw attention to the severe gender disparities that exist with regard to access to resources and assets and the historical discrimination faced by women in access to land, livestock, credit and other productive resources, despite their unpaid and unrecognised contribution to agriculture and farm and non-farm family based economic activities.

Table 13.4 reveals the Gender Equality Index in Mizoram and India.

Table 13.4: Gender Equality Index in Mizoram and India

State	*2006*	
	Rank	GEI
India	112.	0.497
Mizoram	32	0.374

Source: Ministry of Human Resource Development Report.

Another research studies also reveals that in GEI, India ranks 112 out of the138 countries on the Global Instability Index based on 2008 data. Mizoram ranks 32 among the states in India. GEI ranks and scores for the above table indicate that India and Mizoram affluence does not translate into better opportunities for women, and reinforces the fact on gender inequalities.

Gender Equality Index refers to that stage of human social development at which "the rights, responsibilities and opportunities of individuals will not be determined by the fact of being born male or female", in other words, a stage when both men and women realize their full potential.

The Human Development Index (HDI) is a simple average of three dimension indices that measure average achievements in a country or state with regard to 'A long and healthy life', as measured by life expectancy at birth; 'Knowledge', as measured by the adult literacy rate and the combined primary, secondary and tertiary gross enrolment ratio; and 'A decent standard of living', as measured by estimated earned income in Purchasing Power Parity (PPP). The poor status of women is reflected through the Gender Development Index (GDI), which ensures the unequal achievements of men and women. The goals of human development cannot be achieved without the development and empowerment of women.

Gaps between HDI and GDI reflect the existence of gender disparities in translating development into equitable outcomes. The higher HDI, GDI scores indicate the progress in translating its growth into a better quality of life for both women and men. Disparities in access to resources and outcomes are penalised and result in lower levels of attainment on GDI and GEM.

Table 13.5 below describes the HDI and GDI scores and ranks for Mizoram and India.

Table 13.5 : HDI and GDI Scores and Ranks for States in 2006

State/Country	*HDI*	*Rank*	*GDI*	*Rank*
Mizoram	0.688	12	0.687	9
India	0.605	134	0.590	112

Source: Ministry of Human Resource Development Report.

The Gender Inequality Index is a composite measure reflecting inequality in achievements between women and men in three dimensions: reproductive health, empowerment and the labour market. It varies between zero (when women and men fare equally) and one (when men or women fare poorly compared to the other in all dimensions). The health dimension is measured by two indicators: maternal mortality rate and the adolescent fertility rate. The empowerment dimension is also measured by two indicators: the share of Parliamentary seats held by each sex and by secondary and higher education attainment levels. The labour dimension is measured by women's participation in the workforce. The Gender Inequality Index is designed to reveal the extent to which national and state human development achievements are eroded by gender inequality, and to provide empirical foundations for policy analysis and advocacy efforts. It can be interpreted as a percentage loss to potential human development due to shortfalls in the dimensions included. Higher values of the GII indicate worse achievements. The Gender Inequality Index measures the loss in human development due to inequality in reproductive health, empowerment and labour market between women and men. Losses in HDI and the Gender Inequality Index are highly correlated; indicating that unequal distribution of human development is strongly associated with gender inequality.

Table 13.6: The Female Infant Mortality Rate

State/Country	*Total*	*Male*	*Female*
Mizoram	37	37	38
India	53	52	55

Source: Registrar General of India, 2009.

According to Registrar General of India, the total infant mortality rate of Mizoram was 37, out of which MIMR was 37 and IMR was 38 in 2008. The gender gap in infant mortality rate is defined as the difference between the female infant mortality rate and the male infant mortality rate. A positive value of IMR implies higher infant mortality rate among females as compared to males, while a negative figure reflects excess male mortality among infants. The gender gap reveals one excess female not surviving during infancy, as compared to males, among every 1,000 babies born.

Table 13.7: Life Expectancy at Birth in India 1991–2006 (Latest)

State/Country	*Total*	*Male*	*Female*
Mizoram	64.0	64.1	61.6
India	64.5	62.6	64.2

Source: National Health Profile.

The expected years of survival at birth for females has been showing a positive trend over the years. Women live up to an average of 61.5 years in Mizoram and for India is 64.5 in 2009.

Table 13.8: Maternal Mortality Rate 2006 (Latest)

State/Country	*Female*
Mizoram	0.30
India	254

Source: National Health Profile.

The Maternal Mortality Rate (MMR) is calculated as the number of maternal deaths per 1,00,000 live births. This indicator is based on information collected that refers to deaths of women on account of pregnancy, childbirth or within 42 days of childbirth. MMR indicates how safe motherhood is.

Total Fertility Rate: The fertility rate as per the NFHS-II is an average of three babies per woman for the country as a whole.

Table 13.9: Total fertility rate in 2006 (Latest)

State/Country	*Rank*	*Total Fertility Rate*
Mizoram	8	2.9
India	–	2.7

Source: National Health Profile.

Table 13.10: Adult Sex Ratio and Child Sex Ratio

State/Country	*Child sex ratio*			*Adult sex ratio*	
	Rank	*2001*	*2011*	*2001*	*2011*
Mizoram	20	964	971	935	975
India	–	927	945	933	–

Source: Statistical Hand Book of Mizoram.

As on 1st March, 2011, the sex ratio of the total population of Mizoram is 975 which has significantly increased if we compare with 935 of 2001. The state's child sex ratio has increased to 971 in 2011 from 964 in 2001.

Table 13.11: Decadal Growth Rate and Death Rate of Population

State/Country	*1991–2001*			
	Death Rate			*Birth Rate*
	Total	*Male*	*Female*	*Total*
Mizoram	5.1	6.3	3.9	13.4
India	7.4	8.0	6.8	22.8

Source: SRS Bulletin October 2009, Registrar General of India.

The decadal population growth rate for 2001–2011 is 22.78 per cent, out of which male percentage is 20.31 and female is 25.43. The total death rate for Mizoram was 5.1, out of which, the male rate was 6.3 and female rate was 3.9 and birth rate was 13.4 in 2008.

Table 13.12: Gross Enrolment Ratio

State/ Country	*2009*								*2003–2004*		
	Gross Secondary Level			*Gross Tertiary Level*			*Combined Gross Ratio*		*Hr.Edu.*		
	T	*M*	*F*	*T*	*M*	*F*	*M*	*F*	*M*	*F*	*T*
Mizoram	87.70	88.5	86.8	45.6	45.50	45.70	0.61	0.54	11.9	9.64	10.38
India	77.5	80.6	74.1	45.5	49.2	41.4	0.55	0.38	10.59	7.65	9.21

Source: Ministry of Human Resource Report.

Table 13.13: Literacy Rate

State/Country	2001		
	Literacy rate		
	T	M	F
Mizoram	91.58	93.72	89.40 (2011)
India	65.8	54.16	75.85

Source: Census Report.

Table 13.14: Literacy Gender Gap

State/Country	LGAP	RANK
Mizoram	4.56	28
India	21.69	–

Source: Census of India–2001.

Gender gap of literacy rates for Mizoram has come down from 13.78 to 4.56 percentages in 1971 to 2001. This is lower than national average that was from 23.98 to 21.69. India's total literacy rate is 65.8; out of which female literacy rate was 54.16 and for male was 75.85.

Per capita government expenditure on health in the IHR (1999-2000) is Rs. 674 for Mizoram and for India is Rs. 162.

Table 13.15 indicates the Empowering Women through per cent seats held by women in Parliament and in the Gram Panchayats in 2006 and 2009 for 15th Lok Sabha and Rajya Sabha in India.

Table 13.15: Empowering Women in Parliament

State/ Country	2006		2009	
	% seat by women In Parliament	%Gram Panchayats	% seats 15th Lok Sabha	% seats Rajya Sabha (2009)
India	8.3	32.75	10	9.52
Mizoram	–	0.5	–	–

Source: Election Commission Report.

The percentage of Women Age 15–49 who have Experienced Physical or Sexual Violence in 2005–06 is shown in Table 13.16.

Table 13.16: Physical or Sexual Violence 2005–06

	% of Physical or Sexual Violence
Mizoram	25.5
India	35.5

Source: NFHS-3.

The most important sources of disempowerment faced by women are:

(i) Harassment through violence, both physical and sexual; and
(ii) Severe disparities in access to assets such as land and low share of "paid" work and income. Women face physical, mental, emotional and sexual abuse both within and outside their home.

The above analysis gives us clear picture about the equalities and disparities of women existed in Mizoram and India.

How can Economic Empowerment of Women be achieved in Mizoram?

According to the Eleventh Five Year Plan, the following steps and strategies may be experimented to improve the status of women and bring them empowerment with the ultimate objective of making all women economically independent and self-reliant through:

Recommendations for the Service Sector

- A policy of equal opportunity should be formulated to encourage women's increased participation within a time bound frame.
- Women headed enterprises from this sector should be exempt from tax.
- The tax rebate for women employed in this sector should be further increased.
- There should be a tax incentive to encourage women entrepreneurial ventures in industries where there are low numbers of women workers and/or management.
- To encourage enterprises to employ women and to ensure tax incentives for enterprises employing more women.
- Increase the number of vocational training institutes for women. There should be slots in vocational training institutes for the re-training and skill upgradation of women. Recommendations for strengthening women's agricultural capacities:
- Agricultural extension services and other infrastructural support for women farmers should be made available to women farmers.
- Policies should be designed to ensure women's control over complementary resources including credit, forest, fuel, fodder, information and training.
- Training programmes covering areas such as land surveying,

resource mapping, resource management, use of technology, marketing, financial management; cooperative management and organic farming should be made available to women.

- Measures should be taken to remove middlemen in the sale of non-timber forest products and women's cooperatives for directly marketing these products should be formed.
- Ensuring women's effective presence in village decision-making bodies:
- All Joint Forest Management groups should have at least one-third and, if possible, 50 per cent women in their executive committees.
- Increase subsidies to poor farmers and non-farm livelihoods (livestock, fishing, fodder etc.). Providing incentive such as provision of higher subsidies for land development, credit and rebate on transfer fee, house tax, sales tax and stamp duties on women owned land, housing and rural industries.
- Gender equality in inheritance laws governing for tribal women need codification and formalization, in keeping with the principle of gender equality. Customary laws to be reviewed through legislation to ensure the economic and social security of women. This has to be supplemented by providing legal literacy and legal support services for women.
- Recording of women's shares, the NSS, agricultural census and the cost of cultivation surveys should collect gender-disaggregated data on land ownership and use, and origin of the property (viz. purchase, inheritance, lease etc.). All levels of government functionaries to be involved with keeping land records or computerizing and updating records, those women's inheritance shares in land as widows, daughters, etc. are fully and proactively recorded. The recording should be in women's own names, rather than jointly with other relatives.

For Improving Women's Access to Public Land

- Distribution of surplus land and land under all land distribution programmes viz., Land Ceiling Act, should exclusively be to rural landless women workers.

Recommendations for Women in the Small-Scale and Unorganised Sector

- Comprehensive legislation for the unorganised sector is needed with provisions relating to leave, pension, housing and child care, a complaints committee on sexual harassment, regulation of employment, wages and conditions of work, work records, safety and occupational health, work tools and safety equipments, Rights over Resources, dispute resolution bodies at District level and Appellate Body at the State Level.

- There is an urgent need for ensuring regulations in this sector that deal with employment, conditions of service, social security and welfare.
- Social security provisions must be created that encompass the right to health and medical care, employment injury benefit, maternity benefit, group insurance, housing safety measures, and Gratuity and Pension benefits.
- Tripartite Boards for each broad sector with adequate representation for women in the Board including complaints committee for sexual harassment, with 50 per cent workers' representation with proportionate representation to women; boards to be formed at local, taluk, district, state and national levels.
- Budgetary allocation (3%) for the social security needs of the unorganized sector. The funds can be drawn from the cess/levy on the sector itself and contribution from the Central and State Governments. A social security fund should be constituted.
- Promulgation of Government Orders for regularization of Labour of unorganised workers whether casual or contract, with identity card, fair wages, weekly holiday, weekly leave, hours of work, maternity and child care, ESI, pension, P.F., safety and occupational health.

Recommendations on Self Help Groups (SHGs) and Micro Credit

- Given the importance, scope and scale of the SHGs and micro-credit phenomena, a high-level Committee on the Status of SHGs should be constituted to review the existing perspectives, policies and programmes related to SHGs in order to strengthen their potential towards addressing the social, economic and political rights of women. The mandate of the Committee should include recommending the manner in which the State will generate data in order that the performance of micro-credit based interventions may be reviewed and monitored.

- Identification and analysis of existing macro data on indicators that will enable an assessment of the impact of SHGs. This could include macro data related to poverty reduction, distress migration, violence against women, inclusion of economically and socially marginalized communities etc.
- The Committee should also be mandated to recommend the process and to monitor progress in terms of empowerment and equity can be designed.
- The findings of the Committee should be not limited to mere recommendations, which might or might not be incorporated. The Eleventh Five-Year Plan needs to ensure that the recommendations are necessarily reflected in the formulation of new policies and programmes or redesigning of existing ones. Once the indicators are in place all Departments and Ministries should report according to these indicators. The Committee should work within a timeframe and adequate budgetary allocations for this should be made.

Bringing SHG Data in the Public Domain

- The State and other Institutions engaged with SHGs should make available the data related to achievements in poverty alleviation, empowerment and literacy. Such data should be gender disaggregated. With the growing recognition that women are not a homogenous category data should be further disaggregated in terms of other categories like, caste, class, religion, ethnicity, educational status etc. Such data will be extremely useful for planning purposes.

Regulation of the Financial Functions

- The State and the appropriate Ministries should institute a Regulatory framework for the functioning of micro finance institutions in order that there be a limit on the extent of interest rates and the manner of recovery of loans not be exploitative.
- Assets created through micro-credit should be in the name of women.

Addressing Gender Issues and Adopting a Holistic Approach to Empowerment

- Micro-credit should be seen as one part of a broader strategy to enhance women's agency on social, political and economic levels. Policies and programmes should simultaneously seek to increase women's confidence, awareness, negotiation ability, literacy, health, as well as women's vocational, entrepreneurial and management skills, to enable micro finance inputs to translate into sustained empowerment. The costs of enabling that empowerment through extensive training inputs and other strategies need to be considered a necessary and direct cost commitment of all micro-credit based programmes.

- SHGs can be federated and expanded into larger community based organizations. This can enable them to leverage greater amounts of credit and undertake more sustainable livelihood options. In addition these large women's collectives should be empowered to take on gender justice issues and collectively struggle against gender-based discrimination and violence against women.

Capacity Building on Gender Issues

- In order to ensure that issues of gender are adequately addressed the capacity building inputs need to be strengthened, and provided for longer durations and with a long-term focus.
- The capacity building inputs should focus on Building an understanding on gender issues including violence against women.
- Understanding legal provisions *vis-a-vis* violence.
- Enabling women to understand how they can access institutions of justice.
- Information on Government schemes, especially those related to women and gender justice.
- A core curriculum framework should be developed for training at the national level. Those who have expertise in the field of gender as well as SHGs should develop the curriculum framework jointly. A strong training of trainers programme should be designed so that expertise can gradually be available at decentralized levels.
- A substantial literacy programme should be included as part of the SHG programmes.
- All agencies that sponsor SHGs (banks, micro finance institutions and government departments, NGOs, donor agencies etc.) should contribute to a Women's Crisis Fund to be managed by SHGs which will address women's needs related to violence, health, food etc.

SHGs in Governance Structures

- Greater linkages and formal mechanisms between representatives of SHGs and PRI Institutions should be worked out so that the priorities of poor women can inform village planning processes and in order that governance systems are responsive to their demands.

Adoption of Holistic Livelihood Options

- The vision must be broadened from narrowly defined enterprise development activities (which typically include non-viable income generation activities) to a livelihood approach. This should be based on a mapping of existing livelihood options.
- SHGs should not only be conduit for delivery of services but should be strong collective of women. These should be sustainable. These should ensure backward linkages with technology and credit and forward linkages with markets so as to generate both farm and non-farm livelihood opportunities.
- Policies and programmes should design a wide range of financial products and services to meet the needs of poor women. Four broad categories of credit products are recommended: credit for income generating activities, credit for investment in education and health; consumption credit including household needs; and products for social security.
- Adequate capacity building package on livelihoods should be developed.

Recommendations on Women in Information and Communication Technologies (ICTs) Empowerment Programme

- Address and integrate gender perspectives when developing and implementing national policies, legislation, strategies and regulatory and technical instruments in the area of Information and Communications Technologies (ICT) and media and communications, and create monitoring and accountability mechanisms to ensure implementation of gender sensitive policies and regulations;
- Address ICT-related infrastructural and tariff barriers that disproportionately affect poor women and women living in remote and rural areas;
- Support and encourage research on women's information needs,

find ways to adapt ICT to the needs of the poor and especially illiterate women, and study the impact of ICT on women's social, economic and political empowerment;

- Support and encourage gender equality principles and pedagogic perspectives in all aspects of science and technology education.
- Develop policies and mechanisms for increasing the number of female students in science and technology and ICT related fields, and expand training and capacity building programmes for women on the use of new technologies;
- Ensure that women gain access to promising new employment opportunities, including through ICT-based economic activities.
- Strengthen the use of traditional information and communication technologies, such as radio, TV and print, in parallel to enhancing the use of ICT and convergence with new ICT, towards the empowerment of women; Collect, share, positively recognize and widely publicise good practices to counter gender stereotyping and negative portrayals of women in all forms of media and communications.
- Increase efforts to compile statistics on ICT use disaggregated by sex, develop gender specific indicators on ICT use and needs, and generate sex-disaggregated data on employment patterns in media and ICT professions;
- Provide resources for innovative media and ICT projects in support of gender equality and for the production of content that is particularly relevant to women's interests and concerns;
- Ensure mechanisms and resources to safeguard traditional and indigenous knowledge and other intellectual resources that are held as public common good from being appropriated.
- The nodal office of National Commission for Women should be established in each block and district to protect the rights of women, girls and children, voice their issues and concerns and pay undivided attention to monitor the compliance with the existing Laws and establish effective coordination with other related offices.
- Elected women representatives in Panchayati Raj Institutions (PRIs) need to be intensively trained to develop skill, capacity building and knowledge management that can help them generate adequate confidence to participate effectively in decision-making process as well as occupy decision-making positions.

Recommendations on Employment and Poverty Alleviation/Income Generation Activities

Swarnjayanti Gram Swarozgar Yojana (SGSY)

- Reservation for women should be increased from 40 per cent to 50 per cent as the minimum. The women beneficiaries should be drawn from the poor of marginalized sections like SC, ST and minorities. Widows, single women and female-headed households should be given priority. It is necessary to exercise greater vigil to ensure that the allocations earmarked for women are not diverted to other components of SGSY.
- Mere financial assistance does not help the women. They need institutional support on financial inputs in the form of awareness, knowledge, skill training and marketing know-how, etc. should be treated as an integral part of the programme and the mechanism of providing these through convergence with line departments needs to be reviewed. Information on the latest available technology is also key factor.
- The approach of the scheme should be expanded to include an empowerment and right based agenda. 'Swarozgar' should be redefined to include a livelihood approach, the focus should shift from financial management to economic empowerment which would mean going beyond access to credit to strengthening asset creation and ensuring women's access to public resources.
- Based on past experiences, the livelihood options offered at district and block levels should not include unviable micro enterprises and should focus on creating long-term rural livelihood assets and infrastructure for example, ponds, grasslands, community forestry, nurseries, seed and grain banks, etc.
- Rural bank branches should be strengthened with a single window system to address women's needs efficiently.
- Banks should not treat the credit to SHGs as a commercial venture.
- Linkage with RMK may be explored as an alternative source of credit where commercial bank branches are not there.
- As MFIs augment their resources through the savings of poor women members of SHGs, they should invest back in these women. There should be a mandatory social commitment clause from MFIs and other financial institutions working on such programmes.

- Reduced rate of interest should be charged from women SHGs.
- Bank should adopt a single window approach to assist women especially those belonging to marginalized communities, BPL, female-headed households and destitute women so as to overcome the procedural and other barriers to accessing loans.
- Procedures for registered federations and SHGs that are registered or are members of registered federations to access institutional credit should be simplified, with these federations providing the necessary signatures.
- Investment in training of cadres needs to be increased and should include a strong gender component. At present, gram sewaks' interface with the women is low as many amongst them have very little experience of working with women's programmes.
- It should be ensured that at least 50 per cent of the rural development cadres are women, and that vacancies in these departments are addressed to overcome the shortage of worker to ensure quality inputs to the groups.
- Officials need to focus on quality groups, rather than "just forming groups for quality sake".
- Officials need to be trained in rural communication, and before introducing credit programmes, officials need to offer brainstorming sessions on the principles of micro-credit.
- Group members need to act as managers and watchdogs, ensuring discipline on them and reducing dependency on "outsiders" (including NGOs, or non-governmental organisations).

Sampoorna Grameen Rozgar Yojana (SGRY)

Recommendations

- The reservation for women should be increased to 50 per cent. The women beneficiaries should be drawn from the poor of marginalized sections like SC, ST and minorities. Widows, single women and female-headed households should be prioritized. The figure should be applied flexibly (i.e. the figure should not be restricted to 50%) in areas of high male out migration.
- Works that are taken up should be expanded beyond the usual activities like road construction to include building of rural livelihood assets and infrastructure that benefit women such as ponds, storehouses, water post, etc.
- Its scope should be widened to cover also parents of children withdrawn from all occupations (hazardous, non-hazardous and

domestic) in view of the Bill on Child Labour passed by the Parliament.

National Food for Work Programme (NFFWP)

Recommendations

- 50 per cent reservation for women should be provided. Also, priority should be given to parents of children who have been withdrawn from working in industries, houses, etc. The women beneficiaries should be drawn from the poor of marginalized sections like SC, ST and minorities. Widows, single women and female-headed households should be prioritized. The figure should be applied flexibly i.e. the figure should not be restricted to 50 per cent in areas of high male out migration.
- Women's demands for work should be prioritized.

Indira Awas Yojana (IAY)

Recommendations

- All BPL families to be included and priority should be given to SC, ST, OBC, minority communities, female-headed households, widows, homeless aged women, destitute and single women.
- Evolve a credit-cum-subsidy scheme of housing for the non-BPL families.
- Improve access to drinking water to the houses so that women do not have to waste long hours in collecting water when they could be performing more productive activities.
- The policy of public-private partnership/corporate social responsibility should be evolved in undertaking such plans.

Swarn Jayanti Shahari Rozgar Yojana (SJSRY)

Recommendation

- The percentage of women beneficiaries should be made 50 per cent. The women beneficiaries should be drawn from the poor of marginalized sections like SC, ST and minorities. Widows and single women should be prioritized. The figure should be applied flexibly (i.e. the figure should not be restricted to 50 per cent) in areas of high male out migration.

National Rural Employment Guarantee Act/Scheme

Recommendations

- Integrate the implementation of the NREGA with the planning process in general, and specifically with other requirements of rural development, especially those with direct impact on women and girls. Thus, schemes and projects initiated under NREGA could include those that would dovetail with other plans such as provision of universal schooling.

- NREGA must ensure the actual participation of women workers through the statutory provision of 30 per cent of employment opportunities, which must not remain on paper.
- In planning for women's additional employment, women must be treated as entities in their own right and not just as a resource for the family. This is also relevant for the National Rural Employment Guarantee Scheme (NREGA) where their right to employment must not be subsumed within the family card.
- Scheme may be made women friendly. Facilities like wage parity, maternity benefit, shelters, crèches for the children (below 6 years of age) of workers, water and sanitation facilities at the workplace, transport services, security, etc. should be provided.
- It is important to encourage women to apply especially in places where public knowledge and awareness about the scheme may be low. There may be even less knowledge regarding the one-third special allocations for women. The levels of illiteracy amongst unskilled workers (who are the beneficiaries under the scheme), would be especially high in the case of unskilled women workers. It is necessary to spread awareness and knowledge amongst them.
- Failure to observe the rule of non-discrimination in wage payment has been seen in some places–this should be brought to the notice of the authorities.
- There is a provision for setting up Vigilance and Monitoring Committees for every work taken up under the scheme, members of which will be elected by the Gram Sabha. It has to be ensured that women are included in these committees.
- The quorum for the Social Audit Forum, which is to be the same as the Gram Sabha, has to be applied separately for all the groups.

Swa-Shakti

- The objective of the Programme was to bring out socio-economic development and empowerment of women through promotion of women SHGs, micro credit and income generating activities.

Swayamsiddha

- This is an integrated scheme for women empowerment through formation of Self Help Groups (SHGs) launched in February, 2001. The long term objective of the programme is holistic empowerment of women through a sustained process of mobilization and convergence of all the ongoing sectoral programmes by improving access of women to micro-credit, economic resources, etc.

Swawlamban Programme

- Swawlamban Programme, previously known as Norwegian Agency for Development Corporation (NORAD), a women's economic programme, was launched in 1982-83 with assistance to provide training and skills to women to facilitate them to obtain employment or self-employment on sustained basis. The target groups under the scheme are the poor and needy women, women from weaker sections of the society such as Scheduled Castes and Scheduled Tribes etc. In order to ensure more effective implementation and for better monitoring/evaluation of the scheme, it has been transferred to the State Governments from 1st April, 2006 with the approval of Planning Commission.

Globalisation and Skill Development

With the coming of Globalisation and liberalization, new technologies and fast changing markets tend to make existing skills obsolete and require upgradation, new skills and multi-skilling. Support to Training and Employment Programme (STEP) seeks to provide skills and new knowledge to poor and assetless women in the traditional sectors. Skill development is provided in ten traditional skills amongst women. This is a Central Scheme launched in 1987. Further, the possibilities of providing training and skills to women both in traditional and non-traditional sectors and integrating with Rashtriya Mahila Kosh for credit linkages are being considered. A sum of Rs. 240 crore is proposed for the scheme in the Eleventh Five Year Plan.

Women in Tourism Empowerment Programme

Women in Tourism Empowerment Programme will focus on Life Skills, Tourism, Marketing and Entrepreneurship incorporating a Beauty

Therapy component whereby candidates will be trained on applying make-ups, manicures and pedicures in order for them to immediately create small projects as individuals and offer these services to local people and tourists.

Budgeting for Gender Equity

Ministry of Women and Child Development Vision Statement is "Ensuring overall survival, development, protection and participation of women and children of the country" and Mission Statement is "Budgeting for Gender Equity". Together with Gender Budgeting, HDI, GDI and GEM are tools that can be used to identify deep-rooted gender-based inequities which demand that corrective policies, programmes and schemes be implemented in order to achieve gender justice and equitable development outcomes.

Conclusion

"When women moves forward the family moves and when the village moves the nation moves". We can understand now the gap between men and women in terms of economic participation by comparing unemployment levels, the levels of economic activity and remuneration for equal work from this study.

It is clear that the empowerment of women will allow raising women's self-awareness, skill development, creative decision making and it may also lead to produce better citizens and a new and modern Mizoram and India.

Effective implementation and utilization of Women Empowerment Programme in Mizoram and India will safeguard the interests of women. By identifying and quantifying the gender gap, we hope to provide policy-makers with a tool offering direction and focus for the work of significantly improving the socio-economic and political potential of all the citizens of Mizoram and India.

In addition, we hope that this study provides the impetus for policy-makers to strengthen their commitment to the idea of women's empowerment, energy and resources to make gender equality a reality. The above statistics will help in identifying areas that need policy and programme interventions, setting near and far-term goals, and deciding priorities, besides understanding them in an integrated structure.

REFERENCES

Agarwala, Rina (2002): "Working for Autonomy? Differentiating Women's Work in India", *Indian Journal of Labour Economics*, Vol. 45, No. 4.

Agnes, Flavia (1999): "Law and Gender Equality: The Politics of Women's Rights in India", Oxford University Press, New Delhi.

Bannerji, Himani (2001): "Inventing Subjects, Studies in Hegemony, Patriarchy and Colonialism", Tulika Books, New Delhi

Bonita, Alias (2005): "Emergent Women (A Mizo Women's Perspective)", Mittal Publications, New Delhi.

Census of India (1998): State Profile–India 1991, Office of the Registrar General, Table 24, pp. 110–112.

—— (2001): Provisional Population Totals, Registrar General of India, Economic Survey of India, Human Development and Resource Department Reports.

Krishnaraj, Maithreyi (1999): "Women's work in Indian census: Beginnings of Change", *Economic and Political Weekly*, Vol. 25, Nos. 48–9.

Mizoram Economic Survey, 2010.

Mizoram State Commission for Women Act, 2004.

"Mizo Women Today" Tribal Research Institute, Aizawl, Mizoram.

National Commission for Women Reports.

Singh, Amar Kumar and C. Rajyalakshmi (1993): "Status of Tribal Women in India, Social Change". Dec. 23(4). pp. 3–18, Location: SNDT Churchgate.

The World Economic Forum: Study for Women, Geneva, 1971.

U.N. ICPD: International Conference on Population and Development, Summary of the Programme of Action. 1999.

UNDP: Human Development Report, Oxford, 1999.

Visaria, Leela (2000): "Violence against Women: A Field Study", *Economic and Political Weekly*, Vol. 35, No., 20 May 13th–19th World Conferences on Women Reports, Eleventh Five Year Plan Document.

14

Empowerment and Women in the Sixth Schedule Area of Mizoram with Special Reference to Lai Autonomous District Council

Jangkhongam Doungel

Introduction

Women empowerment is the most talk-about issue in different circles in the present generation. It is a historical fact to admit that gender inequality could be found in the tradition of different nations and people whether they are advanced or primitive. However, the degree of gender discrimination is different in different social set-up. Gender inequality could be witnessed in different forms both in the economically backward countries of the Third World as well as in the advanced countries of Europe and America. It is thought provoking to know that women were denied voting right till the early twentieth century even in the western democratic countries, namely, England, France, Switzerland and Portugal. In such a way, there is no cent per cent absence of atrocities against women in different nationalities and sub-nationalities of the world. It is ascertained in the Bible that the census of Israelites excluded women and children in the population record. In the midst of the then on-going issues of women discrimination and the necessary measures for their (women) betterment, women empowerment has been championed in the vigorous form since the late twentieth century and it is further intensified in the twenty-first century. Consequently, the intensified campaign of women empowerment has reached even the remotest corner of the world and it is the most sought after issue now even in the sixth Schedule area of Mizoram.

At the time when Mizoram was a district of Assam, namely, Lushai Hills district, the whole geographical area was a Sixth Schedule area where there were Mizo District Council and the Pawi Lakher Regional Council. However, with the upgradation of the Lushai Hills as Union Territory of Mizoram in 1972; the Mizo District Council was abolished and it was deleted from the list of Autonomous District Council in the Sixth Schedule provision to the Constitution of India. On the other hand, the Pawi Lakher Regional Council (P.L.R.C.) was trifurcated into three Regional Councils, namely, Pawi Regional Council, Lakher Regional Council and the Chakma Regional Council on 2nd April, 1972; and the said three Regional Councils were subsequently upgraded to the status of full-fledged Autonomous District Councils on 29th April, 1972.[1] Contrary to the popular belief of the plain area, there was no much women discrimination in the tribal society in the past as well as at present. And, the like situation could also be found in the tribal dominated Sixth Schedule area of Mizoram. It is not proper to comment that gender inequality is absent in the area, however, it should be admitted that women are not discriminated in the like manner how it was done in some plain areas of mainland India. Despite the absence of unwanted discrimination of women, the impact of women empowerment and women upliftment has rocked the area. As a matter of fact, women empowerment is now intensively initiated in the Sixth Schedule area of Mizoram.

Historical Background

The Lai Autonomous District Council (L.A.D.C.) is the largest in geographical area among the three Autonomous District Councils of Mizoram and its area is 1870.75 sq. km. The Headquarters of the L.A.D.C. is located at Lawngtlai, Sub-Headquarters at Bualpui 'NG' and Divisional Headquarters at Diltlang, Sangau, Vathuampui, Chawngte 'P' and Lungtian. As per the 2008 Statistical and Population Report of the Local Administration Department (L.A.D.) Report of the L.A.D.C., there are 86 villages, 4 sub-villages, 86 Village Councils and 73,820 population in the whole L.A.D.C. area. The structural set-up of the L.A.D.C. is also categorized into three broad organs on the pattern of separation of powers, such as, legislative, executive and judiciary. The L.A.D.C. has 25 functioning department and some other minor departments and it has now staff strength of more than 1659 employees.[2] The L.A.D.C. area is mainly dominated by the Lai tribe and other tribes, inhabiting the area other than the Lai tribe are–Lusei, Hmar, Ralte, Mara, Paite, Bawm, Pang, Chakma and Bru. Other than the above-mentioned tribes, some migratory tribes from Myanmar and Bangladesh are also found in the western belt of the L.A.D.C. area. All the tribes, inhabiting the L.A.D.C. area other than the Chakmas and Brus are kindred tribes of the Chhinlung origin people who are popularly identified as Zo hnathlak (Zo ethnic group of people) in Mizoram. In the like manner how women are treated in the different tribes of the Zo ethnic group in India, Myanmar and Bangladesh; the same treatment has also been meted to women of the Lai tribe in the L.A.D.C. area. Inheritance right was denied to women whether it be family property or chieftainship, as such, women hardly became chief even though they were the daughters of the prominent chiefs from the royal clans.[3] Women were regarded as lower in status than men before; however, such outlook has radically changed now. As a matter of fact, there are remarkable signs of improvement in the status of women in different fields at present.

Present Status and Role of Women in L.A.D.C.

The role and status of women in the L.A.D.C. area at present shall be analysed as given under the following heads.

Government Service

Women are not lagging behind men with regard to employment in government services. The percentage of women employees in District Council office and various departments of the State Government have shown good sign of women empowerment. In the District Rural Development Agency (D.R.D.A.) office at Lawngtlai; out of 19 normal staffs, 10 are males and 9 are females. In the MGNREGS section, there are 10 males and 6 females out of the total employee strength of 16. Whereas there are 10 male and 4 female employees in the BRGF section and there are 2 male and 2 female employees in the IWDP section. Thus, there are 53 employees under various schemes and branches under the D.R.D.A., Lawngtlai which comprise of 32 males and 21 females. There are five Gazetted Officers among the 53 employees who comprise of 3 females and 2 males.[4] In the Deputy Commissioner's office at Lawngtlai, there are 29 regular employees who comprised of 20 males and 9 females. Besides these, there are 10 Muster Roll (M.R.) employees who comprised of 3 males and 7 females. Whereas, there are only 4 employees in the Election branch which has no female employees.[5]

The Block Development Officer (B.D.O.) office, Lawngtlai has 14 normal regular staffs that comprise of 12 males and 2 females. There are also 34 employees in the MGNREGS branch who comprise of 23 males and 11 females. In the Hariyali section under B.D.O. Lawngtlai Rural Development Block, there are 5 employees where there is only a single female employee.[6] There are also sizeable numbers of women employees in other departments under the state government in the district level. The L.A.D.C. has 604 non-plan posts, there are 461 males and 143 females, and it also has 211 plan posts which are filled up by 167 males and 44 females. Thus, the total office staffs of L.A.D.C. comprise 815 where there are 628 men and 187 women. Over and above these, there are 1773 teachers in both Primary and Middle Schools under L.A.D.C. where 1295 are men and 488 women.[7]

Political Field

The participation of women in active politics is not up to the mark till now in the L.A.D.C. area. No women had ever been elected as Member of Legislative Assembly (M.L.A.) and Member of District Council (M.D.C.) from the area till now. No women candidate appeared in the State Legislative Assembly election in the area till now and there was one history setter in the Member of District Council (M.D.C.) election. L.H. Suntlemi happened to be the only women candidate who appeared in the electoral history of L.A.D.C. politics till now. She polled 11 votes each in the fifth and sixth L.A.D.C. general election from Bungtlang Constituency in 1988 and 1992 respectively. She again contested in M.N.F. ticket from Tuithumhnar Constituency in 1997 and polled 125 votes.[8] There are now 86 Village Councils under the L.A.D.C. jurisdiction and there are 594 Village Council members in all the 86 Village Councils. However, there are only 3 women out of 594 members in the Village Councils. It is also interesting to note that only one out of 86 Village Councils has women as Village Council President (V.C.P.) at Council Veng locality in Lawngtlai, but, the only woman V.C.P., Regionthangi was thrown out in no-confidence motion in June, 2011. Thus, there is no woman V.C.P. in Village Councils under L.A.D.C. jurisdiction at present.[9] Women participation in politics has been encouraged by different political parties by establishing women frontal organizations in the district level set-up of the party and corrective measures have been taken up so as to enable women to take proactive engagement in political activities. Political parties, establishing women frontal organizations in the district are Indian National Congress (I.N.C.), Mizo National Front (M.N.F.), Mizoram People's Conference (M.P.C.), Bharatiya Janata Party (B.J.P.)

and the Zoram Nationalist Party (Z.N.P.). Despite the functioning of women frontal organizations and involvement of women in political activities, no political parties encourage women to seek party ticket or to contest election. Out of the four nominated seats in the L.A.D.C., one seat has been reserved for women in each term since the fifth term of 1992. However, yes women are preferred than the capable and potential women even in the nominated M.D.C. seat. It should be recollected that other than K. Zapari who was the nominated M.D.C. from women seat in the fifth and sixth terms of L.A.D.C., the speech or expression of views by other women nominated members of other terms were hardly heard. [10] It is evident that the top brass of the ruling party preferred easy to remote control or yes women than capable women who could voice certain issues in the District Council session as nominated M.D.C. in the women seat. There is good sign of development for women in political field with the adoption of Panchayati Raj in the District Council session by the L.A.D.C. in its emergency session which was held from 3rd–5th June 2011. As per the enacted legislation, one seat each is to be reserved for women in the elected category in each Village Council under the L.A.D.C. jurisdiction. As such, at least 86 women members are expected to be elected in all the Village Councils of L.A.D.C. due to reservation of seats for women.[11]

Economic Empowerment

Women participated tremendously in the socio-economic activities in different tribes of the Zo ethnic group from before. During the era of chieftainship, jhum cultivation was the main occupation where women had to assist their husbands or father in the jhum field from morning till evening. Over and above that, women had to manage the whole household activities and they had to work on the looms when they had leisure time after the harvest season was over. It should be recollected that women in Lushai Hills had contributed more in the socio-economic activities than their fellow Bengali women in the plain. At present, the economic compulsion and the urge for better standard of living have led women to take up all the available employment to supplement their family economic needs and requirements. As per the statistical handbook of Mizoram, 2004, women constituted 43 per cent of the work forces in Lawngtlai District.[12] Like other parts of Mizoram, women in L.A.D.C. area too contribute in the economic activities as government servants, teachers, banking services, business activites, trade and commerce and as labourers in farms, agricultural field and other manual works. Out of the 265 trade licenses, issued by the Revenue Department of the L.A.D.C., there are 180 males and 85 females.[13] So, women presence is found in almost all the economic activities from before till now. It is evident that women presence is not found in the following categories of works, namely, cement mistry, carpentry workshop as well as in driving of commercial vehicles, taxis and auto-rickshaws etc. However, the workforces in government service, trade and commerce, other tertiary activities and manual labourers are now dominated by women.

Church

The Church is understood and popularly known as the community of believers or union of Christ followers. So, Christ believing Church members are determined to be controlled by their Lord and Saviour, Jesus Christ. Therefore, different Churches conduct regular Church services and organize various Church activities to nourish the spiritual growth of the church members.[14] In this regard, ordained Ministers (pastors) and lay preachers (elders and deacons) are entrusted with the responsibilities of looking after the Church administration and Ministry in the parish level as well as in the local Church level. The lay preachers who are entrusted with the responsibilities of looking after the Church administration in the local Church level are Upa (ordained elders for lifetime) and Tual Upa (elders who are elected for a fixed term) in Presbyterian Church of India and Evangelical Church of Maraland, whereas, Upa (ordained elders for lifetime) and Rawngbawltu (Deacon) held the same responsibilities in Baptist Church of Mizoram (B.C.M.) and the Lairam Jesus Christ Baptist Church (L.J.C.B.C.). As the B.C.M. and the L.J.C.B.C. are the two dominant Churches in the L.A.D.C. administered area, the paper mainly deals with the involvement of women in the said two Churches. There are 13 parish or pastorate areas under the administrative jurisdiction of Executive Secretary, Baptist Church of Mizoram, Lawngtlai; where there are 350 male elders but only one female elder. So, just one out of the 351 elders under Executive Secretary jurisdiction of Lawngtlai happened to be woman.[15] The Lairam Jesus Christ Baptist Church which has headquarters at Lawngtlai has 496 male elders and 4 female elders. Thus, there are just 4 female elders out of the 500 elders under the L.J.C.B.C. Assembly.[16] There are also sizeable numbers of female deacons in both B.C.M. and L.J.C.B.C. in different local Churches, however, as record of list of the deacons have not been maintained in offices of the two Churches; list of women deacons could not be highlighted.

Factors Responsible for Women Empowerment in the L.A.D.C. Area

Some of the factors which are responsible for speedy improvement of women empowerment in the L.A.D.C. area shall be analysed as given below.

Church

Different Church programmes are successfully pursued only with the participation of women. Singing fellowship (zaikhawm), Church services, social work and various other programmes, organized by the Church have never been accomplished without women participation. Over and above that, women wing of all the Churches in Mizoram are active in their own way for God's service and in attending the Church services. Despites the little presence of women as elders and deacons in the Church as well as their exclusion from various Church responsibilities, they have contributed a lot from women wing as a constructive platform. Women wing of the Baptist Church of Mizoram could be dated back to1936 where Girl Auxiliary was established under the initiative Miss E.M. Chapman. The various responsibilities and activities of women in regard to the Church was ushered by the Girl Auxiliary and a separate women wing was established after three decades, that was, in 1965 by the B.C.M. Assembly. As a result, Baptist Kohhran Hmeichhe Pawl (B.K.H.P.) or Baptist Women Fellowship was established. As per the 2002 report, the B.K.H.P. has over 370 branches or units and 20,233 members. The B.K.H.P. units in the Executive Secretary jurisdiction of Lawngtlai are also effectively functioning and they rendered many yeoman services to the Church assembly as well as for their own speedy overall growth. The L.J.C.B.C. also has a women wing, namely, Lairam Isua Krista Baptist Kohhran Hmeichhe Pawl (L.I.K.B.K.H.P.) or Lairam Jesus Christ Baptist Church Women Fellowship. The L.I.K.B.K.H.P. has 70 units and over 3500 members. There are 6 women theological graduates and all of them except one serve as full term workers under L.J.C.B.C. Assembly. Lairam Motherless Home, hospital projects, offset and weaving industry are some of the projects of L.I.K.B.K.H.P.[17] Besides guiding women members of the Church in the right spiritual path, women wings of the Churches have also taken up various programmes for personality built-up of their members. As such, seminars, workshops, talks and various fellowship programmes have also been organized so as to make their members aware of their rights and privileges. In a seminar, organized by the All India

Theological Trained Women of India (A.T.T.W.A.) at L.J.C.B.C. Moriah Local Church, Lawngtlai in 19–21 August, 2009; it was deliberated upon by the resource person, a woman herself that women members of the Church should be aware enough to elect their fellow woman in election of the Church elder. And in the event of the absence of the women candidates in the Church elder election, women members should be bold enough not to cast their votes, she added.[18] It is evident that, resource person of the seminar, Dr. T. Vanlaltlani herself, being a woman full term worker of the Church might have faced certain hardship and difficulties in the male dominated Church administration. Yet, balance of views and expression should be maintained as far as practicable even in the campaign for women empowerment so as to enable speedy evolutionary changes in order to avoid reactionary and revolutionary methods.

Political Parties

Political parties all-over India are so concerned about the welfare of women in theory and they also chalked out various programmes for women empowerment because they are eyeing the votes of women. Yet, the practice in real politicking is different. The case in point being the women reservation bill which has been lying in the Parliament for more than a decade now. All political parties whether they are in the category of national, regional or registered; have their own women frontal organisations just to involve women in the political socialization process. Political parties, establishing women frontal organizations in the L.A.D.C. area, namely, Indian National Congress (I.N.C.), Mizo National Front (M.N.F.), Mizoram People's Conference (M.P.C.), Bharatiya Janata Party (B.J.P.) and the Zoram Nationalist Party (Z.N.P.) involve women in political activities which happened to be women empowerment in the indirect process. Despite the non-encouragement of wo.nen ticket seekers in the M.L.A. and M.D.C. election, the involvement in political activities at least helped women to move forward. Further, the reservation of one nominated M.D.C. seat for women in L.A.D.C. since 1992 also has extensively helped women to claim for more rights.

Philanthropic Women Associations

Apart from women fellowship department of the Church and women frontal organization of the political parties, philanthropic women associations have also tremendously contributed to the speedy process of women empowerment. Mizo Hmeichhe Insuihkhawm Pawl (M.H.I.P.) and Lai Women Association (L.W.A.) are the two main women philanthropic associations in the L.A.D.C. administered area. The activities of the M.H.I.P. could be dated back to 1946 as a result of the establishment of the Hmeichhe Tangrual Pawl, however, the proper establishment of the M.H.I.P. was effective only on 6th July, 1974 and its branches spreaded far and wide even beyond the geographical boundary of Mizoram.[19] The Lawngtlai Sub-Headquarters of M.H.I.P. was established in 1976 and it has 37 branches at present with over 3800 members. The M.H.I.P. Sub-Headquarters and branches have contributed a lot in widow upiftment and in claiming of maintenance fund by women who were divorced by their husbands. Over and above that, various women empowerment programmes have also been organized by it in Sub-Headquarters and branch level. The M.H.I.P. Sub-Headquarters has now run Gilead Drop-in-Centre in collaboration with Mizoram Aids Control Society (MSACS) where prevention and care have been provided to drug users and HIV/AIDS infected people. Moreover, proper care has also been given to commercial sex workers and steps have also been taken up to rehabilitate them. The M.H.I.P. Sub-Headquarters is now expecting to open deaddiction centre with the help of the Government of Mizoram.[20]

The Lai Women Association (L.W.A.) was established on 24th April, 1974 at Lawngtlai as philanthropic association of women of the Lai tribe. It has Headquarters at Lawngtlai and it has over 40 branches all-over L.A.D.C. area. The L.W.A. has now over 10,000 members and it is the largest women philanthropic organization in L.A.D.C. area. The L.W.A. has taken up various programmes for ushering women empowerment programme and it has issued guidelines which are to be followed in connection with marriage and bride price. It also issued guidelines which are to be followed by women in various social programmes of the society and it now runs girls hostel to enable the safe stay of girls of the remote area for education and other purposes in Lawngtlai. The L.W.A. also helps the Lairam Motherless Home and Exodus Centre of Life for effective pursuance of the committed works. Over and above that, L.W.A. also often raises its voice for women empowerment in politics.[21]

Impact of Panchayati Raj Institution

As per the provisions of the Panchayats Extension to the Scheduled Areas (PESA), Act, 1996, Panchayati Raj has been enforced in the Scheduled Areas eight states, namely, Andhra Pradesh, Bihar, Gujarat, Himachal Pradesh, Maharashtra, Madhya Pradesh, Orissa and Rajasthan with effect from 24th December, 1996. The nationwide process for extension of Panchayati Raj in the Fifth and Sixth Schedule areas have been vigorously pursued, as such, it is now the ongoing process even in the Sixth Schedule area of Mizoram. Both the Lai Autonomous District Council (L.A.D.C.) and the Mara Autonomous District Council (M.A.D.C.) have enacted the adoption of Panchayati Raj System with certain adjustment in the Village Council set-up of their respective District Council. As per the enacted legislation, the so-called Gram Sabha of the Seventy Third Amendment shall be designated as Village Assembly and election of the Village Council which had been conducted before by the respective District Council will now be conducted by the State Election Commission. Further, one elected seat in each Village Council shall be reserved for women but the norms for women reservation constituency shall only be given in detail only after rules are to be made by the respective District Council.[22] The implementation of the Act will usher greater empowerment for women in politics because it will now be mandatory to elect at least one woman in each Village Council. Women who could not occupy even 5 elected seats in the Village Council election in the whole L.A.D.C area in the past are now facilitated to occupy at least 86 elected seats in Village Councils now. The reason being, there are 86 Village Councils in L.A.D.C. at present and a minimum of one seat each is to be occupied by women in each Village Council. In fact, it is a remarkable political empowerment for women of the Sixth Schedule area in general and the L.A.D.C. area in particular.

Conclusion

Women empowerment is the most hotly debated topic in every nook and corner of the world. Previously, women were not treated as equals of men with respect to inheritance, succession, social status, religious responsibilities as well as in administrative responsibilities. However, there are lots of changes in women's role in different aspects especially in the twenty-first century. At present, women play dominant role in administrative and political decision-making and they are not lagging behind in government service, religious responsibilities and in economic generation of income. The issues of women empowerment which has been prevailing in other parts of Mizoram can also be found in the Sixth Schedule area of the extreme south. Women seemed to be fairly empowered in the field of government servant, politics, and economic empowerment and in Church activities. Yet, their present involvement in politics and Church responsibilities seemed to be not up to the mark which required further empowerment. And some of the factors which ushered women empowerment in the L.A.D.C. area are identified as

Church, political party, women association and impact of Panchayati Raj Institution. It is evident that, not only women but even all the right thinking men are conscious and aware of women empowerment and the menfolk are also interested in ushering the rights and privileges which are due for women. Whatever be the case, custom, tradition and social norms should be taken into account even in the fight for women empowerment. The case in point being, terming a Bible verse in Corinthians which support women's silence in the Church as no longer relevant in the twenty-first century as well as encouraging women not to cast their votes in the election of Church elders if there are no women candidates seemed to be a bit extremist view. Thus, fight for women's right and women empowerment should be pursued without disturbing the ongoing social taboos and culture. In fact, balance is required to be maintained so as to enable the balance growth of women empowerment without disturbing the existing social change. Further, things should be expected to change in an evolutionary process but not in the revolutionary and reactionary process. Revolutionary changes of anything in the social structure are indeed harmful for the society. It is also worthnoting to ponder how the ongoing Women Reservation Bill can be effectively utilized for the benefits of women. Women should first be ready to face the situation. The reason being, women exploitation can further be increased by the Bill only if yes women are preferred than capable women by leaders of political parties. Therefore, whether it be fight for women privileges or women empowerment, it should be balancely done without crossing limit and traditional practices. Women in L.A.D.C. area have now been facilitated with various facilities and provisions but their role in political field and Church responsibilities require further improvement. Whatever be the case, there is greater improvement in the status, privileges and facilities of women but further actions are required to be undertaken in this regard.

NOTES

1. Doungel, Jangkhongam, "Evolution of District Council Autonomy in Mizoram", Spectrum Publications, Guwahati, 2010.
2. "Resource Mobilisation through Local Institutions–Scope and limitations: Comparative Analysis of the three Autonomous District Councils of Mizoram", paper, presented in Workshop on "Resource Mobilization in Autonomous District Councils/Local Bodies" by Dr. Jangkhongam Doungel, organized by the N.I.R.D., Guwahati, 2nd–4th December, 2009.

3. Doungel, Jangkhongam, "An analysis on chieftainship as traditional dominant political Institution of the Lais of Mizoram", U.G.C. Minor Research Project, 2010, Unpublished, p. 25.
4. D.R.D.A. Office, Lawngtlai, Records and Documents, Lawngtlai, 5h July, 2011.
5. Deputy Commissioner's Office, Lawngtlai: Records and Documents, Lawngtlai, 5th July, 2011.
6. B.D.O. Office, Lawngtlai, Records and Documents, Lawngtlai, 8th July, 2011.
7. L.A.D.C. (G.A.D.), Records and Documents, Lawngtlai, 6th July, 2011.
8. Hnialum, R.T., "Road to Lai Autonomous District Council", LADC Publication Board, Lawngtlai, 2010, pp. 83–90.
9. L.A.D.C. (Local Administrative Department), Records and Documents, Lawngtlai, 7th July, 2011.
10. Doungel, Jangkhongam, "Evolution of District Council Autonomy in Mizoram", *op. cit.*, 90–99.
11. Observance of the L.A.D.C. emergency session from the gallery, Session Hall, L.A.D.C., Lawngtlai, 2nd June, 2011.
12. Lalhmasai Chuaungo, "Women's contribution to socio-economic development with particular reference to Mizoram" in Lalneihzovi's (ed.) *Changing Status of Women in North Eastern States*, Mittal Publication, New Delhi, 2009, pp. 76-78.
13. L.A.D.C. (Revenue Department), Records and Documents, Lawngtlai, 19th August, 2011.
14. Vanlaltlani, T. "Participation of women in the Church–with reference to North East India", in Lalneihzovi's (ed.) *Changing Status of Women in North Eastern States*, *op. cit.*, pp. 129–130.
15. Executive Secretary Office, B.C.M., Lawngtlai, Records and Documents, Lawngtlai, 8th July, 2011.
16. L.J.C.B.C. Office, Lawngtlai, Records and documents, Lawngtlai, 7th July, 2011.
17. Vanlaltlani, T., Mizo Hmeichhete Kawngzawh, Synod Press, Aizawl, 2005, pp. 84-95.
18. Deliberation of the seminar at L.J.C.B.C. Moriah Local Church, Lawngtlai.
19. *Op. cit.*, pp. 225–227.
20. Interview with Vanlalhlupuii Fanai, General Secretary, M.H.I.P. Lawngtlai Sub-Headquarters, Lawngtlai, 19th August, 2011.
21. (a) 10th Anniversary Souvenir of Lai Women Association, K.R. Chhingpui (Ed.), Lawngtlai, 2006. (b) Sources from F. Hranglungchhungi, General Secretary, Lai Women Association, Headquarters, Lawngtlai, 2011.
22. Draft copy of the Lai Autonomous District Council (Village Council) Amendment Act, 2011.

15

Economic Contribution of Women in Mizoram

Irene Colbert

Introduction

In Mizoram on the surface, women seem to enjoy greater freedom than other Indian females. Educationally, females have also come up and have occupied various important posts. There is no change of identity after marriage; women still maintain their surname, no dowry in terms of gold and huge sum of money, no purdah system, no prescribed way of dressing. But Mizo society is basically patriarchal and patrilineal in character. This contributes to women's inferior position in all walks of life, be it politics, religion, society, family, as well as economy.

Mizo women contribute immensely to the economy of the state. Their economic contribution can be understood in terms of paid and unpaid services rendered by them. In the traditional Mizo society the fate of a woman seemed to have been determined and divided right from birth (Lalrinchhani, 1998: 21). Right from her childhood days the tiny girl made herself available to the parents. She assisted her parents as much as she could. She had to take care of her younger brothers and sisters, draw water, cook and do any other works whatever the family needed. Sometimes, accompanying her mother she fetched firewood. In this way, the girl helped her parents when she was still young (Sangkima, 2004: 90). Girls of the traditional Mizo society practically had no time to rest. At the same time, a girl of *tlawmngaihna* (self-denial moral code of conduct possessed by Mizos) would see to it that she maintains a restrain in food habits, eating as little as possible, especially while eating in places other than her own home. "The extent of work they did with the little amount of food they consumed", said Challiana, "made one wonder how it was possible for the Mizo girls to remain healthy and strong (Kipgen, 1996: 71)." A Mizo woman has multiple roles to play and is overburdened with household chores and outside her home too. She is always very hard-working, has much hard work to do, and has all too little time available for any profitable leisure The *Lushai* mother will continue to work at her usual duties, even wood and water collection, up to the very day of delivery, there still being a sneaking belief that in this way the chances of a speedy delivery are greatly enhanced. In the cultivation seasons the women will go off for the day to their fields, often taking their babies on their backs, if they have none with whom to leave them safely (McCall: 171–175).

With the inclusion of Mizo women, "the vast majority of rural and urban women work more than 14 hours a day." (Balasundaram, 1993: 7). Earlier, working the whole day at the *jhum* along with others she found no time for taking rest even when she reached home late in the evening. She had to spend the whole night with various engagements. It was customary among married and unmarried women to engage themselves with cotton works. Besides, the unmarried women had to perform a well-established social custom by receiving young men who came to spend time in amusing themselves after toiling the whole day at the *jhum*. This custom is called *Inleng* (courting). When the next day dawned she had to rise early to start life afresh for the whole day. In the early morning she proceeded to the spring (waterpoint) to fill bamboo tubes with water, finish husking the rice by pounding in a mortar and cook breakfast. She has to finish all these tiring jobs before sunrise while the husband and the other male members were still asleep. Then after the meal the real work of the day began. All these pre-day engagements were performed by the young woman and the mother in the house. If the mother had no daughter she had to do these duties single-handed. When the weeding season was over, there autumn set in. That was the season when the men engaged themselves with hunting. Those who did not go for hunting they roamed about helping the family. But for womenfolk it was the busiest season of the year. During this pleasant season set her daily in two features. The first part of her work in a given day was to fetch firewood from the jungle. It was her duty to stock firewood for the next rainy season. The other part included making of clothes for the coming winter (Sangkima, 2004: 90, 91). She was also expected to provide the males with nicotine water called *tuibur* whenever needed and therefore had to produce it by smoking all the time through a small container with a pipe attached. Even if women said, "We are not doing anything", they were busy throughout the day without having the time to rest at all. Their leisure time would be spent for spinning yarn (Selet Thanga, 1979: 16). When there were neighbours who could not pound rice and carry water, it was their duty to help such people. Even to look after the pigs, poultry and other household works were told by their parents to help, which were willingly done by them (Dokhuma, 1992: 205). They played an essential role as food earners of the family.

Till today, women have multiple burdens to shoulder both at home and work. In the sample survey conducted by the paper presenter, 61.33 per cent (19.34 % males, 41.99 % females) admit that Mizo men do not share the responsibilities of looking after children, household duties and earning livelihood, while 38.67 per cent (25.97% males, 12.70% females) think they do. Moreover, 80.42 per cent (37.03% males, 43.39% females) agree that market economy is dominated by women in Mizoram, while 19.58 per cent (10.58% males, 9% females) do not agree. Mizo women, in addition to working outside the home–in the *jhum* or office, all the responsibilities of the home rest with the women–washing and ironing clothes, buying and preparing food, cleaning and beautifying of houses and campus, fetching water and wood, caring for domestic animals like pigs and poultry, kitchen gardening, rearing of children–feeding, clothing, studies, medicating, looking after husband and his belongings, giving instructions and so on and so forth which are never ending, right from early morning till late at night. She has to bear and implement all these responsibilities without having authority.

Mizo women, in spite of their being the main workforce of the family and without whose untiring labour can the family flourish, are often taken for granted by the family members. The unpaid services rendered by them throughout the day often go unnoticed. If she doesn't earn money, her husband may sometimes call her *chawmhlawm* (complete dependent, reliant) in times of quarrelling. She also considers herself as fully dependent on her husband and hesitates to ask for money to buy her smallest necessities. Even if she has monetary earnings, "there are many instances where a mother's income is misused and controlled by the husband" (Hnuni, 1988: 5).

Mizo women are engaged in all kinds of business activities. Many educated women work in offices, schools, colleges, etc. while majority of villagers continue to work in the *jhum*. The result of the sample survey of women and men workers in offices, shops, etc. in Aizawl by Vanengliana, reveals that except for the meat shops, women are in the majority (Vanengliana, 1991: 3–6). From eyewitnesses, we can say that the situation has not changed till today.

Table 15.1: Shop keepers at Bazaar, Bawngkawn, Aizawl (on 28.9.1991)

Sl. No.	*Name of food items sold*	*Males*	*Female*	*Total*
1.	Beef	7	3	10
2.	Fish	–	8	8
3.	Pork	8	1	9
4.	Chicken	3	1	4
5.	Vegetables, etc.	32	281	313
Total		**50**	**294**	**344**

Source: Vanengliana, *Khawiahnge Mizo Mipate?* (*Where are the Mizo men?*) (Aizawl: Synod Social Front, 1991).

The main Bazaar (i.e. the New Market) in Aizawl Town looks like a women's market, as in other markets of Mizoram. Most of the shopkeepers and hawkers are females. We hardly ever see men carrying and selling vegetables in the houses, on the way to markets and even inside the markets. But among the non-Mizos, it is not wrong to say that vendors are men only (maybe with the exception of a very few females). Women also run their petty business and small entrepreneurship–handloom and handicraft, floriculture, tailoring, beauty parlour, etc. There are Mizo women, more in numbers than men going to Delhi, Kolkata, Mumbai, Madras, Kathmandu and Thailand for business. Moreover, within Mizoram itself, there are more females working and earning in offices, bazaars, tea stalls, hotels and other business places. Females who do not work hard are considered lazy and lethargic and if unmarried, such a person may find it difficult to get a good partner, hence, she will conceal her ill-health as much as she can, unless absolutely unavoidable (Vanlaltlani, 2005: 53, 54). In Mizo society, women are very much marginalized and are put in subordination as far as their participation in the Churches, politics and in the society are concerned, yet, they are given much freedom in the field of economics. Hotels, restaurants, tea stalls, etc. are managed and run by mostly females. Besides running shops and other business one can see that women are also employed in large numbers in departmental stores. In most of the Government registered shops, societies and Government fair price shops, majority of the employees are women. They engage themselves as agents and sub-dealers in supplying kerosene oil, gas, etc. But being a patriarchal society, the father is the head of the household and the shop is usually registered in his name. Family property and bank account are also in the father's name.

Table 15.2: Comparison between Males and Females in Government Departments, Aizawl, made between May and October 1991 and the Results

Sl. No.	*Name of Office*	*Occupation*	*Males*	*Females*	*Total*
1.	Civil Secretariat	LDC (Lower Divisional Clerk)	43	147	190
		UDC (Upper Divisional Clerk)	54	80	134
		Asst. (Assistant)	82	87	169
2.	D.C. Office, Aizawl	LDC (Lower Divisional Clerk)	41	63	104
		UDC (Upper Divisional Clerk)	23	25	48
		Asst. (Assistant)	1	1	2
3.	Directorate of School Education	LDC (Lower Divisional Clerk)	1	7	8
		UDC (Upper Divisional Clerk)	6	4	10
		Asst. (Assistant)	5	5	10
		Supdt. (Superintendent)	1	1	2
4.	Directorate of Adult Education	LDC (Lower Divisional Clerk)	1	7	8
		UDC (Upper Divisional Clerk)	2	1	3
		Asst. (Assistant)	1	2	3
5.	SDEO (E)	LDC (Lower Divisional Clerk)	1	5	6
		UDC (Upper Divisional Clerk)	–	1	1
6.	Directorate of AH & Vety.	LDC (Lower Divisional Clerk)	1	8	9
		UDC (Upper Divisional Clerk)	3	4	7
		Asst. (Assistant)	5	1	6
		Supdt. (Superintendent)	1	1	2
7.	Dist. Social Welfare Officer (E)	LDC (Lower Divisional Clerk)	–	2	2
		UDC (Upper Divisional Clerk)	–	2	2
8.	DSWO (W)	LDC (Lower Divisional Clerk)	–	2	2
		UDC (Upper Divisional Clerk)	–	1	1
9.	Directorate of Social Welfare	LDC (Lower Divisional Clerk)	–	5	5
		UDC (Upper Divisional Clerk)	2	6	8
		Asst. (Assistant)	4	4	8
		Supdt. (Superintendent	2	–	2
10.	Controller of Accounts	LDC (Lower Divisional Clerk)	1	8	9
		UDC (Upper Divisional Clerk)	1	3	4
		Asst. (Assistant)	1	2	3
11.	Directorate of Agriculture	LDC (Lower Divisional Clerk)	3	31	34
		UDC (Upper Divisional Clerk)	4	18	22
		Asst. (Assistant)	5	4	9
		Supdt. (Superintendent	2	–	2
12.	Assembly Secretariat	LDC (Lower Divisional Clerk)	6	9	15
		UDC (Upper Divisional Clerk)	8	10	18
		Asst. (Assistant)	5	7	12
		Supdt. (Superintendent)	3	1	4
		Translator	–	6	6
		Total Per cent	319 36%	570 64%	889

Source: *Vanengliana, Op. cit.*, pp. 434–43.

Women are discriminated with regards to distribution of wages. For daily work which consists of around 7 hours of field work from 9:00 A.M–4:00 P.M women are paid in urban areas, Rs. 150 and for similar 7 hours daily work period men are paid Rs. 200 (in rural, Rs. 120 and Rs. 150). In 1976, the Government of India promulgated an Equal Remuneration Act (ERA) No. 25 of 1976. As per this law it became "the duty of employer to pay equal remuneration to men and women workers for same work or work of similar nature". It also provides for no discrimination on the ground of sex at the time of recruiting men and women workers. This Act covers any employment carried on by or under the authority of the Central Government or a railway administration, or in relation to a banking company, a mine, oilfield or major part of any corporation established by or under. Females should be made aware of this Act to avoid discrimination against them.

In Mizoram, females concentrate in primary sectors as cultivators, household workers and agricultural labourers. Moreover, female annual growth rate is quite high and almost doubled males growth rate in agricultural labourers (11.59%: 6.86%); in household industry workers (12.04%: 7.4%) and other workers (12.21%: 5.8%). (*see* Table 15)

Even after four decades of development and planning, majority of women in Mizoram are still concentrated in a narrow range of occupations characterized by low level of skill thereby low wages and income. Though their contribution is substantial, it is a fact that the labour put in by women in discharging their economic and non-economic activities do not get their due recognition. (Lalthansangi, 2004: 51, 52). The labour which does not produce surplus cannot be calculated in terms of money. Because they are not paid, it does not enter into the market. Therefore, the hardest job of women, the job which sustains the family, has been considered by men as a natural role, best fitted to the lives of women. It is this male exploited ideology that Maria Mies called the 'housewifization' of women. This means women's labour is considered as a natural resource, freely available like air and water (Maria Mies, 1986: 110). We can rightly say that women are the main workforce in Mizoram, yet, it is evident from the following facts that they are enjoying a much lower status than their male counterparts–

1. Mizo women is almost invisible in the formal political institutions of Mizoram–in the chiefdom, Advisory Council (1948–51, only 3 women), Mizo District Council (1952–72, 2 women), Pawi–Lakher Regional Council (1953–72, no women), LADC (1972–2010 August–3 women, all nominated), MADC (1972–2010

Table 15.3: Distribution of Main Workers as Cultivators, Agricultural Labourers, Household Industry Workers and Other Workers in Total Workers of Mizoram: 1971–2001

Census Years	Total Workers			Cultivators			Agricultural Labourers			Household Industry Workers			Other Workers		
	P	M	F	P	M	F	P	M	F	P	M	F	P	M	F
1971	151619	87858	63761	126652	65171	61481	558	385	173	488	375	113	23921	21927	1994
1981	206064	129011	76453	145545	75556	65989	5118	3465	1653	1758	959	799	53643	45628	8015
1991	290317	178011	112306	178101	94878	83223	9527	6181	3346	2958	1997	961	99731	74955	24776
2001	469597	264162	205435	253161	128829	124332	27494	13010	14484	6572	3164	3408	182370	119159	63211
G	3.84	3.74	3.98	2.34	2.3	2.4	13.9	6.86	11.59	9.05	7.4	12.04	7.01	5.8	12.21

Source: Lalthansangi, *Situational Analysis of Women in the State of Mizoram* (New Delhi: National Commission for Women, 2004), p. 49.

P = Persons, M = Males, F = Females

Main Workers are those who have worked for 183 days or more in a year.

G = Annual Average Growth Rate (%).

Table 15.4: Sex-wise Distribution of Employees in Mizoram, 1998–2003

Sl. No.	Statutory	Year	Group-A				Group-B (G)				Group-B (NG)			
			M	F	Total	% of F	M	F	Total	% of F	M	F	Total	% of F
1.	State Govt.	1998	1884	470	2354	19.97	66	26	92	28.26	4916	1985	6901	28.76
		1999	1972	518	2490	20.80	308	54	362	14.92	4915	2345	7260	32.30
		2000	1928	483	2411	20.03	308	58	366	15.85	5027	2273	7300	31.13
		2001	2047	428	2475	17.29	419	85	504	16.87	4870	2292	7162	32.00
		2002	2203	446	2649	16.85	272	184	456	40.35	5168	2266	7434	30.48
		2003	2252	558	2810	19.86	231	76	307	24.76	5202	2499	7701	32.45
2.	Central Govt.	1998	66	13	79	16.46	34	01	35	02.86	71	11	82	13.41
		1999	166	37	203	18.23	89	07	96	07.29	49	22	71	30.99
		2000	157	36	193	18.65	84	07	91	07.69	42	16	58	27.59
		2001	169	38	207	18.36	78	07	85	08.24	54	18	72	25.00
		2002	164	42	206	20.39	68	05	73	06.85	67	18	85	21.18
		2003	184	46	230	20.00	80	07	87	08.05	58	26	84	30.95
3.	Semi-Govt.	1998	151	28	179	15.64	04	00	04	00.00	46	33	79	41.77
		1999	63	08	71	11.27	02	00	02	00.00	40	31	71	43.66
		2000	59	07	66	10.61	01	00	01	00.00	36	27	63	42.86
		2001	61	09	70	12.86	11	02	13	15.38	36	26	62	41.93
		2002	58	07	65	10.77	07	04	11	36.36	48	34	82	41.46
		2003	59	09	68	13.24	06	05	11	45.45	49	36	85	42.35
4.	Banking and Insurance	1998	151	29	173	16.76	04	01	05	20.00	133	78	211	36.97
		1999	63	28	168	16.67	17	05	22	22.72	136	72	208	34.62
		2000	59	27	168	16.07	18	04	22	18.18	133	69	202	34.16
		2001	61	31	173	17.92	18	04	22	18.18	60	11	71	15.49
		2002	58	45	243	18.52	20	04	24	16.67	57	28	85	32.94
		2003	59	46	246	18.70	24	04	28	14.29	49	29	78	37.17

5. Autonomous District Councils	1998	144	29	173	16.76	00	00	00	00.00	153	29	182	15.93
	1999	140	28	168	16.67	15	02	17	11.76	165	34	199	17.09
	2000	141	27	168	16.07	22	03	25	12.00	169	34	203	16.75
	2001	142	31	173	17.92	102	10	112	08.93	108	24	132	18.18
	2002	198	45	243	18.52	74	07	81	08.64	148	23	171	13.45
	2003	200	46	246	18.70	107	11	118	09.32	123	25	148	16.89

Source: Lalthansangi, *Situational Analysis of Women in the State of Mizoram* (New Delhi: National Commission for Women, 2004), p. 50.

Table 15.5: Sex-wise Comparison of Employees (Group-wise) of Different Statutories in Mizoram for the Period 1998–2003

		1998	*1999*	*2000*	*2001*	*2002*	*2003*
Group A	M	2334	2429	2373	2511	2762	2791
	F	564	595	557	509	543	665
	Total	**2880**	**3024**	**2930**	**3020**	**3269**	**3456**
	% F	**18.96**	**19.68**	**19.01**	**20.27**	**16.61**	**19.24**
Group B(G)	M	108	431	433	628	441	448
	F	28	72	68	108	204	103
	Total	**136**	**505**	**499**	**736**	**645**	**551**
	% F	**20.59**	**14.26**	**13.63**	**14.67**	**31.63**	**18.69**
Group B (NG)	M	5319	5305	5407	5128	5488	5481
	F	2136	2504	2419	2371	2369	2615
	Total	**7455**	**7809**	**7826**	**7499**	**7857**	**8096**
	% F	**28.65**	**32.07**	**30.91**	**31.62**	**30.15**	**32.30**
Group C	M	19173	19470	20082	8281	20952	20615
	F	5840	6279	6603	6399	6391	6455
	Total	**25013**	**25749**	**26685**	**24680**	**27343**	**27070**
	% F	**23.35**	**24.39**	**24.74**	**25.93**	**23.37**	**23.85**
Group D	M	10068	10684	10531	9796	9848	9637
	F	1122	1279	1288	1634	1610	1612
	Total	**11190**	**11963**	**11819**	**11430**	**11458**	**11249**
	% F	**10.03**	**10.69**	**10.90**	**14.30**	**14.05**	**14.33**
Over all Summary	M	37002	38219	38826	38038	39455	38972
	F	9672	10725	10939	11021	11117	11450
	Total	**46674**	**48944**	**49765**	**49059**	**50572**	**50422**
	% F	**20.72**	**21.91**	**21.98**	**22.46**	**21.98**	**22.71**

Source: Lalthansangi, *Situational Analysis of Women in the State of Mizoram* (New Delhi: National Commission for Women, 2004), p. 51.

August–out of 1 elected and 4 nominated women, 1 EM), CADC (1972–2010 August, out of 1 elected and 2 nominated women, I EM), Lok Sabha and State Assembly of Assam (1952–72, no women), Village Council (very few comparatively to men) and Legislative Assembly (out of 5 women, only 1 Minister of State, no female from 1987 election). So far we have never had women speakers, Chief Ministers and MPs. We had 1 party President (1967). After 1987, women are invisible in the Assembly. Women's economic conditions may not permit them to participate in politics.

2. Religiously women are at a disadvantage. Though the missionaries improved the conditions of Mizo women, they brought with them

the patriarchy of the 19th and early 20th century western societies and Churches. While the women missionaries worked among the local women, the Churches established were entirely under the control of the men missionaries–and, in due course, local men leaders (Hnuni, 1999: 151-52). In the structure of the Baptist and Presbyterian Churches, right from the highest level, the Synod/Assembly, down to the level of the local Church, women have been excluded–except in their own Women's Fellowship. It excludes and ignores women who represent (or more than half in many Churches) its members in all matters in which important decisions are made concerning its life. Women members are simply subject to the decisions of male members (R.L. Hnuni: 68–70). Many women and men study theology in Mizoram. After finishing their studies, when the churches invite applications for workers as Pastors, the women are disqualified straightaway, no matter what her qualification maybe, or even if they had done much better than the men, just by virtue of her being a woman, she is rejected. Qualified and competent women theologians are given posts which can be performed by untrained people. Moreover, they do not enjoy the same pay scale as ordained Ministers. For the Baptist ordained Ministers, their tenure is up to the age of 65 while for the theologically trained women, it is only up to 60. Mizo women are denied ordination and also in most Churches even the use of pulpits which are made with money contributed by them. The Presbyterian Pro Pastors cannot be ordained if their wives occupy government job (Presbyterian Church of India, 2005: 58). Moreover, they do not ordain women not only as Pastors but also as Elders. The Baptists can ordain women, only as Elders but this is also a very rare case. The Baptist Pastors' wives, who are not even the employees of the Baptist Church of Mizoram, have to leave their hard earned jobs by 2015 (Baptist Church of Mizoram, 2008: 20). Right to work given by the Indian Constitution is denied to them. In the case of Baptist female missionaries, when they get married, in many cases, they are forced to give up their job even if their post was a substantive post and even if they had worked earnestly for many years. Though women contribute a lot for the works of the Churches in Mizoram, they function under the subjugation of male egoism and their usefulness is overlooked when it comes to their ordination.

3. The usage of Mizo Customary Laws (since 1927), backed by the society and government, is the revelation of women's inferior position in the family and society. In spite of being the main workforce, according to such Laws, women can inherit only through a 'will'. Inheritors are to be from the male siblings who reside in the ancestral home, and among them the youngest is given first preference as he is expected to look after the parents till death. In case he has left the house, he will be succeeded by the next youngest and so on. If at all there aren't any such persons to do so, the daughter who looks after them will be the inheritor (Mizo Hnam Dan, 2005: 83–85). In Mizo society, since linear and inheritance are through the males, property belongs to the father and to the mother in case of death of her husband, as long as she looks after their children and grandchildren. Such a woman is considered as a righteous, faithful, respectful and holy, worthy to be praised. Otherwise, she will not inherit anything (Mizo Hnam Dan.2005: 85). A young widow is not given a chance to remarry. A man distributed his property among his children and said that no one was to disturb his wife while she was alive. The wife definitely stayed in their house but the husband already distributed all his property, as soon as she died, the property was to be distributed and so the wife had no right to neither sell nor dispose them off. Though she looked as if she had lots, but she was really poor. Sometimes, there are instances of the mothers being kicked off from their own homes and because of daughter-in-laws some live more as strangers in their own homes. After death of both parents, in case of court case between brother and sister regarding heirship, the son is sure to win the case as in the Mizo Customary Laws, only males are given first preference (Lucy Lalrinthari, 2005: 4). In the case of earning high income by both the husband and wife, the money is used in accumulating land, constructing building, etc. which will later be inherited by the sons only. This is also an indirect process of economic exploitation (Shimray in R.L. Hnuni (ed.) 1999: 48). Some parents who are educated and have a broader outlook have on their own began to think about a share for their daughters. They divide their property among both sons and daughters. But the majority, especially in rural areas, maintains the traditional practice.

Mizo women suffer prejudice even with regards to divorce. Women, being purchased with a bride price of Rs.400—Rs.500, can be divorced at husband's wish with no claims for anything except her own properties brought by her to the husband's house at the time of marriage, if the husband and the wife are still residing in the husband's house, as everything belongs to the husband's father including those earned by both the husband and wife. Some people feel that the meagre Rs. 20 security deposited by the groom which has been practised since earlier times is the cause of speedy divorce rate and therefore should be changed to at least one lakh to prevent the husband divorcing his wife at will, Magistrate Lucy Lalrinthari said that one female's husband died, they had put all their income in the father's name in the bank. The court gave heirship certificate to the children and the mother guardianship. The court did not allow her to take out money from the bank even for looking after the children. She had to take prior permission of the court for withdrawal (Lalrinthari, 2005: 5).

In Mizo Customary Laws, there is no penalty for a man who commits adultery and is not so looked down by the masses as women who commit the same. On the other hand, a woman may lose her reputation if she commits adultery and she is termed as *Uire* (adulteress). In such instances, if her husband does not forgive, she has to leave her house empty handed, with no claims of her own properties including her own children. She has to refund the bride price and can leave the house only with what she is wearing (Mizo Hnam Dan, 2005: 37). After the death of her husband, the woman is still considered *Uire* if she sleeps with another man before performing an *inkaihchhuah* ceremony. If such a thing happens, then her children or her husband's relatives may kick her out of the house. If her children want to continue staying with her, she may be allowed to do so, but she will not be permitted to sleep in the master bed. On the other hand, if the husband commits adultery and if he divorces his wife, she will take out with her one-third of their earnings, except if they still live in a joint family and in such a situation she is entitled to take with her only her belongings (Mizo Hnam Dan, 2005: 37).

If a man has a child with a girl outside the wedlock, he has to pay a pittance of the bastards' price of Rs. 40 (Lalhriatpuii, 2004: 1). Such a small amount does not hinder a person to commit such act. If a larger amount is to be fined, it is expected that such crime will definitely be minimized.

Scrutiny of the realities of the situation reveals that because women do not have control of properties acquired through their hard earned labour, resulting in very unsound economic conditions, they are naturally at a disadvantaged position in other walks of life. They cannot afford not to be at their husbands beg and call, unless they want to suffer the consequences of hardship under separation/divorce.

Suggestions

Certain suggestions need to be mentioned for the improvement of the economic conditions of women, so as to bring about their all-round development, such as–

1. Monetary unpaid services rendered by the females at home need to be considered and women therefore should be made to jointly control the finances, etc. of the household.
2. Joint or single bank account should be opened. Not only working and earning should belong to women, but also owning.
3. Ownership of property should be equally distributed like land, gas connection, shops, cars, etc., so that she will be economically sound and self-sufficient in case of disasters like death, divorce, etc.
4. Customary Laws should be revised with regard to inheritance of property, divorce laws and other loopholes. Females should be allowed to inherit even without a 'will.' Bride prize should be increased. Security deposit of Rs. 20 by the bridegroom should be increased to Rs. one lakh at the minimum. Prize of an illegitimate child should be increased from Rs. 40 to at least one lakh.
5. Churches should not hesitate to give ordination to deserving women as Pastors and Elders, keeping in mind the trends with other parts of the world. More women should be allowed to participate in the important decision-making bodies of the Church. Right to work should be allowed to the wives of the Pastors.
6. Quality education should be imparted to minimize gender gaps. Gender related studies should be included in the syllabus of the academic institutions in Mizoram.
7. Reservation of seats should be introduced, so that more women will be inducted into the Ministry to run the administration of the state. Educated females should be encouraged to take part in the politics of Mizoram. This should be the duty of the existing political parties to invite such persons. This will enhance their economic condition.
8. Awareness generation programmes should be organized, to equip the Mizo females of their rights.

REFERENCES

Balasundaram, Franklin J.(1993): "Women Concern in Asia" (Madras: C.L.S,), p. 7, cited by Shimreingam Shimray, *Women and Economy*, in *Transforming Theology for Empowering Women,* edited by R.L. Hnuni Jorhat: Women's Studies, Eastern Theological College, 1999.

Baptist Church of Mizoram Assembly (2008): *vawi 112–na minute 2008*, Serkawn: Baptist Church of Mizoram Headquarters.

Dokhuma, James (1992): *Hmanlai Mizo Kalphung*, Aizawl: J.D. Press.

Hnuni, R.L. (1999): "*Transforming Theology for Empowering Women*", Jorhat: Women's Studies, Eastern Theological College.

—— (1988): "Women and Development", a paper presented in the Seminar organized on *Development* organized by North East India Committee on Relief and Development on 15th November in Dimapur (Unpublished).

Kipgen, Mangkhosat (1996): "Christianity and Mizo Culture", Jorhat: The Mizo Theological Conference, Mizoram, Eastern Theological College.

Lalhriatpuii (2004): "Economic Empowerment in the Context of Mizo Women", paper presented in State Consultation Meeting on *State Policy*, at State Guest House, Aizawl on 23-24 March (organized by Mizoram State Commission for Women) (Unpublished).

Lalrinchhani, B. (1998): "Christianity and Women in Mizoram: A Study of the Impact of Christianity on Women in Lunglei District" (Unpublished M. Phil. Dissertation, Department of History, North Eastern Hill University, Shillong.

Lalrinthari, Lucy (2005): "Mizo Hmeichhiate leh Mizo Customary Law", paper presented in a Seminar organized by MHIP Sub-Headquarters, Lunglein (Unpublished).

Lalthansangi (2004): *Situational Analysis of Women in the State of Mizoram,* New Delhi: National Commission for Women.

McCall, A.G. (1977): *Lushai Chrysalis,* Aizawl: Tribal Research Institute.

Mies, Maria (1999): "Patriarchy and Accumulation on a world Scale Women in the International Division of Labour", Zed Books, London, 1986, p. 110, cited by Shimreingam Shimray, *Women and Economy*, in *Transforming Theology for Empowering Women,* edited by R.L. Hnuni, Jorhat: Women's Studies, Eastern Theological College.

Presbyterian Church of India (2005): *Synod Bu Vawi 81–na* Aizawl, The Mizo Presbyterian Church Synod.

Sangkima (2004): *Essays on the History of the Mizos*, Guwahati: Spectrum Publications.

Shimray, Shimreingam (1999): "Women and Economy", in *Transforming Theology for Empowering Women,* edited by R.L. Hnuni (Jorhat: Women's Studies, Eastern Theological College.

Thanga, Selet (1970): *Pi Pu Len Lai*, Aizawl: Lianchhungi Book Store.

The Mizoram Gazette Extra ordinary, *Mizo Hnam Dan (Mizo Customary Laws)*, Notification No.H.12018/119/03–LJD/62, the 4th April 2005.

Vanengliana (1991): *Khawiahnge Mizo Mipate?* (*Where are the Mizo men?*), Aizawl: Synod Social Front.

Vanlaltlani, T. (2005): *Mizo Hmeichhiate Kawngzawh*, Aizawl: Mizoram Publication Board.

16

Role of Mizo Women in Economy

J Zorema

Debates on women's issues have been since the last few decades assumed prominence on the global agenda. Women's rights and issues have always been a subject of serious concern and are topics of meetings and conferences around the world. Women represent half the resources and half the potential in all societies. The empowerment and autonomy of women and the improvement of their social, economic and political status is essential for the achievement of sustainable development in all areas of life.[1]

In the less developed countries, rural women continue to struggle with dual responsibilities of economic production and domestic labour, and most are confronted by poverty, illiteracy, high health risks and inadequate access to productive resources.[2] Hence, rural women in their dual roles as producers in the farm and caretakers at home need appropriate technologies to ease their work stress and to improve their productivity. The importance of women's unpaid work in the home and farm production systems should be recognized.[3]

India has a predominantly an agrarian economy. 70 per cent of her population lives in rural areas and out of this 60 per cent is engaged in agriculture as their main source of income. Of all agricultural workers, 99.4 per cent work in the informal sector.[4] In rural India, women agricultural workers are occupying very low positions in the agrarian hierarchy. In terms of gender, rural women bear the burden of poverty and exploitation more heavily than men.[5] Although there are some women who earn a good living from agriculture and can assure family food security or generate surplus sales, most women tend to be among the lower resource farmers. This is not because they are deficient in farming skills, but because they lack access to labour, land, credit, training and mechanization. Stereotypes about women's place often prevent planners and implementers of development projects from incorporating women into plans and programmes.[6] As long as gender is an important indicator of economic, social and political roles, there is a need for special policies targeted to rural women for their education and training, technology transfer and credit facilities.[7]

An attempt is made in this paper to know how far Mizo women are involved in the economy of the state. An attempt is also being made to identify factors that hinder their development and to bring light on how women are affected by programmes, projects and policies that are instituted by the government and otherwise, how best to take advantage of such initiatives and how to minimize their negative impact on women.

Background

In the pre-colonial era, the Mizos lived in a village–based society. The prevalence of inter-tribal feud and inter-clan warfare had perhaps compelled them to live together in villages. Shifting of villages to new areas was done as soon as the surrounding jhum lands were worked out.[8]

The Mizo means of livelihood was mainly through cultivation. Due to the absence of flat lands, they had developed a slash and burn method of cultivation popularly known as 'Jhumming system'. Therefore, the permanency of a village was determined by the facilities afforded for cultivation in the neighbourhood. When all the land within easy reach was exhausted, the village was shifted to a fresh site.[9] In fact, their economic system was interwoven with everyday life, social, cultural and religious practices. Production initially was meant for family consumption. They were greatly dependent on the forest products. All the materials needed for building their houses–wood, thatch, cane and bamboo came from the forests.[10] The pre-colonial Mizo economy was not monetized.

The Mizo society was patriarchal. Marriage took place out of mutual agreement and was a civil contract. In fact, a man bought his wife and so regarded her as a possession with which he could do as he liked.[11] All children belonged to the father and the father's family. Women did not inherit any property. According to Chapman and Clark, "A woman had no rights at all. In body, mind and spirit she belonged from her birth to her death to her father, her brother and her husband. Her menfolk could treat her as they liked and a man who did not beat his wife was scorned by his friends as a coward. A woman possessed nothing not even the few clothes she wore".[12] Even then, Mizo women were bagged down with all household works–husking of paddy, cooking, domestication of animals, collection of water and firewood, looking after the children, weaving and stitching of clothing for the entire family and working in the jhum fields all the days. Therefore, they played an important role as food-earners of the family. Hence, when choosing a wife, a man would give priority to health, strength and skill at work of a woman.[13]

The situation, however, has undergone a tremendous change–both socially and economically after the advent of the colonial rulers and Christian missionaries. The colonial and post-colonial period witnessed a great transformation in the position and status of Mizo women. The introduction of western civilization, Christianity and western education were the main instruments by which these changes were brought about. Women have actually made significant contributions in all aspects of Mizo economy especially in the agricultural and service sectors. Presently, more Mizo women are now getting out of their home jobs into paid jobs and are bagged with a combination of their work at home and their jobs outside the homes.

The engagement of women in economic activities in Mizoram is widespread, ranging from the formal to the informal sectors. Women's participation in the formal sector is improved with their access to education and hence as more women get educated and acquire the requisite skills, they are increasingly being engaged in the formal sector and a number of them are holding the managerial positions. Today many educated women work in offices, schools, colleges and even in the universities. A number of them are engaging themselves in a variety of business activities while majority in rural areas are still clinging to the traditional jhumming system. The result of the sample survey of women and men workers in offices, shops etc. in the state capital, Aizawl conducted by Vanengliana, reveals that except for the meat shop, women are in the majority.[14] However, while considering that women make up the majority of workers in the Government service sector, it is disheartening to note that their impact on the decision-making process is still limited. This is due to the fact that they are found at the receiving end of the decision-making process and hence they have little or no influence on the decisions that affect them.

Women have also been doing quite well in running their petty business and small entrepreneurship such as in handloom, tailoring, floriculture, beauty parlour and so on.[15] Mizo women, especially those of rural women, are engaged in a wide variety of occupations especially in the unorganized sectors. In the rural unorganized sectors, women care for cattle, sowing, transplanting, harvesting, weaving, working in the handlooms and producing handicrafts mostly as low-paid wage earners or unpaid family workers. They are also engaged in producing and selling a variety of goods such as vegetables, fruits, flowers, cooked food, groceries etc.[16] Even today Mizo women are marginalized with regard to distribution of wages. For a day's work of unskilled labour women gets Rs. 100 while men are paid Rs. 150. Hence, the Equal Remuneration Act (ERA) No. 25 of 1976, which enshrines "the duty of employer to pay equal remuneration to men and women workers for the same work or work of similar nature" is not fully implemented especially in the private sector.

Even today the Mizo women are much marginalized and are placed in subordination as far as their participation in the Churches, politics and in the society are concerned. However, it is surprising that they are given much freedom in the field of various economic activities. In many families women are bread-earners while a number of the male members are sitting idly. Traditionally, the Mizo woman is a busy housekeeper and worker.

There can be no doubt about the fact that women have formed a very crucial and important part of the Mizo economy, because in a primarily agrarian and subsistence economy, the labour of entire household is essential for the sustenance of the economic activities. It is impossible to accept that they were passive observers in the process of production. If we look into the history, we come across a number of stories which refer to the women weaving, husking the rice, working in jhum, carrying water and wood. Women have worked hand in hand with men to keep the economy going. This means that both men and women are equally involved in providing the necessary economic sustenance.

Within the service sector, the fastest growing sector, women's participation is highly skewed towards wholesale and retail trade sub-sector. This conforms to the traditional conception of women as traders, cooks and caretakers at home and in the community at large. Those having their small entrepreneurship, like running shops and selling vegetables on the road side, market place or door to door, are faring well. Mizo women, apart from running shops and doing other business, are also employed in large number in Departmental Stores and as housekeepers. In most of the Government registered shops, societies and Fair Price Shops, majority of the employees are women. They also engage themselves as agents and sub-dealers in supplying and distributing oil, gas etc.[17] In all parts of the state, there are more female workers than males to be seen in shops, restaurants and other variety of stores.[18]

There is a significant relationship between women and nature and this is shaped by the ways in which they interact with the environment.[19]

Given that the process of production, reproduction and distribution vary by gender among other things. Women and men will understand and experience the environment differently and hence are likely to define and be affected by it differently. Women in most societies play a crucial role as food producers, providers and managers. In Mizoram, the role of women in agriculture cannot be overemphasized for they are involved in almost all sectors of agriculture–farming, processing and distribution. On the whole, women contribute more than men in terms of labour input in farming. Apart from this, they are solely responsible for household management duties. However, the income accruing to them is not commensurate with their tasks in the household. Household income distribution is always and often skewed in favour of men.

Even after four decades of development and planning, majority of women in Mizoram are still bagged in a narrow range of occupations characterized by low level of skill and income. Adding to these, the unpaid strenuous works rendered by them clearly show that Mizo women are more or less economically exploited.[20]

It is estimated that almost half of the economically active people in Mizoram is made up of women. They are engaging in various economic activities and predominate in the informal micro–small and medium scale agriculture, industry and service sectors of the economy. However, their contributions to economic growth and development are not fully represented because their activities are in the informal low-growth-low-return[21] areas and are basically subsistent. Unfortunately, most of the work that women do are not considered as economic activities but are rather seen as traditional chores to which they are duty bound to perform.[22] This tends to underrate the women's contribution to economy and thus invariably understate the Gross Domestic Product.

Another significant drawback is that although women are taking active part in the economic development of the state, especially in growing and marketing cash crops, yet, they do not have control over the niches in agricultural cycle.[23] They have been marginalized and disadvantaged as farmers. They have been treated as minors where finance and decision-making are concerned. Mostly their role in farming has been relegated to that of suppliers of labour while acquisitions of productive resources such as land, finance and extension services have virtually neglected them. These programmes generally and very often overlooked the major role that women play in agricultural production, marketing and management. In fact, they are often side-tracked from development interventions involving capacity building and technology transfer.[24]

With the increasing rate of rural to urban migration coupled with growing population, there is an urgent need to enhance women's effort at sustaining the rural farming sector. A survey of the use of appropriate technology devices revealed that rural women in the state were either generally not aware of the possibilities that existed or they considered the available technologies to be too expensive or inappropriate to their need.[25] As a remedial measure to this situation, it is suggested that Training Centres be established for rural women and involvement of women professionals be increased in the design and dissemination of appropriate technologies. It is asserted that these improvements would bring significant progress in their productivity. Hence, the adoption of strategies such as formation of women's cooperatives, introduction of modern farm inputs, diversification of farming enterprise and intensification of extension services are genuinely suggested. Therefore, the overall goal is dynamic understanding, at different levels, of the situation of women in agriculture in order to improve their status and enhance their contributions in economy. Equally important is the integration of women's concern in the economic agenda of the state.

So far, many projects for women are pure welfare projects. The ultimate objectives should be to increase their productivity and self-reliance.[26] As such, women's cooperatives should be promoted as a strategy to expand their access to information, increase their comparative bargaining power, and create opportunities for collective actions to access economic inputs. In reality, however, persisting gender biases, deep seated community dynamics and time constraints prevent them from actively participating in these organizations intended to bring about social capital benefits and female empowerment.[27] Strategies to address the impediments to women's empowerment at the societal and economic levels should go beyond the welfare, poverty alleviation, efficiency and model. Power of decision and choice of alternatives should be made available.

NOTES

1. Shahin Razi, "Social Face of India: Bridging Divides", in *Kurukshetra*, Vol. 55. No. 10, August 2007, pp. 11-12.
2. "Enhancement of Women Farmers' Role in the Development of Rural Asia", A Seminar organized by Rural Development Administration (RDA), Korea on 16.1.2008. http://www.agnet.org.
3. *Ibid.*
4. Reema Nanavaty, "Women Agriculture Workers". www.India–Seminar.com.

5. A.K. Rajula Devi, "Women in Agriculture and Rural Areas–India", Working Paper 183, April 1989. http://www.wid.msu.edu.
6. Anita Spring, "Women Farmers and Food Issues in Africa: Some Considerations and Suggested Solutions", Working Paper 139, September 1987. http://www.wid.msu.edu.
7. A.K. Rajula Devi, *op. cit.*
8. N.E. Parry, *The Lakhers*, Shillong, 1932, Reprint 1976, p. 6.
9. T.H. Lewin, *Wild Races...* p. 136.
10. Chapman and Clark, *Mizo Miracle*, p. 9.
11. *Ibid.*
12. *Ibid.*, p. 13.
13. R.L. Hnuni, "Impact of Christianity on the Hill Women of North East India", A paper presented in a Seminar on "*In the North and North East*" organized by Serampore College, Jorhat 12th May, 1997, p. 5.
14. Vanengliana, "Khawiah nge Mizo Mipa te?" (Where are the Mizo Men?) in *Khawtlang Nun Hruaina.* Published by Synod Social Front, Aizawl, 2000, pp. 3–6.
15. Lalhriatpuii, "Economic Empowerment in the Context of Mizo Women", A paper presented in the State Consultation Meeting on State Policy at Aizawl on 23-24 March, 2004, organized by the Mizoram State Commission on Women, p. 3.
16. Indrabushan Singh and Usha Kumari, "Rural Development and Women Empowerment" in *Kurukshetra*, Vol. 55, No. 5, March 2007, p. 4.
17. "Mizo Women Today" published by Tribal Research Institute, Directorate of Art and Culture, Government of Mizoram, Aizawl.
18. Vanengliana, *op. cit.*, p. 436.
19. Nora Judith Amu, *The Role of Women in Ghana's Economy*. ISBN 9988-0-2606-4. p. 29.
20. Jagadish K. Patnaik, *Mizoram Dimensions and Perspective–Society, Economy and Polity*, New Delhi, 2008, p. 354.
21. Nora Judith Amu, *The Role of Women in Ghana's Economy*. ISBN 9988-0-2606-4. p. 28.
22. *Ibid.*, p. 31.
23. Ma Elena Chiong–Javier, "Women in Agriculture and Marketing: Evidences and Lessons from the Philippines and Vietnam". http://www.cid.harvard.edu
24. *Ibid.*
25. Rosebud V. Kurwijila, "The Role of Appropriate Technology in Reducing Women's Workload in Agricultural Activities in Tanzania", Working Paper Abstract–208, July 1990. http://www.wid.msu.edu
26. Frank Ellis, *Agricultural Policies in Developing Countries*. Cambridge University Press. Books.google.com., p. 292.
27. "Enhancing the Role of Women Farmers in the Development of Rural Asia". http:// www.agnet.org

17

Socio-economic Empowerment of Mizo Women through Rashtriya Mahila Kosh:
An Analysis

C. Vanlalkulhpuia and *Elangbam Nixon Singh*

Introduction

Mizoram is one of the states of India having total area of 21,081 sq km. The currently density per sq. km in Mizoram is 52 per sq.km. According to 2011 Census of India, Mizoram's population has reached approximately 10.91 lakh, an increase of 22.78 per cent from the past decade. Mizoram feeds approximately 0.09 per cent of India's total population. As per census report of Mizoram, of the total population figures 10,91,014 male and female were 5,52,339 and 5,38,675 respectively. As per preliminary report of Census 2011, Mizoram has a literacy rate of 91.58 per cent which is above the national average of 74.04 per cent. Total 8,47,592 people were found literate in Mizoram as per 2011 census report. In literacy, of the total 8,47,592 literate population, 4,38,949 were male while remaining 4,08,643 forms female. In percentage, male were 93.72 per cent literate while female were having 89.40 per cent literacy. With regards to Sex Ratio also known as Gender Ratio, Mizoram surpasses the average Sex Ratio of India. As of 2011, India's average Gender Ratio stands at 940 while Mizoram's Sex Ratio stands out at 975. The State Director of Census Operations Mizoram, H.P. Sahu highlights that since 1901 to 1961, Mizoram's Sex Ratio crossed the 1000 mark varying from the highest at 113 in 1901 to the lowest at 1009 in 1961 and continued to decline during these decades. From the year 1961, the Sex Ratio of Mizoram declined to 946 in 1971 and 919 in 1981. However, from Census 1991, the number of females per 1000 males has continuously increased till 2011, he said. The data shows that population of Mizoram in 2011 was 10,91,014 as against 8,88,573 in 2001 census.

Table 17.1: District-wise Break-up of the State's Population

District	*Male*	*Female*	*Total*
Aizawl	2,01,072	2,02,982	4,04,054
Lunglei	79,252	74,842	1,54,094
Champhai	63,299	62,071	1,25,370
Lawngtlai	60,379	57,065	1,17,444
Mamit	44,567	41,190	85,757
Kolasib	42,456	40,598	83,054
Serchhip	32,824	32,051	64,875
Saiha	28,490	27,876	56,366

Source: Indian Population Census 2011.

Table 17.1, clearly shows that literacy rate of Mizoram population, female literacy rate in the district of Aizawl is higher than men while other districts men literacy rate is higher than women. Gender bias has been and still continues to be one of the major social evils in the society at large. However, with the passage of time, we witness in our modern world of today the emergence of the so-called weaker gender rising to positions of high status and power. Historically speaking, women have always been subdued and considered incapable and unworthy of greater tasks, and mostly subjected to affairs of the home. In recent times, women have come out of these homes to prove their worth even in the realm of politics which has been and still is considered a man's arena. Highlighting this phenomenon is the landmark decision of the Mizoram Government allotting 33 per cent reservation for women in the upcoming Municipal Council Elections.

In Mizoram, the women's group and organizations like the MHIP believe that the developments taking place in the municipality elections is none other than the product achieved out of the year of 'Women Empowerment' (1997–2011). Women in Mizoram are grateful and welcome the first and only time where women are given reservation in the political scenario. It is a landmark achievement indeed and though still seen as an experiment, it is hoped that it will help women in confidence building, creating awareness and having faith in their abilities, capabilities and their intelligence and foresight in the tasks that lay ahead.

Micro-finance: An overview

Today, more than one million SHGs have been credit linked across the country and they are able to mobilize about thousands of crores as credit from the formal financial institutions. It is mostly women who are now organising SHGs. Though the average size of the loan today is very low, the potential is very large (Adams, Dale W. *et al.,* 1992). Of late, there is a paradigm shift in the rural credit delivery system in India. Self-Help Groups (SHGs) especially of women are emerging in different parts of the country as grass roots mechanism to provide credit out of group funds. The money saved by the members are pooled and used as a revolving fund to provide credit for consumption and production purposes. Loans are advanced to the members based on priority determined by the group (Chatterjee, Shankar: 2004). There is no denying the fact that micro finance that helps borrowers is necessary but is not a sufficient condition for micro enterprises promotion. Other inputs are required especially in a market-led approach for sustainable development of micro enterprise. Several small entrepreneurs fail to achieve sustainable projects because a major share of their project funds are diverted to debt servicing. In this context, management of group funds by the poor especially Women providing sustainable livelihood opportunities through micro enterprise development becomes important (Kotaiah, P.: 1997). Experience in many countries demonstrates that poor women make investments wisely and earn returns. However, the flow of financial assistance to them was too marginal, if at all, to enable them to cross the poverty line. The need to create grass roots organizations to enable women to come together, to analyze their issues and problems themselves, and to fulfil their needs was strongly advocated. In fact, experience shows that some of the successful 'group-based participatory programmes' have made significant improvement in the living conditions of poor women (Malyadri, P.: 1997). In India, major funding agencies for micro credit programmes have been NABARD, Rashtriya Mahila Kosh (RMK) and Nationalized Banks.

Literature Review

Tandon, Jannavi *et al.* (1997) in their study examines the major objective of the Kosh as a promoter of credit as an instrument of socio-economic change for the development of women. Studying the socio-economic and demographic profile of women applying for loans; the repayment schedules; and the soliciting of views regarding the entire loan system, found that women felt that the loan amount should be increased and they should be assisted in marketing their goods.

Premchander, Smita and Vanguri, Pramila (2007), in their policy paper states that the Indian Government has paid special attention to women's empowerment in both the National Policy for Empowerment of Women (NPEW) 2001 as well as the Tenth Five Year Plan which illustrates its commitment to women's empowerment and welfare. Due to lack of employment opportunities for women, support for self-employment and women's enterprises are recognized as essential for releasing women's economic potential. Many NGOs have taken on the task of women's empowerment through micro-enterprises in recognition of the impact it can have on women, their families and poverty alleviation. Social empowerment aims to provide women easy and equal access to all the basic minimum services to enable them to realise their full potential. Economic empowerment aims to make all women economically independent through training, employment and income generation activities, allowing women to enjoy not only the *de jure* but also the *de facto* rights and fundamental freedom at par with men in all spheres.

ICPRD (Independent Commission for People's Rights and Development, 2003) in their proposal for micro finance found that economic empowerment is the first step towards the goal of equal participation of women in local communities. In implementing micro-credit programmes for poor women, several issues need to be taken into account. The credit plus activities are vital links in transforming women into entities of empowerment rather than mere clients of micro finance interventions. Several micro finance institutions have been criticized for failing to reach the poorest of the poor. It was seen that apart from the roles of reproduction and home management, micro credit programmes became the triple burden in poor women's lives. The micro credit group or SHGs often became a vehicle for providing security. Not only were business opportunities learnt through SHGs, but also collective marketing, self-care health services, adult literacy classes, and awareness generation programmes were often taken up in the absence of state provided services. The emphasis on savings and loans rather than the group process was the weakest link. The poorest often dropped out due to the pressure to save, and often defaulted. It was therefore found necessary to develop micro finance agencies or institutions that have organized collective action as well as ensure high repayment, i.e. uphold the twin agenda of women's empowerment with financial viability. This requires special interventions that are tailor-made, and based on a grass roots approach to planning, along with a well organised structure of layered credit groups, along with regular thrift training to workers.

Objectives of the Paper

The most prominent National level micro finance apex organization providing micro finance services for women in India is the National credit fund for women or the Rashtriya Mahila Kosh (RMK). The present paper attempts to analyse Rashtriya Mahila Kosh (RMK) in the socio-economic empowerment of Mizo women.

The objectives of the present study are as follows:

(i) To highlight the importance of Rashtriya Mahila Kosh (RMK).
(ii) To analyse the achievement and performance of Rashtriya Mahila Kosh (RMK) in Mizoram.
(iii) To offer some suggestions for the socio-economic empowerment of Mizo women through Rashtriya Mahila Kosh.

Methodology

The present paper is based on secondary data. Secondary data has been collected and analysed from various reports and publications of the Ministry of Women and Child Development, Rashtriya Mahila Kosh. Data for RMK for the state specific i.e. Mizoram is not available. As far as possible, data available for the North East states are taken into account for consideration of the present study.

Rashtriya Mahila Kosh (RMK): An Overview

The National Credit Fund for Women or the Rashtriya Mahila Kosh (RMK) is working exclusively for poor women. Its loans are available solely and entirely to this target group. The reasons for this are several:

(i) Among the poor, the poor *women* are the most disadvantaged, they are characterized by lack of education and access to resources, both of which are required to help them work their way out of poverty and for upward economic and social mobility.
(ii) The problem is more acute for women in countries like India, despite the fact that women's labour makes a critical contribution to the economy–this is due to low social status and lack of access to key resources.
(iii) Evidence shows that groups of women are better customers than men–they are better managers of resources–benefits of loans are spread wider among the household if loans are routed through

women-mixed groups are often inappropriate in Indian society–record of all-male groups is worse than that of all-women groups, everywhere. It has been felt for some time in India that the credit needs of poor women, particularly in the unorganised sector, have not been adequately addressed by the formal financial institutions in the country. The vast gap between demand for and supply of credit to this sector established the need for a National Credit Fund for Women. The National Credit Fund for Women or the Rashtriya Mahila Kosh (RMK) was set up in March 1993 as an independent registered society by the Department of Women and Child Development in Government of India's Ministry of Human Resource Development with an initial corpus of Rs. 31,00,00,000— not to replace the banking sector but to fill the gap between what the banking sector offers and what is needed by the poor.

Main Objectives of RMK

(i) To provide or promote the provision of micro-credit to poor women for income generation activities or for asset creation.

(ii) To adopt a quasi-informal delivery system, which is client friendly, uses simple and minimal procedures, disburses quickly and repeatedly, has flexibility of approach, links thrift and savings with credit and has low transaction costs both for the borrower and for the lender.

(iii) To demonstrate and replicate participatory approaches in the organisation of women's groups for thrift and savings and effective utilisation of credit.

(iv) To use the group concept and the provision of credit as an instrument of women's empowerment, socio-economic change and development.

(v) To cooperate with and secure the cooperation of the Government of India, State Governments, Union Territory administrations, credit institutions, industrial and commercial organisations, NGOs and others in promoting the objectives of the Kosh.

(vi) To disseminate information and experience among all these above agencies in the Government and non-government sectors in the area of micro finance for poor women.

To receive grants, donations, loans, etc., for the furtherance of the aims and objectives of the Kosh. The office of the Kosh is situated in New Delhi. The Kosh does not have any branch offices. The Executive

Director is the chief executive officer of the Kosh. The Executive Director functions under the overall supervision, direction and control of the Governing Board. The Governing Board comprises 16 members consisting of senior officers of the Government of India and State Governments, specialists and representatives of NGOs active in the field of micro finance for women. The Governing Board is chaired by the Minister in-charge of the Department of Women and Child Development in the Government of India. The General Body of the Kosh consists of all members of the Board, institutional members and individual members.

Main Roles of RMK

Wholesaling Role:

(i) It acts as a wholesaling apex organisation for channelising funds from government and donors to retailing Intermediate Micro finance Organisations (IMOs).

(ii) The Kosh has so far received only a one-time grant from government and has not needed to raise funds from any other sources.

Market Development Role

(i) It develops the supply side of the micro finance market by offering institution building support to new and existing–but–inexperienced IMOs by structures of incentives, transfers of technology, training of staff and other non-financial services.

(ii) The Kosh realises that it can play a value adding wholesaling role only when a sufficiently large and well established micro finance sector already exists–this depends on the number of IMOs and the sustainability of IMOs–subsidised institution building increases the equity of any IMO as much as grants do–large and premature disbursement of funds to the IMO can reduce the effectiveness of any institution building effort.

Advocacy Role

RMK acts as an advocate or agent for influencing development and micro finance policy and creating a more enabling policy and legal environment for spread of micro finance activities in India. Being a creation and a representative of the government, RMK has a particular advantage in this area.

Eligibility Criteria

(i) NGO/VO/VA should have Experience in Micro credit for a minimum of 5 years.

(ii) NGOs/VOs/VAs having availed loan of '.50 lakhs and above from Rashtriya Mahila Kosh would be considered.

(iii) NGOs/VOs/VAs should have adequate infrastructure and training capabilities for implementing RMK's various schemes.

(iv) Proposal for appointment as Nodal Agency of Rashtriya Mahila Kosh would not be considered from defaulting NGOs/VOs/VAs.

(v) NGOs/VOs/VAs should have resource Personnel having experience in micro credit/social activities/law/accounting etc.

(vi) Dynamic young persons having experience in micro credit, accountancy, capacity building, preparation of financial statements, annual report etc., sponsored by NGOs/VOs/VAs designated as Nodal Officer (NO) for implementing RMK's scheme and the organisation represented will be accorded the Status of NOA.

(vii) The above eligibility criterias may be relaxed in deserving cases by the Executive Director.

Rashtriya Mahila Kosh and Women's Financial Inclusion

According to the 1995 World Bank estimate, in most developing countries the formal financial system reached only the top 25 per cent of the economically active population–the bottom 75 per cent having no access to financial services apart from moneylenders. In India, the formal financial institutions have not been able to reach the poor households, especially the women, in the unorganised sector. Structural rigidities and overheads led to high cost of making small loans. Organisational philosophy being such, it has not been oriented towards recognising the poor as creditworthy. The problem has been compounded by low level of influence of the poor, either about their creditworthiness or their demand for savings services. Micro finance programmes have often been implemented by large banks at the behest of the government. Low levels of recovery have been further eroded due to loan waiver programmes leading to institutional disenchantment with lending to small borrowers.

All these gave rise to the concept of micro credit for the poorest segment along with a new set of credit delivery techniques. With the support of NGOs, an informal sector comprising small Self-Help Groups (SHGs) started mobilizing savings of their members and lending these resources among the members on a micro scale. The potential of these SHGs to develop as local financial intermediaries to reach the poor has gained recognition due to their community based participatory approach and sustainability–recovery rates have been significantly higher than those achieved by commercial banks in spite of loans going to poor, unorganised individuals without security or collateral. Success stories in neighbouring countries, like Grameen Bank in Bangladesh, Bank Rakiat in Indonesia, Commercial and Industrial Bank in Philippines, etc., gave further boost to the concept in India in the 1980s (Yunus, Mohammad: 2004).

The Global Summit on Micro Finance held in Washington in February, 1997 set a global target of covering 100 million poor families with credit by 2005–it was expected that 25–30 million of these could be in India alone. The poor in India define the micro finance market. According to The Planning Commission estimate of 1993-94, 36 per cent of the population or 320 million people live below the poverty line–which means there would be 140–150 million women alone living below the poverty line. Assuming that only 30 per cent of the country's poor women are ready to adopt micro finance as a method of poverty alleviation, it is estimated that 40–45 million poor women would need credit. As against this, it is estimated that all agencies in India engaged in the provision of micro finance services, would have together covered barely 1 million poor people by the close of 1998-99. The most prominent national level micro finance apex organisation providing micro finance services for women in India is the National Credit Fund for Women or the Rashtriya Mahila Kosh (RMK).

Table 17.2 tries to analyse the overall cumulative details of sanctioned, release/disbursement made by RMK in the country to different schemes with figures as on 31.03.2011. There are 1464 new NGOs coming up along with the repeated 452 NGOs. The total number of borrowers is 6,87,512, amounts sanctioned 30,752.09 lakhs and the total amount disbursed 25,181.78 lakhs.

Performance of RMK in North-Eastern Region

In order to remove the uneven presence of micro-credit in the country which is witnessed mostly in North Eastern region due to poor presence of banking network, lack of infrastructure and awareness, RMK has formulated a concessional package for the voluntary organisations of the North Eastern region for easy access of credit from RMK to meet the credit needs of the poor women of the region. The relaxations are:

The organization having completed one year of its registration (presently 3 years) can apply for the loan.

(i) Margin on loan reduces from 10 per cent to 5 per cent.
(ii) The grace period on repayment of loan enhanced from 6 months to 12 months.

Table 17.2: Cumulative Details of Sanctioned, Release/Disbursement with Figures as on 31.03.2011

(' in Lakhs)

Sl. No.	*Name of the scheme*	*No. of NGOs New*	*No. of NGOs Repeat*	*No. of Borrowers*	*Amount Sanctioned*	*Amount Disbursed*
1.	Main Loan	758	246	464676	20659.96	16061.32
2.	Revolving Fund		100	154605	4311.50	3997.20
3.	Loan Promotion	296	53	27579	911.20	610.00
4.	Housing Loan		6	1600	281.00	212.50
5.	Gold Credit Card		17	30289	2410.00	2387.71
6.	Franchisee	2	6	6677	1409.00	1295.00
7.	SHG Development	405	14		369.88	305.50
8.	Marketing		7		37.25	37.25
9.	Refinance	3	1	586	203.30	153.30
10.	Working Capital Term Loan		2	1500	159.00	122.00
	Total	**1464**	**452**	**687512**	**30752.09**	**25181.78**

Source: Ministry of Women and Child Development Rashtriya Mahila Kosh Annual Reports.

Table 17.3: Cumulative and Year-wise Achievement of RMK (up to 31.03.2011)

(' in Lakhs)

Year	*Loan Sanctioned*	*Loan Disbursed*	*No. of NGOs*	*No. of SHGs*	*No. of Women beneficiaries*
2005-06	1930.9	2068.42	82	2731	27305
2006-07	3071	2410.6	88	3469	34692
2007-08	3228.8	2557.74	52	3583	35827
2008-09	3030.45	2647.7	44	3617	36166
2009-10	1471	1563.03	23	1540	15404
2010-11	1278	1249.15	22	1336	13362
Total	**14010.15**	**12496.64**	**311**	**16276**	**162756**

Source: Ministry of Women and Child Development Rashtriya Mahila Kosh Annual Reports.

(iii) The repayment period of loan enhanced to five years invariably for all schemes.

(iv) The NGOs to be supported with 10 per cent of the loan sanctioned as capacity building assistance.

(v) To provide second class sleeper rail fare and where there is no rail link, cheaper class to and fro Air Fare to the members of NGOs (up to 2 numbers) for coming to Delhi for execution of document.

Table 17.4: Cumulative and State-wise Achievement of RMK in North East India (up to 31.03.2011) (Rs. in Lakhs)

Name of State	*Amount Sanctioned*	*Amount Disbursed*	*No. of NGOs*	*No. of SHGs*	*No. of Women beneficiaries*
Arunanchal Pradesh	10	5	1	10	100
Assam	475.9	444.9	12	623	6225
Manipur	284.05	216.04	36	842	8421
Mizoram	4	2	1	7	70
Meghalaya	Nil	Nil	Nil	Nil	Nil
Tripura	Nil	Nil	Nil	Nil	Nil
Nagaland	74	45.5	8	79	859
Total	**847.95**	**713.44**	**58**	**1561**	**15675**

Source: Ministry of Women and Child Development Rashtriya Mahila Kosh Annual Reports.

From Table 17:4, it can be seen that amongst the states of the North East, the state of Mizoram lags far behind with regard to the performance and achievements of the Rashtriya Mahila Kosh (RMK). With regard to the amount of loans sanctioned, the state of Assam occupies the highest position and Manipur second, while Mizoram has the lowest with only Rs. 4 lakhs. It is pertinent to mention here that Meghalaya and Tripura had not received any loan from RMK till date. Also, with regard to the amount of loans disbursed, the state of Assam occupies the highest position even though it has only 12 numbers of NGOs and 623 nos. of SHGs while the State of Manipur which occupies the second position has many as 36 no. of NGOs and 842 SHGs. It is deplorable that Mizoram has only 1 (one) number of NGOS and 7 SHGs under the Rashtriya Mahila Kosh (RMK) and the amount of loan disbursed being only Rs. 2 lakhs. The state of Arunachal Pradesh whose position stands/remains closest to that of Mizoram also has only 1 NGO and 10 SHGs but was able to disburse loans amounting to Rs. 5 lakhs.

RMK and Mizo Women

After analysis of the performance and achievements of RMK in the North East, it is clear that Mizoram still needs to surge forward in using RMK for the socio-economic empowerment of women. This may be possible through rousing public awareness of the important/workings/programmes of RMK. Even though the literacy rate of women in Mizoram is not low as compared with the rate of men literacy rate and also with the other whole country but, knowledge and involvement to the RMK is not satisfactory as compared with the other states of North East India. This result clearly shows that women in Mizoram still need to be guided and shown the way to make beneficial use of the RMK.

Moreover, even those women beneficiaries have been given loans under RMK faces the problems of low recovery. Another important drawback that RMK faces is that there is only one main office located in New Delhi, and no branch offices in the states.

1.7 Conclusion and Suggestions

Taking into consideration the overall workings, performances and achievements of the RMK with special reference to Mizo women, the following suggestions may be taken into consideration to ensure its effective functioning:

(i) Creating awareness regarding the workings and benefits of RMK in the state especially amongst Mizo women.

(ii) Establishment of branch offices in the state so that RMK would be more accessible and this in turn would eliminate low-recovery rate.

(iii) Implementation of regular trainings and workshops in the North Eastern states, so that these states would be able to compete with other parts of the country. RMK proposes to undertake different programmes in the future, but the effective implementation of these programmes also depends on the concern and due recognition given by the state governments. The scheduled programmes are:

- (i) Conduct impact studies and feasibility studies
- (ii) Skill training of women
- (iii) Enterprise development training of women and NGO staff
- (iv) Product and market development
- (v) Development of data bases and trade related information systems
- (vi) Acquisition of computer and institution of Information Management System.

Women play an important role in the socio-economic development of country, but since time immemorial they have been the neglected lot. So, in 21st century there is a need for the women empowerment to attain highest level of socio-economic growth. In this direction several policies and programmes have been introduced by the Government of India. These programmes play an important role in the upliftment of women. But, the effective implementation part has to be taken care of to make women more independent and socially as well as economically empowered. The wide spectrum of emerging models of SHG-based institutions reflects the effort of NGOs and other stakeholders in addressing the challenge of sustainability. The multiple constraints and opportunities that determine the types of institutions promoted include: (i) the legal and regulatory provisions in the states of operation; (ii) the origins of the programmes and the broader vision for the community; (iii) the capacity of the NGO to support micro finance; (iv) poverty contexts and social conditions in different areas; (v) the availability of physical and financial infrastructure and external support. RMK has a strategic vision to expand its programme uniformly all-over the country to empower more and more economically poor women of the country in a phased manner. The Mizo women should not be lagging behind as far as RMK programmes are concerned as it will help to empower them socially as well as economically.

REFERENCES

1. Adams, Dale W. and Pischke, J.D. Von (1992): "Micro enterprise Credit Programmes", *World Development*, 20(10), (October), 1463–1470.
2. Chatterjee, Shankar (2004): "Empowering women through micro finance: A study", *Women's Link*, 10(3), (July-Sept): 15–21.
3. http://www.sinlung.com/2011/04/37pc–of–mizoram–population–lives–in.html#ixzz1X6TTPMc
4. http://mizoramexpress.com/index.php/2011/04/population–of–mizoram–released/#ixzz1X6T2RjhP
5. Independent Commission for People's Rights and Development (2003): "Demand Survey for Micro finance in Central Eastern India: A Proposal", New Delhi: ICPRD.
6. Kotaiah, P. (1997): "Banking on micro entrepreneurs–Innovative lending and credit programmes", *National Bank News Review*, 13(2), (April-June).
7. Kumar, Udaia (2004): "Branding micro finance", *Shelter*, 17(1), (January).
8. Malyadri. P (1997): "Financing Rural Non-Farm Sector", *Khadi Gramodyog*, May, Vol. 43, No. 8, 442–448.
9. Ministry of Women and Child Development, Rashtriya Mahila Kosh Annual Reports 2010-11.
10. Nangkyntiew Kimi Wason (2009): "The 21st Century Mizo Women on the Rise", *The North East Today*.
11. Premchander, Smita and Vanguri, Pramila (2007): "Micro finance and Women's Empowerment: Programme and Policy Review", New Delhi: CARE India.

12. Tandon, Jannavi *et al.* (1997): "Impact study of Rashtriya Mahila Kosh credit facilities to poor women through non-governmental organisations", Varanasi: Banaras Hindu Univ., Faculty of Social Sciences, Centre for Women's Studies and Development.
13. Yunus Mohammad (2004): "Grammeen Bank Micro-credit and millennium development goals", *Economic and Political Weekly*, September 4, 4077-4080.

18

Empowerment of Women through Entrepreneurship:

A Study of Mizo Women

R.K.P.G. Singha

Introduction

Empowerment of women has become an important issue at the present context. The economic empowerment of women is being regarded these days as one of the best devices for the socio-economic upliftment and progress of a country. So, the issue of economic empowerment of women is of paramount importance to political leaders, Government, researchers, NGOs, social scientists and planners and a matter of great debate and discussion. From Fifth Five Year Plan onwards there has been a marked shift in the approach to women's issues from welfare to development and women empowerment has been recognized as the central issue in determining the status of women. Keeping this in view, the Central and State Governments have been implementing many programmes and schemes to empower women economically, socially, politically and legally with special emphasis on those who are in rural areas. The ultimate objective of all these efforts is to make women economically independent and self-reliant.

Men and women both are two wheels of society and contribution of both is essential for building healthy nation. Even after 60 years of independence women in India are struggling for entrepreneurial freedom. She has to seek permission from her family members. She has to face various socio-economic problems even after getting permission from family. That is why women as entrepreneurial resource have not been widely recognized in India. There has been increasing trend in number of women owned enterprises in India but despite government efforts, substantial growth could not be achieved. Through the development of entrepreneurship, women are becoming economically independent and providing employment opportunities to others. The emergence of women entrepreneurs and their contribution to the national economy and overall women empowerment is quite significant. Women entrepreneurship has gained momentum in the last few decades with the increase in the number of women enterprises and their substantive contribution to economic growth particularly after economic reform in India. In this globalized world, women entrepreneurs are crucial part of the global quest for sustained economic growth and social development. In India, though women have played a vital role in the society, their entrepreneurial ability has not been properly tapped as our society is still male-dominated and has lower status in the society. The development of women entrepreneurship has become an important part of our plan priorities. Various policies and programmes are being implemented for the development of women entrepreneurship in India.

With the objective of promoting Women entrepreneurs, SIDO organizes Entrepreneurship Development Programmes, Management Development Programmes, Skill Development Programmes etc. that provide training and technical schemes for the setting up SMEs units. A number of programmes/schemes are in operation with an objective of economically empowering the women, particularly in rural areas. The third All India Census of Small Scale Industries (2001-02) revealed that 10.11 per cent of the SMEs are owned by women entrepreneurs. This report further highlighted that 9.5 per cent of the total units are managed by women.

Coming to Mizoram the status of entrepreneurship development of women is not different than any other North Eastern states of India rather it is yet to occupy a place on the industrial map of India as it is still identified as "no industry area" at the national level. It is a clear fact that if we see from the high ratio of government jobs in proportion to total population of the state and at the same time growing unemployment is also another reason for women participation in entrepreneurship. So, at the present juncture and in the changing scenario more and more women entrepreneurs are coming to participate in the field of business, trade and commerce. High literacy rate among the women entrepreneurs in Mizoram is also very encouraging.

Objective of the Study

1. To critically study the importance of women empowerment and entrepreneurship in Mizoram at the present context.
2. To study the various aspects of women entrepreneurs in Mizoram.
3. To critically examine the problems faced by the women entrepreneurs.
4. To offer some suggestions for women empowerment through entrepreneurship.

Meaning of Women Entrepreneur

Women entrepreneur may be termed as a women or group of women who initiate, organize, and run a business enterprise. The Government of India has defined women entrepreneurs based on women participation in equity and employment of a business firm. Accordingly, a women entrepreneur is defined as "an enterprise owned and controlled by a women having a minimum financial interest of 51 per cent of the capital and giving at least 51 per cent of the employment generated in the enterprise to women. As an entrepreneur, a women entrepreneur has also to perform all the functions involved in establishing an enterprise. These include idea generation and screening, determination of objectives, project preparation, product analysis, determination of forms of business organization, completion of promotional formalities, raising funds, procuring men, machine and materials and operation of business. In short, women entrepreneurs are those women who think of a business enterprise, initiate it, organize and combine the factors of production, operate the enterprise and undertake risks and handle economic uncertain embroil in running a business firm. Initially, women tend to go in for traditional and home based projects and the common perceptions even today is that women go in for garments, pickles, etc. this, however, is far from the truth, with the changing times, a large and growing number of women take up non-traditional projects and succeed as entrepreneurs. Women entrepreneurs have been making a significant impact in all segments of the economy all-over the country. The areas chosen by women are retail trade, restaurants, hotels, education, insurance, readymade garments.

Entrepreneurship Development in Mizoram

The status of entrepreneurship development in general in Mizoram is more or less similar with other North Eastern states; rather it is yet to find a place on the industrial map of India. Owing to various constraints, setting up of a large scale industry is yet a dream. Presently, among the various industries of Mizoram, one or two are of medium scale, and the rest are from small-scale, tiny, village and cottage, handloom and handicrafts category with very little investment only. Moreover, among the common features of all the Public Sector Enterprises in Mizoram, operational revenue was significant, no efforts were made to raise the same, overheads were mounting, employees had a mindset of government department's working and failed to recognize the existence of their respective corporations, concept of accountability and firm commitment was absent which is also true in other North Eastern States, the additional capital contributed by the Government of Mizoram could not be put to productive use rather it was consumed to wipe off annual loss, the management was conservative in approach and did not benefit from capital gearing which led to cost and time overrun as to project implementation, failed in promoting ancillarization in their respective field and could not occupy the central position as leader among prospective/private entrepreneurs of future were prominent.

Mizoram did not make headway in industrial development and the people by and large depending on government jobs. Therefore, there is a need to change the mindset of new generation particularly under at this globalised world by opening up of their horizons and by bringing a change in their thought through orientation which is a challenge for the policy makers.

Women Entrepreneurship in Mizoram

In Mizoram interesting development is participation of more and more women entrepreneurs in trade, business and commerce and they are doing very well in terms of performance comparing to their male counterparts. Women entrepreneurs have been making a significant impact in all segments of the economy. The important motives for women to become entrepreneurs are such as economic needs of pressures, utilization of own experience and education, husband's or family's interest or support, availability of free time and finances, desire to become independent, unemployment and personal ego and satisfaction of doing something of their own. Today we find women in different types of micro enterprises, traditional as well as non-traditional, such as retail trade, foreign goods retail trade, restaurants, beauty parlours, second-hand garments shop, electronics, readymade garments, fabrics, eatables, handloom and handicrafts, poultry, plastics, soap, drugs, tailoring, knitting etc. what motivates women to aspire for a career in business is an interesting thing to explore and analyze in this remote part of the country. According to Mclelland and Winter, motivation is a critical factor that leads one towards entrepreneurship. This apart, the challenge and adventure to do something new; liking for business and wanting to have an independent occupation are some of the attractive leverage for women. These factors indicate a relatively deeper commitment to entrepreneurial profession on the part of entrepreneur. Responsibility thrust, due to death of a keen, break of family or incapacitation of a near relation are the push factor. Apart from these, special qualifications attained for running a concern, identifying the demand from the market, external motivation, employment to needy and destitute to set-up an ancillary unit, business already in the family are some of the factors which gave stimulus to women entrepreneurs to start business in this remote part of the country. At the same time, growth of women entrepreneurship is slow in Mizoram due to various constraints such as lack of education, dual role of women, lack of aptitudes and training, lack of freedom to choose a job according to ability, custom and family burden, small market, financial problem etc.

Education plays an important role in entrepreneurship development in the context of Mizoram. The literacy rate of female in Mizoram is very commanding comparing to other parts of the country, Mizoram being attained 2nd highest literacy rate (2001 census) in the country in general. The educational attainments of women in the state are very much comparable with the men (Table 18.1). The urban women are more literate than the rural. A critical perusal of Table 18.1 shows that the female literacy rate was only 16.7 per cent in 1951 and it stood at 86.71 per cent in 2001 which is very encouraging. Women are not behind than the male counterparts and that leads to women empowerment and overall socio-economic development in the state of Mizoram.

A cursory view of Table 18.2 highlights the main and marginal workers in Mizoram. Analysis of Table 18.2 reveals that the proportions of workers in rural areas were higher being 57.20 per cent than in urban areas being 47.87 per cent. The proportions of male and female workers to total workforce work out to 56.30 per cent and 47.70 per cent respectively in the year 2001. Thus, it shows that women participation in workforce in Mizoram is quite significant which contribute to the state economy.

Table 18.1: Literate Population and Literacy Rate through Decadal Census

Year	*Literate Persons*			*Literacy Rate*		
	Male	*Female*	*Total*	*Male*	*Female*	*Total*
1951	44,375	16,718	61,093	46.15	16.7	36.23
1961	70,743	46,354	1,17,097	53.4	34.7	44.00
1971	1,03,324	74,469	1,78,793	60.49	46.71	53.79
1981	1,65,812	1,29,873	2,95,685	79.36	68.61	74.26
1991	2,51,551	2,10,379	4,61,930	85.61	78.6	82.27
2001	3,50105	3,11,340	6,61,445	90.71	86.71	88.80

Source: Statistical Abstract 2007, Directorate of Economics and Statistics, Mizoram.

Table 18.2: Main and Marginal Workers in Mizoram (1991 and 2001)

Workers	*1991 Census*			*2001 Census*		
	Main Workers					
	Rural	Urban	Total	Rural	Urban	Total
Male	99722	78289	178011	120662	104766	225428
Female	69615	42691	112306	80937	56085	137022
	Marginal Workers					
Male	7048	8322	15370	18193	19387	37580
Female	13962	17696	31658	36252	30887	67129
Total Workers	190347 (51.19)	146998 (46.23)	337345 (48.9)	256044 (57.20)	211115 (47.87)	467159 (52.6)
Total Persons	371810	317946	689756	447567	441006	888573

Source: Economic Survey of Mizoram 2007-08.

Note: Figures in the brackets show percentage of total workforce.

Table 18.3 depicts the participation of women in management ownership in SSI sector in Mizoram in various districts. It can be inferred from the table that number of enterprises managed and owned by women differs from district to district in Mizoram. There are numerous reasons for such disparity like population of the districts, educational level and other opportunities available to the women entrepreneurs. Aizawl district ranked first followed by Champhai and Lunglei respectively in women ownership in SSI sector. The position of Mamit district ranked last from the foregoing analysis.

Table 18.4 displays the female employment in SSI sector in various districts of Mizoram. The average female employment is about 23 per cent which is quite promising. Four districts i.e., Kolasib, Aizawl,

Table 18.3: Participation of Women in Management/Ownership in SSI Sector

Districts	*No. of Enterprises Managed by Woman*	*No. of Women Enterprises*	*Ranks of Women Enterprises*
Mamit	10	6	8
Kolasib	29	24	5
Aizawl	535	118	1
Champhai	44	46	2
Serchhip	15	15	6
Lunglei	43	43	3
Lawngtlai	15	11	7
Saiha	35	27	4
Total	**726**	**290**	

Source: R.K.P.G. Singha, 2010.

Table 18.4: Share of Females in Employment, District-wise in SSI Sector

Districts	*Total*	*Female*	*Percentage*	*Rank*
Mamit	103	18	17.48	7
Kolasib	359	85	23.67	4
Aizawl	6951	1726	24.83	3
Champhai	464	85	18.32	6
Serchhip	169	32	18.93	5
Lunglei	545	97	17.80	8
Lawngtlai	128	48	37.05	1
Saiha	294	85	28.91	2
Total	**9013**	**2176**	**23.37 (Average)**	

Source: R.K.P.G. Singha, 2010.

Lawngtlai and Saiha have more than average women employment in the sector out of 8 districts in Mizoram. Again the table also portrays that in terms of rank in women employment in SSI sector in the state, Lawngtlai stood first and followed by Saiha, Aizawl, and Kolasib respectively and Lunglei district being the last.

Table 18.5 highlights the employment profile of Rural Micro Enterprises in Mizoram. Women employment in rural micro enterprises is also quite significant comparing to urban set-up in Mizoram. Rural women are not lagging behind in terms of entrepreneurship in the state. Analysis of the table depicted that Lawngtlai district ranked top in terms of female employment in rural micro enterprises being 80 per cent followed by Kolasib district 38 per cent and Mamit district at 20 per cent respectively. Surprisingly, there is no women employment in Saiha district.

Table 18.5: Employment Profile of Rural Micro Enterprises in Mizoram

	Number of persons Employed in Rural Micro Enterprises				
Districts	*Male*	*Female*	*Total*	*Female Percentage*	*Rank*
Mamit	39	10	49	20	3
Kolasib	25	15	40	38	2
Aizawl	395	42	437	10	6
Champhai	115	25	140	18	4
Serchhip	33	6	39	15	5
Lunglei	45	4	49	8	7
Lawngtlai	5	12	17	80	1
Saiha	14	—	14	0	—
	671	**114**	**785**	**15**	

Source: Third Census of Small Scale Industries in Respect of Mizoram State, Directorate of Industries, Aizawl.

Problems associated with Women Entrepreneurs

Developing entrepreneurship especially women entrepreneurship is not so easy. It is constrained with several problems. Some of the problems are general in nature and the others are specific to women entrepreneurs as we live in a complicated social structure. The problems are highlighted as hereunder:

1. The greatest problem to women entrepreneur are that they are women. Indian society is patriarchal and women in India are generally regarded to be homemakers and not 'businesswomen'.
2. Indian society is a complex one. Women are not treated equal to men. They are not given equal opportunity to play the vital role in the society though the Indian Constitution provides equality between sexes. Thus, in practical women face many challenges to enter into business, trade and commerce in this part of this country.
3. Women generally lack support, encouragement and motivation from others due to various known and unknown reasons. Sometimes, men discourage to take any venture in trade and commerce by women and are jealous of their success in business.
4. Another important fact is that generally women are considered that they have low-level management skills and they cannot handle properly the business affairs.
5. Another argument against women is that they are less mobile than men. In business affairs mobility of the entrepreneur is very crucial to manage the business. It is generally accepted that the

confidence in women to travel day and night to various places is lacking compared to male counterparts. The same problem is faced by the women entrepreneurs in Mizoram.

6. Another important issue is that financial institutions are not favourable to women entrepreneur and they are dubious about the entrepreneurial capabilities of women. Financial institutions are reluctant to lend money to women entrepreneurs and they put many conditions before they lend money to them.
7. High production cost of business operation prevailing in Mizoram is a big hurdle for the development of women entrepreneurs in this part of the country.
8. Women are always busy with their domestic duties and are always an impediment to their success in business career.
9. There are many other problems which women come across while running a business. Problems are such as high competition, lack of infrastructure, power shortage, shortage of raw materials, lack of self-confidence, exploitation by middlemen, social attitude towards women, and so on which are also faced by women entrepreneurs in Mizoram.

Concluding Remarks

Women comprise half of human population. They have been identified as key agent of sustainable development and women's equality is as central to a more holistic approach towards establishing new patterns and process of development that are sustainable. The contribution of women and their position in the family as well as in the economic progress and social transformation are very crucial. The micro entrepreneurship is strengthening the women empowerment and removes gender inequalities. They are economically empowered and attaining status in family and community. The women are empowering themselves technically to cope with the times and productively using their free time and existing skills for setting and sustaining enterprises. This will not only generate income for them but also improve the decision-making capabilities that led to overall economic empowerment.

In Mizoram, the emergence of women entrepreneurs and their contribution to the state economy as well to the women empowerment is quite visible in the recent past and more and more entrepreneurs are starting their new ventures. In the context of Mizoram, education of women played a very critical role in the development of women entrepreneurs and running successfully in their venture. In future, more and more entrepreneurs will join in business and trade. For the socio-economic development of Mizoram particularly women in line with other parts of the country many aspects like infrastructure, initiative to promote investment and entrepreneurship with proper marketing strategy is need of the hour. The focus of women entrepreneurship should be on business opportunities on trade with neighbouring countries, agro and food processing, sericulture, handloom and handicrafts etc. as the establishment of large scale industry is not feasible due to various constraints in the state and through this venture women will be empowered for overall and sustainable development of the state.

REFERENCES

Hussain, Syed Vazith and Sivasankar, P.R. (2005). "Women Empowerment and Prime Minister Rojgar Yojana", *Indian Journal of Commerce*, Vol. 58, No. 2, April–June.

Kabra, K.C. and Singha, R.K.P.G. (2006). "Border Trade in Mizoram: Emerging Trends and Future Prospects", in: David R. Syiemlieh *et al.* (eds). *Challenges of Development of North East India*, Regency Publication, New Delhi.

Khanka, S.S. (1999). "Entrepreneurial Development", S. Chand & Company Ltd., New Delhi.

Laskar, B.I. (2010). "Industrialization in Mizoram: Problems and Prospects", New Central Book Agency (P) Ltd., Kolkata.

Lipi (2009). "Women Empowerment: Globalization and Opportunities", in *Empowerment of Rural Women in India*, Kanishka Publishers, New Delhi.

On All India Third Census of Small Scale Industries in Respect of Mizoram State, Directorate of Industries, Mizoram, Aizawl. (2001-02).

Prabha Singh (2009). "Rural Women and Development of Entrepreneurship with Special reference to Punjab", in *Empowerment of Rural Women in India*, Kanishka Publishers, New Delhi.

Prasad, Hanuman and Verma, V.L. (2005). "Women Entrepreneurship in India", *Indian Journal of Commerce*, Vol. 58, No. 2, April-June.

Rastogi, Harsha (2003). "Entrepreneurship Development", King Books, Delhi.

Singha, R.K.P.G. and Kabra, K.C. (2006). "Entrepreneurship and Information Technology in Mizoram", In: Prasain, G.P. (ed.). *Entrepreneurship and Small Scale Industries*, Akansha Publishing House, New Delhi.

—— (2006). "Problems and Prospects of Rural Entrepreneurship with Special Reference to Mizoram", In: Ahmed, J.U. (ed.). *Development Vision of North East India*, Concept Publishing Company (P) Limited, New Delhi.

Statistical Abstract–2007. Directorate of Economics and Statistics, Mizoram.

Vasanthagopal, R. and Santha, S. (2008). "Women Entrepreneurship in India". New Century Publications, New Delhi.

Website visited: http://www.enotes.com/business/q–and–/whar–major–problems–faced–by–women–entrepreneurs–55369 accessed on 25-7-2011.

SECTION V

Women's Empowerment: Barriers and Strategies

19

Political Empowerment of Women in Mizoram:

Barriers and Strategies

Bilal Ahmed

Introduction

Women work two-third of the world's working hours. They earn only 10 per cent of the world's income and own less than 1 per cent of world's property. Where laws or customs prevent women from having the right to inheritance, they have no assets for economic stability. Around two-third of adult illiterate world wide are women. In many societies around the world women never belong wholly to themselves, they are the property of others throughout their lives. Their physical well-being—health, security and bodily integrity—is often beyond their control. Around the globe, home and community are not safe heavens for girls and women. At least one in three females on earth has been physically or sexually abused. Poverty and exclusion push some girls and women to engage in sex work, almost always the desperate last choice. Systematic rape as a weapon of war has left millions of girls and women traumatized, forcibly impregnated, and/or HIV positive. So women's subordination or disempowerment is a universal factor. Therefore, their empowerment becomes a necessity. Women empowerment offers a pathway towards dignity and security—for women, their families and the whole communities.

Of all empowerment with importance, political empowerment is considered the most important one. The political empowerment is meant for participating in political decision-making process. And women political empowerment has to do with political influence of women and the institutionalization of the participation in political decision-making process (Gangmei, 2010). The political empowerment for women is regarded as the key driver for their economic and social empowerment. Their enhanced participation in governance structures is viewed as the key to redress the gender inequalities in societies.

Background (World)

Women all-over the world have remained out of political realm for quite a long time. For centuries they were not welcomed at the helm of political affairs. However, with the increasing recognition of women's historic exclusion from structure of power among international community, a global commitment has been made to redress gender imbalance in politics. The global debate on the promotion of women's political participation/ representation has been surrounded by different approaches. One group of theorists argue for equal participation of women in politics from the human rights perspective. For them, women constitute half of the world's population and therefore, it is only fair that they should have equal participation and representation in world democracies. The other group opines that men and women are essentially different. Women have different vision and concepts of politics owing to their sex and gender roles as mothers. Therefore, it is assumed that women in politics will bring a special caring focus and female values to politics. Though differ in their approaches, all theorists agree that women must be included in politics (Bari, 2005).

Despite the pronounced commitment of the international community, reinforced by the Convention on Elimination of All Forms of Discriminations Against Women (CEDAW) and the Beijing Platform of Action there is no significant change in the situation. Study shows that the percentage of women in world Parliaments has dropped over the years. Their representation is quite disproportionate to their population. Strangely enough, ten Parliaments in the world do not have even a single women parliamentarian. According to a recent study, the percentage of women parliamentarians in the world is only 13.28 (Faridi and Parveen, 2011). In South East Asian countries the female participation in politics ranks somewhere between 6 to 13 per cent. The 30 per cent aim stipulated by the United Nations for 1995 is far beyond reach (Bruns, 1999).

India

Women participation in formal politics in India reveals that there has been a marked increase in their voting turnout and election campaigning. But they continue to be under-represented in legislative bodies both at the national and state level and in political parties. The percentage of women members in 2009 Lok Sabha is 10.86, while in the Rajya Sabha it is only 8.57 per cent (Faridi and Parveen, 2011). Similarly, the number of female representation in legislative bodies in most of the states in India is below 20 per cent mark reflecting a pan-Indian gender exclusion from electoral participation (Rai, 2011). The Women Reservation Bill (WRB), which proposes 33 per cent reservation for women in both Union and States Legislature, has survived many years of animated debate within and outside Parliament. Though the Bill has been placed in the Parliament on several occasions, it has been withdrawn in one plea or the other. Even the political parties, which claim to be in favour of 33 per cent women reservation, do not give more than 10 to 15 per cent seats to women. The Election Commission had earlier come up with the suggestion that political parties should implement one-third reservation in their own parties first. But there were not many takers. All this suggests that the Indian female marginalization from electoral participation stems mainly from political party competition, as national and regional political parties discriminate women not only in terms of seat allotments in the electoral battle, but also in the party rank and file and chain of command. So it is argued that the electoral process in India is filled with male patriarchy and dominance that act as impediments to women participation (Rai, 2011).

However, the 73rd and 74th Constitutional Amendments have brought significant changes in the grass root level politics in India. The Amendments provided for one-third (33.33 per cent) seats reservation for women in the Panchayati Raj Institutions (PRIs). This has enabled large numbers of women to enter politics at the grass roots level. While women through the PRIs are making the state sensitive to the issues concerning poverty, inequality and gender injustice, they are also helping to change women's perceptions of themselves. They have infused confidence and inculcated a sense of empowerment by enabling them to exercise control over the resources. That is why to some theorists, the increased participation of women in electoral competition in the 1990s as voters and sharing of political power at the grass roots level reveal that electoral politics in India is no more gender exclusive but is quite inclusive (Rai, 2011).

With this background, the present paper, based on secondary sources, will try to explain the factors which hinder political empowerment of women in Mizoram. It will argue that political empowerment of Mizo women need a combined strategy along with the reservation. It will also attempt to suggest some possible ways which may help in political empowerment of women in Mizoram.

Mizoram

Like most societies, the Mizo society is patriarchal where women are by nature inferior to men. The only political institution in the traditional Mizo society was Chieftainship, which was completely dominated by men. Barred by custom, women become rulers only when they had a chance. In some occasions women became rulers after the death of their husbands. Ropuliani became a chief after the death of her husband and established her hegemony over surrounding villages. She fought against the British colonialism and ultimately became a heroine in Mizo history. These were exceptions, but it proved that the Mizo women were capable of handling political power even in the traditional society.

The formation of women's organization called Mizo Hmeichhe Tangrual on 16th July, 1946 was an important landmark in an emerging politics in Mizoram. The organization was formed with a view to promote the status of women in the society, but gradually the leaders convinced that their objectives will fulfil better if they take active part in politics. The organization took a significant decision in this regard when it passed a resolution, which said that the organization will take part in politics whenever it deems fit. After the formation of District Council in Mizoram, one of the main concerns of the Tangrual organization was to take part in the village level administration. When the President of Tangrual organization, Hmingliani was nominated as a member in the Second Mizo District Council, she played a significant role in changing the customary law of the Mizos. Because of her relentless effort, the Mizo women have a right to inherit the family property (Sangkima, 2004). This is another example of the capability of Mizo women. But after 1962, the Tangrual organization gradually alienated itself from active politics. During the period from 1962 to 1972, till attainment of Union Territory (UT), no woman elected or nominated in the District Council.

In the assembly election of UT in 1972 no party had any women candidate. The Mizo Union, however, nominated one woman. In 1975 Brig. T. Sailo's People's Conference (PC) appointed a woman as one of its secretaries. But, it was Mizo Democratic Front (MDF) which had made a woman as its President. So for the first time a woman became the leader of a political party in Mizoram (Sangkima, 2004). In the second Legislative Assembly election of Mizoram in 1978 only one woman candidate, Thanmawii of PC party contested and elected. She was the lone woman candidate out of the total 113 contestants, and she was the first elected woman member in the Mizoram Legislative Assembly (Sangkima, 2004). In the election of 1987 Lalhlimpuii was elected on the Mizo National Front (MNF) ticket. She became a Minister in Laldenga's Ministry, thus becoming the first women Minister in the Mizoram Assembly (Sangkima, 2004). In 1998 election while 33 per cent seat reservation for women was being debated in India, no major party in Mizoram allotted seats to women except MNF (Nationalist) which allowed a woman candidate. This election was important because as many as eight women contested election, though no one was elected (Sangkima, 2004). Similarly, there were only four women among 192 candidates contesting the Assembly poll in 2003 (Mahapatra, 2008). The recent scenario reflects the same story. In the Village Council election of 2006 only 36 women were selected as members from 556 villages and out of which only 3 are elected as Presidents (Lalhriatpuii, 2010). There is not even a single women member in the present Mizoram Legislative Assembly.

Thus, Mizo political life is male dominated, and women, by and large, continue to remain out of politics. Today, the women of Mizoram are largely educated, and they play a significant role in the socio-economic and cultural life of the Mizo society. But in the field of politics and political participation, they are miserably lagging behind of their counterparts in other states. On the whole, in Mizoram, women's representation in any political decision-making process, in both Village Council and Assembly, is abysmally low.

Barriers

The most important factor which prevents women to participate in politics is the patriarchal value system and patriarchal mindset. Patriarchy as a system of male domination shapes women's relationship in politics. It transforms male and female into men and women and constructs the hierarchy of gender relations where men are privileged. The gender role ideology is used as a tool by patriarchy to place women within the private arena of home as mothers and wives and men in the public sphere. The way women are defined by their culturally attributed roles as mother, wives and daughters—only still constitute one of the largest obstacles for women to enter politics nationally and locally (Bruns, 1999). In Mizoram also, patriarchal values are mainly responsible for minimal participation of women in politics (Mahapatra, 2008; Gangmei, 2010; Laldenga n.d.). Throughout the ages, the Mizo women are assigned to the role of mothers, wives and daughters. Their role was confined to domestic or so-called 'private' arena. They had little chance to involve themselves in public activities.

If the male domination is basically responsible for exclusion of women from political representation in Mizoram, women themselves are equally ignorant to their political rights. Majority of the Mizo women are not aware of the opportunity of equal excess to political structure provided in the Indian Constitution. Most of the time women themselves think that politics is beyond their domain of activity. They do not have much interest in political participation or representation. The Mizo women generally participate in politics only by casting their votes and supporting their husband and relatives at the time of their election campaign (Lalhriatpuii, 2010). Even while casting their vote, they are always under the influence of their husband or father. By and large, Mizo women have remained 'passive voters' in elections and their polling behaviour is determined by the decisions that the male members take. Study reveals that women with their own voting decisions show a higher voting participation than women whose decisions were influenced by others (Rai, 2011). Autonomous women's organizations of Mizoram can play a vital role in this regard. But even the Mizo Hmeichhe Insuihkhawm Pawl (MHIP), the biggest women organization in Mizoram, could not make any noticeable impact in the political field (Laldenga n.d.).

Strategies

In such a situation the political empowerment of women in Mizoram become a difficult task. Gender quotas or reservation of seats for women seems to the only way out. Gender quota has emerged as a global fast tract strategy to redress the exclusion of women from the formal political arena. There is a clear cut consensus that gender quota is an effective tool in addressing women's exclusion and ensuring their presence in formal structure of politics. The reason for higher women representation in the Parliaments of Afghanistan (27%), Iraq (25.45%) and Pakistan (21.35%) is mainly due to reservation of seats for women (Rai, 2011). Similarly, it was only after the passing of 73rd Constitutional Amendment Act that huge number of women have entered in the decision-making process of grass roots (Panchayat) level politics in India (Faridi & Parveen, 2011). So, in Mizoram also, gender quota is very much essential for political empowerment of women (Laldenga n.d.).

But it was pointed out that without addressing the structural constrains to women's political exclusion; their inclusion through gender quota cannot lead to an effective representation. When gender quotas are instituted, they do not necessarily bring gender equality. When women enter politics through gender quotas they are forced to play on male's terms (Bari, 2005). It is a fact that women candidates are generally fielded from 'losing' constituencies where the party does not want to 'waste' a male candidate (www.fes.de). Interestingly enough, while a women quota is always an easy target in many countries, other quotas (such as regional, ethnic etc.) are never opposed in the same way (Bruns, 1999). Long lingering of WRB in Indian Parliament is an example of this. It has also been found that the elected women representatives are treated as 'puppets' in the Panchayati Raj Institutions. Most of them remain mute spectators to the proceedings of the Panchayat meetings and rarely participate in discussions (Faridi & Parveen, 2011). So it was concluded that without the transformation of the wider politics, gender quotas cannot lead to women's political empowerment (Bari, 2005). Advanced legislation on women issues may exist, this does not automatically ensure full women participation or fully equality. It is the task to pressure for further implementation into effective laws and law enforcement which in the long run ensure political participation (Bruns, 1999). The experience of all South Asian countries shows that women's political empowerment can be achieved only by a combination of several strategies. This is also relevant for the political empowerment of women in Mizoram.

Reservation or gender quota is very much essential for Mizo women to start in politics, but it will not automatically put them on equal power. Simple participation in elections will not enable them to be a part of the political decision-making process. To get equal representation in the political arena the women of Mizoram must act. They should make themselves aware of the political rights provided by the Constitution. They must be able to think independently while casting their vote. The women of Mizoram must develop interest in politics, should realize the importance of their vote. Women's organizations of Mizoram can play a big role in creating an 'enabling environment' where the Mizo women can get aware of their rights. Where they can realize the importance of their vote and developed interest in politics. Women must think that women and politics are not opposites. Women can handle power. And they should.

The women's organizations of Mizoram can also come together to form an exclusive women's political party. Attempt to form a feminist political party may not be successful, but it can be used as a tool to pressurize the bigger political parties to concede more space for women.

Concluding Remarks

Socially and economically, the women of Mizoram have earned an honoured place in today's Mizo society. But their participation in political decision-making process is still a far away cry. So there in an urgent need for political empowerment of women in Mizoram. Reservations or quotas are very essential for Mizo women to make a start in politics. It should not be an end in itself but a step forward in promoting their political participation. After all gender quotas or reservations do not automatically guarantee the final political empowerment. So it is necessary on the part of Mizo women themselves to take the responsibility and to develop self-esteem. Therefore, it can be concluded that a combined strategy is necessary for the political empowerment of women in Mizoram.

REFERENCES

Bari, Farzana (2005): "Women's Political Participation: Issues and Challenges", www.un.org, Accessed on 2-8-11.

Bruns, Gabriele (1999): "Political Empowerment of Women", www.unescap.org, Accessed on 2-8-11.

Faridi, H.M and Ghazala Parveen (2011): "Dynamics of Women's Participation and Empowerment in 21st Century", *MAINSTREAM*, Vol. XLIX, No. 11, pp. 25–28.

Gangmei, Benjamin (2010): "Political Empowerment and Tribal Women of Manipur", www.hmar.in, Accessed on 5-8-11.

Laldenga: (n.d.): "Status of Mizo Women", www.zogamonline.com, Accessed on 5-8-11.

Lalhriatpuii (2010): "Economic Participation of Women in Mizoram", Concept Publishing House, New Delhi.

Mahapatra, Padmalaya (2008): "Status of Women: Some Reflection" in J.K. Patnaik (ed.), *Mizoram: Dimensions and Perspective: Society Economy and Polity,* Concept Publishing House, New Delhi, pp. 379–387.

Nageshwar, K (2010): "Political Empowerment of Women", www.countercurrents.org, Accessed on 5-8-11.

Rai, Praveen (2011): "Electoral Participation of Women in India: Key Determinants and Barriers", *Economic and Political Weekly*, Vol. XLVI No. 3, pp. 47–55.

Sangkima (2004): "Women and Politics in Mizoram Through the Ages" in Sangkima (ed.), *Essays on the History of the Mizos,* Spectrum Publication, Delhi/Guwahati, pp. 159-172

"Women Empowerment: The Debate on Political Representation", www.fes.de, Accessed on 5-8-11.

20

Barriers to Women's Empowerment in the Mizo Society

K. Zohra

"Woman is the companion of the man gift with equal mental capacities. She has the right to participate in the minutest details of the activities of man, and she has the same right of freedom and liberty as he... By sheer force of vicious custom, even the most ignorant and worthless men have been enjoying a superiority over woman which they do not deserve and ought not to have" (Gandhiji, *Young India*, 1918).[1]

Meaning of Empowerment of Women

The term '*empowerment of women*' has become popular especially after 1980s. It refers to the process of strengthening the hands of women who have been suffering from various disabilities, inequalities and gender discrimination.

The term '*empowerment of women*' refers to the process of providing power to woman to become free from the control of others that is to assume power to control her own life and to determine her own conditions.

The term '*empowerment of women*' could also be understood as the process of providing equal rights, opportunities, responsibilities and power positions to women so that they are able to play a role on par with men in society.[2]

Women cannot be empowered by a magical manner. It is not an automatic or a spontaneous process but require deliberate and consistent efforts. It is through the combined and coordinated effort of the government, people and the women, the task can be fulfilled. Women cannot be effectively empowered by statutory provisions or governmental effort alone. Women are empowered through women emancipation movement, education, communication, media, political parties and general awakening.[3]

The dictionary meaning of the term *empowerment* is to give power or authority. Hence, *empowerment* is the act of giving power. Thus, women's empowerment is the act of empowering women, i.e. to give them the power or authority. *Empowerment* is not necessarily only at the workplace or at home, but in general, it means the control which women have overall the resources. The term *empowerment* has different meanings to women of different classes. Any programme which aims to deal with empowerment of the poor and with women empowerment in particular must begin with an understanding and the causes for the lack of power.[4] *Empowerment* is a multi-dimensional process which should enable individual or a group of individual to realize their full identity and power in all spheres of life. Development with justice is expected to generate the force that lead to empowerment of various sections of the people in a country and to raise their status.[5]

In the Mizo family and society, women appeared to enjoy more freedom and liberty than their female counterparts elsewhere in India, but on deeper scrutiny they are not so. The status of early Mizo women, especially in the pre-Christian days was very low both in the family as well as in the social life. In the traditional Mizo society, the status and position of a woman was determined and divided right from birth. When the male child was born he was blessed by the *upa* (elder) as *'Mipa huaisen sai kap tur'* which means *'a valiant, the would-be elephant killer.'* At the same time, the birth of a female child was greeted with the words, *'Se man tur'* meaning '*one who would cost a mithun.*' Even today, the Mizo women are not liberated and they are regarded as subordinate to men and they are very much discriminated in various aspects of life.[6]

Patiarchal System

The family, religion, culture, tradition, media, etc. are the pillars of a patriarchal system and structure in the Mizo society. The well-knit and deep-rooted socio-cultural system makes patriarchy invincible and feasible in the family and society. The Mizo family is a strict patriarchal one, completely dominated by male authority. Hereditary and lineage are reckoned through male only.[7] In the family, father is the head of the household, and he controls all members of the family, all properties and other economic resources. He makes all major decisions and he is recognized as more superior to woman, and the son is customarily treated more important than the daughter in the family. Thus, in the family woman is under the control of man, and the wife is considered part of the husband's property. Traditionally, it is clearly held the view that the women or wives are purchased with prices and therefore they belong to men or husband. The status and position of wife or woman is defined in the family and the society. E. Chapman and M. Clark thus observe as follows:[8]

> "*A woman has no right at all. Body, mind and spirit, she belonged from her birth to her death, to her father and her husband. Her menfolk could treat her as they liked and a man who did not beat his wife was scolded by his friend as a coward*".

In the Mizo family and society, woman is treated as '*weaker sex*', and thus, there is a clear cut division of labour or separation between male and female from the childhood.[9] N. Chatterji says that unlike the male child who by custom and convention, had to move very early in his life to the *Zawlbuk* discipline, the female child continued to exist in the family constellation. This by itself provided a greater psychological reinforcement to the parents in favour of the female child.[10] Among the Mizos, there are several indigenous myths and traditions which have been used to justify the women's subordination or their inferiority in the family and society. There are many phrases and idioms which reflect the traditional attitude of men towards women, and some of them are given as below:[11]

(a) *Hmeichhe finin tuikhur ral a kai lo*, which means that women's wit does not cross the water point.
(b) *Hmeichhia leh palchhia chu thlak theih an ni*, which means that wife and old fence can be changed at any time.
(c) *Hmeichhia leh chakai in sakhua an nei lo*, meaning that women and crabs do not have religion.
(d) *Chakai sa, sa ni suh, hmeichhie thu thu ni suh*, meaning as crab's meat is not counted as meat so also women's word is not counted as word.
(e) *Nupui vau loh leh vau sam loh chu an pawng tual tual*, meaning that unthreatened wife and unthreatened creepers of the field are both unbearable.

Gender Inequality

The principle of gender equality is clearly enshrined in the Constitution in its preamble, Fundamental Rights, Fundamental Duties and Directive

Principles. The Constitution not only grants equality to women but also empowers the state government to adopt measures of positive discrimination in favour of women. And accordingly, Mizoram State Commission for Women was established by the Mizoram State Assembly on November 8, 2004.[12] Gender discrimination is still prevailed in the Mizo society though the Constitution of India [Articles 14, 15 (i), (ii) and 16] guarantees the right to equality and non-discrimination on the basis of sex or gender.[13] Women are, however, denied as legal personhood and they are refused on certain cases unless they produce the authorization of their husbands or fathers. Gender inequalities and biological differences in sex have deep historical roots, which are considered as indigenous practice or tradition in the Mizo society for the past many centuries or generations. From historical point of view, gender inequalities and differences are accepted as a fact due to social stratification and gender discrimination in the family and society. They have different views, needs and interests, and also have unequal power and opportunities in leadership and decision-making. The women's roles and responsibilities in the family and society are largely focused on caring and nurturing the children, and these roles are sometimes ignored or are assigned little value. Women and men have different and unequal roles and responsibility in the family and society.[14]

Gender discrimination or injustice is still prevailed in the Mizo society especially in the public and Church leadership. Gender inequality occurs in various aspects of the socio–cultural life of the Mizos, particularly in the family, society and Church, and women are looked down by the Church leaders.[15] Gender inequality, gender discrimination and gender injustice bring about exclusiveness and separation between the two sexes. Gender inequality is not Biblical. Male and female inclusivity is clearly found in the Scriptures. According to Bible (Genesis 1: 27), *"...In the image of God, he made them, male and female he created them...", and in Galatians 3: 28, "There is no longer.....male or female for all of you are one in Christ."*[16] Galatians 3: 23–29 may be considered as a *Magna Carta* for equal right and freedom especially *between and among the Jew and Greek; slave and free; male and female* (Galatians 3:28). However, there is no gender base instruction or expectation in this passage. This passage or verse does not denote a loss of identity for women and men. It acknowledges the real identity which includes sexual orientation as a part of identity, and rejects any form of separation.[17]

Isolation, separation and subordination are the most popular words which bring about the patriarchal mindset in the Church. Partnership and gender equality is justified by the scientific study on genetics which gives us reliable information that in humans 99.9 per cent of the genes are biologically the same in everyone. There is a great degree of similarity among the people of different ethnic groups, race, gender, class, caste, etc. There are very few genes less than 1 per cent to be exact that determine sex, colour of skin, facial feature, etc. Similarity of 99.9 per cent between women and men suggests that both sexes are genetically similar.[18] Gender sensitization is very important in bulding up the equitable partnership between women and men, but gender cannot be addressed in isolation or separation. However, the Mizo Christians partly fail to maintain or fulfil the Biblical principle or teaching of gender equality or partnership between the two sexes especially in Church leadership (Church government/ ministry) and ordination of women.

Biblical scholars, theologians and Church leaders mix up the poor male-oriented translations of certain verses of the Bible with the prevailing phrases and traditional socio-cultural stereotypes for women and men in the family and society. Therefore, the Churches in Mizoram still face critical situation where women are not accepted as leaders. Gender inequality or gender bias in the Church hierarchy also lead to deny women equal access to leadership position and ordination.[19] The interpretation of some Biblical text are often used to legitimize and limit the roles and responsibilities of women within the Church. Thus, women are often denied to play prominent roles especially in the ordained ministry and Church leadership. There is clear cut division between male and female. Women are responsible for certain social works and activities like cleaning and decoration of the Church buildings, preparing and serving meals and snacks, fund-raising, charity, teaching children in Sunday School, etc. and men on the other hand, occupy primarily the male-mainstream of the ecclesiastical activities.[20] Gender biased discrimination and injustice are culturally accepted in Mizo society by following the Hebrew way of life[21], and this conceptual dictum thus prevent women from enjoying personal liberties and full citizenship. The Mizo Christian community has been slow in recognizing the issue of gender justice and gender equality in Church leadership and ordination of women. Gender roles defined by society are founded on tradition and culture. The images and views of many Churches in Mizoram are also strongly influenced by culture and tradition. Culture is prominently used as a cover-up or an excuse for not taking action on violence and discrimination against the women. Moreover, culture is being used to maintain the difference between women and men. We need to recognize or understand that there are good and bad aspects of culture and that culture is a powerful force. It is true to say that the Gospel must prevail above the Mizo indigenous culture and tradition. The theological view held by *Jesus or Gospel above the culture*[22] is the key factor to remove certain barriers connected with the empowerment or women leadership in the Mizo society.

Re-enforcement by Christianity

The early Mizos worshipped different gods and goddesses and believed in the existence of different goddesses such as *Khuanu, Van chung Nula, Chawngtinleri* and *Lasi*. These female deities had great influence in the socio-religious life of the early Mizos. These goddesses were believed as the sources of blessing for mankind and also defenders of men.[23] This indigenous religious belief suggests that there is certain gap or difference between the male and female deities, which shape the socio–religious life of the Mizos. In performing religious ceremonies and other sacrificial rites, the women did not have a part to play. All these rites are performed by male members only. A woman could not become a religious head or a priest called *Bawlpu* or *Sadawt*.[24] The early Mizos also believed that only the wives of the *Thangchhuah* men could enter *Piaral* (heaven). Thus, the women could not attain a status of importance by their own.[25] The women can become subordinate or follower of their husbands in the next world after death.

The contribution of the Christian missionaries towards social transformation in Mizoram is valuable, and they have also made many positive contributions towards the liberation of women. However, social transformation did not change certain socio-cultural system or practice in the Mizo society and some degrees of patriarchal values were rather re-enforced by Christianity. It is clearly stated that the missionaries themselves who came from the patriarchal culture and male-dominated Church structure enriched and appropriated certain patriarchal culture of the Mizos and the early missionaries also rather imposed some of the western patriarchal values or Christian culture among the converts. One of the early Christian missionaries observed:[26]

> "*You look like the descendants of the Jew... But your faces are not like the Jews, you look a bit different. But you have the same way of doing things.... Every nation can join them as we white people do. You are nearer to them we white people... Your way of living, custom, culture are like it is said in the Bible.*

> *In the Bible it's written–do this, don't do it. These (commandments) are already taught by your ancestors. There are no other people like you (anywhere) in the world. But you are different from Israel because you don't know your God...*"

From the early period, Christianity did not encourage women's leadership except in the field of school education and health service. Again, Christianity did not encourage ordination of women. Even today, many Churches uphold this tradition and culture. Christianity re-enforced the clan-based elder (male) village administrative pattern in the Church. The highest decision-making body of a local congregation or Church is permanently constituted by male elders. Women are excluded from the Local Church, the decision-making body. Women should attend the worship services, participate in fund raising and so on, but should not participate in decision-making or should not demand ordination. Christianity re-enforced a male biased theology.[27] The whole Christian tradition is interpreted from the experience of male's experience. Christianity has given an ideology of male duty, inferior status of women and an exclusive male dominated Christian ministry. Traditionally, socio-cultural view on women coincided exactly with the view held by the Church in the early Christian era.[28]

Re-enforcement by Modernity

Historically, it was the British who had introduced the process of modernization in this region, Mizoram since the last part of the 19th Century A.D. (after 1890) under the influence of two outside forces-government and mission.[29] However, the advent of the British and Christian missionaries broke down the tribal seclusion or isolation of the hill region, and the British had introduced new civil administration, new economic system (cash economy), western education, new housing pattern, western dresses, etc. In fact, modernity had brought about many negative impacts especially on women through the British authorities and Christian missionaries. One of the most peculiar characteristics of modernity is business with massive industrial capitalism. The primary objective of production is to maximize project through competition and accumulation of capital resources. This situation makes women powerless, completely dependent on men who control capital resources. Cash economy and industrial development thus bring the male oriented business system. This modernity or modernism within socio-political and economic life does not help or encourage the Mizo women to avail decision-making authority and leadership in the family and society especially in the public and Church platforms. Irene Colbert clearly mentions recent socio-economic development in which the Mizo women took active part in certain areas like offices, schools, colleges, shops, hotels, restaurants, tea-stall, etc.[30] After analyzing the real problems of the women's empowerment, Batliwala clearly makes remarkable conclusion, which is also relevant to the Mizo society; thus he says:[31]

> The Government and various agencies feel that by providing various resources.... women can be empowered. But economic empowerment does not always lead to total empowerment or enhanced status. Some of the women belonging to affluent families may have the resources but have no decision-making authority in their families and thus are not empowered. Thus, lack of resources is not the causes of dis-empowerment but it is the result of dis-empowerment. The causes are historical factors like low status of women, male-dominated society, etc.

Some Biased Terms: There are several Biblical words which have been interpreted based on indigenous culture and tradition. Traditionally, social view on the women coincided exactly with the view held by the Church in the early Christian era.[32] Misinterpretation or misunderstanding of the following words thus bring gender injustice and inequality which hampered or lowered the status of women in family and society.

Head/Headship

Head or *headship* of the husband or male is clearly found in the Bible from Ephesians 5:23 (*...the husband is the head of the wife...*) and 1Corinthians 11:3 (*...the head of the women is the man...*).[33] The word head is thus interpreted as *authority of man or male over wife or woman.* This interpretation brings about gender discrimination between the sexes, and the male authority over the wife or woman makes the position of the wife or woman inferior in the family and society. This may easily lead to gender injustice in the Church ministry and society. This interpretation is biblically unacceptable because it is literally defined to justify the socio-cultural system of the patriarchal supremacy in the society and family.

In *Greek, kephale* (head) is not used in the sense of ruler or chief, but it is sometimes used in the sense of *source or origin as the source* or *head of a river.*[34] *Head or headship* language or word is meant to be a metaphor pointing to the closeness of husband and wife as paralleling the closeness of body and head. It is great significant for the interpretation of head in Ephesians 5:23 that the combination of headship, authority and union is known to Ephesians, 5.[35]

Submit/Submission

In Mizo family and society, the word *submit* or *submission* is very important criterion for a woman to become good wife. Traditionally, a wife is expected to recognize the supremacy of her husband. Scripture clearly mentions that the wives must submit to their husbands (Ephesians 5:22; Colossians 3:18:1Peter 3:1: Genesis 3:16).[36] The word *submit* or *submission* is interpreted as total surrender of the wife under the power and authority of her husband. The word *submit* comes from Greek *huppo* (next after) and tasso (it arrange), which does not refer conditional submission but the voluntary surrender to self-interest for the sake of others. The instruction *submit* or *submission* is basically reciprocal, nourishing the relationship between husband and wife.[37]

Helper

Scripture clearly says that the Lord God said, "*It is not good for the man to be alone. I will make a helper suitable for him*" (Genesis 2:18).[38] Some scholars and theologians in Mizoram have interpreted the word *helper (women) as subordinate, inferior being or lower gender*, which has established gender discrimination or gender injustice in the Church. This misinterpretation brings a gap between women and men, leading to the patriarchal superiority in the Church and society.

Biblical scholars have shown that the language of the classical text from the creation stories, Genesis 2:18 where women's roles or status has been translated as helper does not in fact require to be subordinate. Jesus included women in his teaching ministry just as he included the male disciples. The best textual evidence suggests that Junias was a woman who was an apostle (Rm.16:7), Nymphe was a house Church leader (Col. 4:15), Phoebe was a patron, a deacon or minister; he was a leader of the Church in Cenchrae (Rm.16:1). There are many other female partners or workers in the ministry of Paul, their names have been mentioned in the Bible (Romans 16).[39] Knowledge of the Biblical languages or words break through gender stereotypes reflected in the poor translations of the text.

Bible Commentary mentions that '*so solitariness is not good for him*; v.18 refers both sexes equally. Since God's creative purpose involved from the first both male and female (1:27), the first step to cure aloneness was the creation of the women to be his partner; the Hebrew implies the fitting into a unity in which the other equally'.[40] The basic purpose of the creation of women is a cure solitariness or aloneness of man through partnership or unity between them.

Bible (NIV) also mentions that 'Woman is the glory of man. She has a place of her own in God's creation, but her place is not the man's. Her place is by the side of man, highly exacted as his queen. She reigns in majesty by the side of man as his glory. In God's order and organization, man is a ruler and woman is the ruling queen by his side. God created woman from the rib of man (Genesis 2: 21f)...God created woman as a companion to man (Genesis 2:18).[41]

Beside Women and Children

Scripture clearly mentions that '*And they that did eat were four thousand men, beside women and children*' (Mathews 15: 38).[42] The attendance or participation of the women and children in this feast is neglected or not taken into the account. Mathews has written this from the Jewish perspective, showing how the Jews treat their women and children in the family and society. Jewish attitude towards the women was discriminatory in their family and social life. Quotations are often cited from Jewish writings. For instance, the Rabbis were encouraged not to teach women and not even to speak to them. This may be epitomized in the passage: '*From garments cometh a moth and from a woman the iniquities of a man. For better is the iniquity of a man than a women doing a good turn*'.[43] Gender discrimination and subordination or inferiority of women in the Jewish society is mixed up with the indigenous patriarchal culture of the Mizos. Many scholars, theologians and Church leaders have accepted and justified the Jewish culture within the Mizo Christianity and thus they apply it to the Mizo women by upholding the critical sentences '*....beside women and children*'.

Pauline theology tries to improve and rectify the gender discrimination, status of women or subordination of women among the Jews or Greeks by imposing equal rights between the two sexes. Scripture clearly mentions that *there is neither Jew nor Greek, there is neither bond nor free, there is neither male nor female*...(Galatians 3: 28).[44] '*No male and female*' theology brings a healthy interdependence between male and female, which form close partnership between the two sexes, and women become partners, not subordinates. The Bible affirms God's perception of the equality of women and men, and as the time went on society and culture created a wide gap between the roles of women and men.[45]

Thaibawi (Henpecked)

The term *thaibawi* is the prominent word or phrase which has many negative impacts on psychology, mentality and socio-cultural life of the Mizo men. It is literally defined as follows: '*Nupui thu awih*' meaning *obeying the command of the wife*; '*Nupui thuhnuai awm*' meaning *submission to the authority of the wife*.[46] Till now, the term *thaibawi* is relevant and applicable in the Mizo family and society.

Thaibawi-man is looked down by both sexes in the Mizo family and society. Therefore, it is very disgraceful and shameful for the husband to be submissive or remained under the control of the wife. Men have great interest to expose the male-superiority and authority over the women in the family and society. The Mizo society is dominated by male-stream. The term *thaibawi* is considered as culture or traditional practice, which has deep roots in the family and social life of the Mizos. The term is also considered as a symbol of femaleness or surrender of the male value under the control of the women. The husbands who have no courage to beat or scold their wives are treated as *thaibawi* (henpecked).[47] Thus, the term rather encourages husbands or men to commit various forms of misbehaviour or violence against their wives or women. The term *thaibawi* creates big gap between the two sexes, and thus, it is very difficult for the Mizo women to hold leadership in the public and Church.

Stereotypes

Culture and tradition are enriched by literature both oral and written through which the status and position of women and men are clearly shown. There are also several words that stereotype women and men and the following lists provide examples of stereotypes of the status and position of women and men in the Mizo family and society.

Women	Men
Weak	Strong
Housewives	Breadwinners

Emotional	Rational
Nurturing	Decision-making
Gentle	Assertive
Followers	Leaders
Caring	Forceful
Delicate	Strong
Fearful	Brave
Aggressive	Competitive
Old maids	Bachelors
Hysterical	Calm

Negative Images of Women

In the Mizo Christian culture, the woman is portrayed as the source of human iniquities, and the role or responsibility of the woman in the fall of humanity in the Garden of Eden is also emphasized as being greater than the role of the man. The woman is again described as a temptress and a trouble-maker, and thus negative images of woman have been developed through misinterpretation the Bible text. The fall of humanity is completely ascribed to woman, and sin commission is considered as female oriented. In this regard, the early Christian missionaries in Mizoram did not improve the status of Mizo women through teaching.[48]

In the Mizo culture and tradition, the women are viewed as procreative agents, the beast of burden and sex objects. These have created different negative images of the women in the family and social life of the people. Such negative images of the women are deep-rooted in tradition and socio-cultural life of the Christian Mizos. The following story tells certain examples of the negative images of the women, and the text runs as follows:[49]

> "*On the gate of Mithikhua (Dead Man's Village) Pu Pawla (a giant) with a huge pellet bow met all spirits of the deceased. If a man had not performed a ceremony 'Thangchhuah' Pu Pawla shot him severely which remained painful effect for many years. But Pu Pawla did not dare to shoot 'Thangchhuah' men at all. He did not shoot even infants dead at birth known as Hlamzuih. He may not shoot a young man who has enjoyed three virgins nor at one who has enjoyed seven different women, even if they were not virgins, but women, whoever they may be he always shoot at.*"

The negative images of women are communicated through various means such as culture, tradition, literature, story, etc. and the images of women have been misinterpreted as sex symbol. This implies that physical beauty is the most important thing for woman. The negative images of women thus lead to violence and harassment against women rape, wife battering, sexual assaults, etc. Table 20.1 shows the sexual crimes committed on the women in Mizoram.[50]

S. No.	*Crimes/Offences*	*2009*	*2010*
1.	Rape	27	12
2.	Molestation	29	13

Ordination of Women

At present, ordination of woman is the most important burning issue among the different Churches in Mizoram. Gender perceptions and stereotypes have deep roots in the indigenous religion, culture, tradition and social system. These perceptions and stereotypes have contributed significantly to women's marginalization in the Church and society. Some of the denominational Churches in Mizoram reject ordination of woman (pastor or elder) due to certain grounds and the more prominent causes are noted as follows: low status of women in the family and society, gender discrimination and injustice, inequality, misinterpretation of some Biblical texts.[51] The Baptist Church of Mizoram had accepted only ordination of woman for elder in 1952 and at present there are about 18 women who have been ordained as elders.[52] The Evangelical Church of Maraland had also accepted ordination of woman for elder in 2010.[53] Outside India, many different Churches have accepted ordination of woman (pastor/minister), the more prominent Churches are—Lutheran Church, French Reformed Church (1965), Church of Scotland (1966), Congregational Church (1917), Baptist Church, Methodist Church, Anglical Church (1975), Church of South India (1982), Church of North India, etc.[54] The Mara Evangelical Church (Myanmar) had also accepted ordination of woman (pastor/minister), in 2006, etc.[55]

Public Leadership

In political leadership, the Mizo woman had a chance to become a village ruler only when her husband died who had no successor or heir. The more prominent women leaders who became regents or rulers were: Lalhlupuii, Pibuki, Rothangpuii, Vanhnuaithangi, Darbilhi, Ropuiliani, Neigpuithangi, Darhlupuii, Darchhohpuii, Darsuakpuii, Suaki and Sumkungi.[56] The British occupation of Mizoram which took place in 1890 and the fall of Ropuiliani in 1893 had gradually changed the roles played by the Mizo women in politics. The formation of the political parties like *Mizo Union* (11 April 1946) and *United Mizo Freedom Organisation* (1946) brought about new pattern of political movement. Thus, the Mizo women also formed women's organization known as '*Mizo Hmeichhe Tangrual*' on 16th July, 1946 with a view to promoting the status of women. Organized itself on the pattern and model of the political party the '*Mizo Hmeichhe Tangrual*' resembled the Mizo Union in many ways. The women leaders were boldly inspired to take active part in politics.[57]

Different voluntary associations like *Mizo Hmeichhe Tangrual Pawl* (16th July, 1946), *Mizo Hmeichhia Insuikhawm Pawl* (6th July, 1946), *Mizo Hmeithai Association* (20th October, 1987), *Evangelical Nurses Fellowship of India* (12th April, 1975), *Young Women's Association* (1985), etc.[58] were formed by the Mizo women and these organizations were basically female oriented bodies, which brought about a big gap and difference between women and men in the Mizo society. This exclusiveness in organization became the weak-point of the women leadership in Mizoram. Mizo women gradually alienated themselves from active leadership in politics due to separation and gender differences between women and men and practically they partly failed to preserve their leadership roles as a result of disturbances following the outbreak of 1966 under the leadership of the Mizo National Front. Hence, the *Mizo Hmeichhe Tangrual* completely divorced politics in its life and activities. The whole set-up of *Mizo Hmeichhe Tangrual* was badly hurt by the political upheaval of 1966, thereby losing its position as an organization representing women in the Mizo society.[59]

In spite of various attempts made by different women's organizations to raise the status of women and leadership, the Mizo women failed to achieve their objectives. In the political history of Mizoram, women took minimal participation in leadership right from the pre-Christianity era. The problems of women leadership and their status in the public and Church ministry have deep roots in history, culture and tradition, which influence the patriarchal mindset being prejudiced against women's leadership in Mizoram.

NOTES

1. Agrawal, Rashmi and B.V.L.N. Rao, *Gender Issues: A Road Map to Empowerment*, Shippra Publication, New Delhi, 2004, p. xii.
2. Shankar Rao, S.N.: *Sociology Principles of Sociology with An Introduction to Social Thought*, S. Chand & Company Ltd., New Delhi, 2006, Reprint, p. 844.
3. *Ibid.*, p. 847.
4. Sethi, Jetindra S.S., Venkatachalam and Manjit Singh (*ed*): *Society and Stratification: Gender Differentiation and Ethnicity*, Indira Gandhi National Open University, New Delhi, 2007, Reprint, p. 25.
5. Agrawal, Rashmi and B.V.L.N. Rao, *op. cit.*, p. xiv.
6. Colbert, Irene: *Women and Politics in Mizoram* in Jagish K. Patnaik (*ed*) *Mizoram Dimension and Perspectives Society, Economy and Polity*, Concept Publishing Company (P) Ltd., New Delhi, 2008, p. 341.
7. Lalrinchhani, B., *A Gender Study of the Socio–economic History of the Early Mizo* in the Historical Journal Mizoram by Dr. Sangkima and Zochungnunga, ed. (Mizo History Association), St. Joseph Press, Aizawl, 2001, p. 11.
8. Chapman, E. and M. Clark, *Mizo Miracle*, Majorie Sykes (ed), The Christian Literature Society, Madras, 1968, pp. 90-91.
9. Thanga, Lal Biak: *The Mizos: A Study in Racial Personality*, United Publishers, Gauhati, 1978, p. 23.
10. Chatterji, N.: *The Early Mizo Society*, Tribal Research Institute, Aizawl, 1975, p. 2.
11. Sangkima, Mizos *Society and Social Change*, Spectrum Publications, Guwahati–Delhi, 1992, p. 31. Hereafter, it is cited as Sangkima, *Mizo Society*.
12. Irene Colbert, *op. cit.*, p. 369.
13. S.N. Shankar Rao, *op. cit*, p. 850.
14. Sangkima, *Mizo Society, op.* cit. p. 30.
15. Major Lalsawmliana, *Hmeichhe Dinhmun, Chachin Tha Engah*, Aizawl, 2009, p. 9.
16. *The Scofield Study Bible* (King James Version), Oxford University Press, Korea, 2003, pp. 4, 1551.
17. World Alliance of Reformed Churches (WARC), *Created in God's Image: From Hierarchy to Partnership, Workbook for Participants*, WARC, 150 Route de Ferney, 1211 Geneva 2, Switzerland, 2003, p. 111, Herefater it is cited as *WARC Workbook*.
18. *WARC Workbook*, *op. cit.*, p. 16.
19. Vanhnuaithanga, R.: *Zalenna Thurin leh Mizo Hmeichhiate*, Lengchhawn Press, Aizawl, 2007, p. 72.
20. World Alliance of Reformed Churches, *Created in God's Image: From Hierarchy to Partnership, A Church Manual for Gender Awareness and*

Leadership Development, WARC, 150 Route de Ferney, 1211 Geneva 2, Switzerland, 2003, p. 18. Hereafter it is cited as *WARC Manual*.
21. Major Lalsawmliana, *op. cit.*, 12.
22. Eddie Gibbs, *I Believe in Church Growth*, Hodder and Stoughton, London, 1981, p. 90.
23. Rag, Chitta Ranjan: *The Mizo Society in Transition*, Vikas Publishing House, Pvt. Ltd., New Delhi, 1993, pp. 47–49.
24. Sangkima, *Essays on the History of the Mizos*, Spectrum Publications, Guwahati–Delhi, 2004, p. 94.
25. B. Lalrinchhani, *A Gender Study of the Socio-economic History of the Early Mizo* in Dr. Sangkima and Zochungnunga, (*editors*). The Historical Journal Mizoram (Mizo History Association), St. Joseph Press, Aizawl, 2001, p. 16.
26. Samra Myer, *Judaism in Minipur and Mizoram By product of Christian Mission* in J.V. Hluna, Sangkima and Ramesh Buragohain (*editors*), *Studies on the Minority Nationalities of North East India–The Mizos*, International Seminar Organised by Directorate of Higher and Technical Education, Government of Mizoram, Aizawl, Muka Printing Press, Aizawl, 1992, p. 64.
27. A. Wati Longchar, *A liberated Women in Captivity* in Narola Imchen, *Women's Issues in the 21st Century*, Eastern Theological College, Jorhat, 2001, pp. 117-118.
28. Sangkima: *Essays on the History of the Mizos, op.* cit., p. 88.
29. Ray, Animesh, *Mizoram Dynamics of Change*, Pearl Publishers, Calcutta, 1982, p. 65.
30. Colbert, Irene *op. cit.*, pp. 347–349.
31. Sethi, Jetindra S.S., Venkatachalam and Manjit Singh (*ed.*): *op. cit.*, pp. 26-27.
32. Sangkima: *Essays on the History of the Mizos, op.* cit., p. 88.
33. *The Scofield Study Bible, ibid.*, pp. 1523, 1562.
34. Zamir, Lima: *Man and Women Relationship: Pauline Perspective* in Narola Imchen (*ed.*), *Women's Issues in the 21st Century*, Eastern Theological College, Jorhat, 2001, pp. 62, 64.
35. *Ibid.*
36. *The Scofield Study Bible*, pp. 9, 1562, 1574, 1632.
37. Zamir, Lima: *op. cit.*, p. 64.
38. *The International Inductive Study Bible*, Harvest House Publishers, Oregon, 1995, p. 6.
39. Gordon, Dr. J. Dorcas: *Life in Fullness*: *Gender Justice A perspective from North America* in the Celebrating Hope for Life in Fullness: Challenges for the Church, World Alliance of Reformed Churches, 24th General Council Accra, Ghana, 2005, p. 36.
40. *New International Bible Commentary* (NIV), Michigan, 1979, p. 117.
41. *The Preacher's Outline and Sermon Bible* (NIV Version), p. 754.

42. *The Scofield Study Bible, op. cit.*, p. 1265.
43. Walter A. Elwell, *Evangelical Dictionary of Theology*, Baker Academy, Michigan, 2007, pp. 1282-83.
44. *The Scofield Study Bible, op. cit.*, p. 1551.
45. *WARC, Workbook, ibid.*, p. 16.
46. Major Lalsawmliana, *ibid.*, p. 3.
47. Colbert, Irene *op. cit.*, p. 341.
48. Major Lalsawmliana, *op. cit.*, p. 12.
49. Shakespear, Lt. Col. J.: *The Lushei-Kuki Clans*, Tribal Research Institute, Aizawl, Reprint, 1988, p. 62.
50. Government of Mizoram, *Statistical Handbook 2010*, Directorate of Economics and Statistics, Mizoram, Aizawl, 2010, p. 78.
51. Vanhnuaithanga, R.: *op. cit.*, pp. 222–234.
52. Vanlaltlani, Dr. T.: *Mizo Hmeichhiate Kawngzawh*, Synod Press, Aizawl, 2007, p. 100.
53. Mrs. K. Pari was ordained as elder on 5th December, 2010 at *Presbytery Conference* held at Tisopi village, Saiha District. This information is provided by Mr. Pheiki Solo, a resident of Saiha Vengpui, on 9th August, 2011.
54. R. Vanhnuaithanga, *ibid.*, pp. 66, 135–137.
55. Mrs. C. Maiki was ordained as pastor on 12th March, 2006 at *General Assembly* held at Tisi village, Myanmar. This information is provided by Rev. Dr. M. Zakonia, ECM Moderator, a resident of New Saiha, on 20th August, 2011.
56. Sangkima, *Mizo Society, op. cit.*, p. 160–162.
57. *Ibid.*, p. 163.
58. Vanhnuaithanga, R.: *op. cit.*, pp. 178–185.
59. Sangkima, *Mizo Society, op. cit.*, p. 169.

21

Empowerment of Women at the Grassroots:
Relevance of New Panchayati Raj Institutions in Mizoram

Harendra Sinha

I. Introduction

The empowerment, equality and autonomy of women are globally recognized as a key factor to achieve progress in socio-economic and political spheres. It is one of the eight Millennium Development Goals to which world leaders agreed at the Millennium Summit held in New York in 2000. In India, the principle of gender equality is enshrined in the Indian Constitution in its Preamble, Fundamental Rights, Fundamental Duties and Directive Principles. The Constitution not only grants equality to women, but also empowers the State to adopt measures of positive discrimination in favour of women. The 73rd and 74th Constitution Amendments (1993) have served as a breakthrough towards ensuring equal access and increased participation in political power structure for women which laid a strong foundation for their participation in decision making at the grassroots levels. The provision of not less than one-third of the total seats for membership as well as office of chairperson of each tier of Panchayati Raj Institutions (PRIs) to be reserved for women is very significant. It is significant in minimising marginalisation of women and strengthening democracy by bringing women in policy formulation and implementation. With no provision of reservation of seats in the traditional Village Councils—the local self-governing bodies in Mizoram and the patriarchal values prevalent right from earlier times, there is lesser presence of women in the village administration. The present paper explores on the trends of woman's participation in the Village Councils, tries to identify the causes of marginalisation of women and analyses the relevance of implementation of new PRIs in Mizoram. This paper is organized from published and unpublished works, findings of some scholars and field-work findings of the author which is required for this study. The present paper is organized as follows. Section II presents new PRI and women's empowerment, section III focuses on women in Village Councils and the causes of marginalisation of women, section IV discusses the relevance of new PRI in Mizoram, section V focuses on the question of quality versus quantity debate followed by conclusion.

II. The New Panchayati Raj (73rd (Constitution Amendment) Act, 1992)

Government of India brought the historic Constitution (73rd) Amendment, which was passed by Parliament on 22nd December, 1992 and notified through Official Gazette on April 20, and came into force on April 24, 1993. This Act revolutionise the PRIs by giving constitutional status and more power to the people at the village level especially women through reservation in the PRIs. It added a new part relating to PRIs in the Constitution of India under Article 243. The state governments now required to take appropriate action under it. Some states have taken action in this respect and in other states as well statutory amendments have been made accordingly. Madhya Pradesh has become the first state in India by introducing PRI on 20th August, 1994 (Avasthi, 2002:532). The 73rd Amendment has created a scope for accomplishing development with social justice, which is the mandate of the new Panchayati Raj System. There can be no real progress if women of a country are not made partners in this process of development. Mahatma Gandhi also believed that full and balanced development of the country and establishment of a just society is possible only when women participate actively and fully in the political deliberations. Article 243D (3) of the Constitution (Seventy-third Amendment) Act, 1992, reads: Not less than one-third (including the number of seats reserved for women belonging to the Scheduled Castes (SC) and Scheduled Tribes (ST)) of the total number of seats to be filled by direct election in every Panchayat shall be reserved for women and such seats may be allotted by rotation to different constituencies in a Panchayat. Clause (4) has the following provision: ...not less than one-third (including the number of offices of chairperson reserved for women belonging to the SC and ST) of the total number of offices of chairpersons in the Panchayat at each level shall be reserved for women: provided also that the number of offices reserved under this clause shall be allotted by rotation to different Panchayats at each level (Maheshwari 2010-11:184). Consequent upon the 73rd Constitution Amendment Act, 1992 significant reorganisation of the panchayats were made in almost all the states of India. At present, there are about 3 million elected representatives at all levels of the panchayat, one-third of which are women. These members represent more than 2.4 lakh Gram Panchayats, about 6,000 intermediate level tiers and more than 500 district panchayats. Spread over the length and breadth of the country, the new panchayats cover about 96 per cent of India's more than 5.8 lakh villages and nearly 99.6 per cent of rural population (http://en.wikipedia). This is the biggest experiment in decentralised governance and in bringing largest number of women at the grassroots level in the history of humanity. Further, in a path-breaking move to empower women at the grassroots level, a meeting of the Union Cabinet, chaired by Prime Minister Manmohan Singh, decided to bring a Bill to amend Article 243(D) of the Constitution to enhance reservation for women in panchayats at all tiers from the current one-third to at least 50 per cent. The enhanced reservation would be applicable to the total number of seats to be filled by direct elections, the offices of Chairpersons, and the seats and offices of Chairpersons reserved for Scheduled Castes and Tribes. The amendment would cover all states and union territories except Nagaland, Meghalaya, Mizoram, tribal areas of Assam, Tripura and hill areas of Manipur. These States and the tribal areas excluded form the 73rd Amendment due to the existence of traditional local self-governing bodies. In Mizoram, there is no reservation of seats for women in the traditional Village Councils resulted to male dominance of the self-governing bodies.

III. Women in Village Councils in Mizoram

The Administration of Lushai (Mizo) village by a hereditary Chief has been replaced by the Village Councils after independence. The Lushai Hills District Council (Village Councils) Act, 1953 was passed under the Lushai Hills Act. No. V of 1953 on the1st December, 1953. Similarly, the Pawi-Lakher Regional Council (Village Council) Act was passed in September, 1954 to streamline village administration in the Pawi-Lakher region. By the Lushai Hills Autonomous District (Administration and Justice) Rules, 1953, the District Council Court was established and Pawi-Lakher Autonomous Region (Administration of Justice) Rules, 1954, the Village Council Courts were constituted in the Pawi-Lakher Region (Singh-1994:149). The Village Councils are still functioning in the state and it has been exempted from the 73rd Constitutional Amendment. There is no provision for reservation of seats for women in the Councils. As a result, Village Councils have been dominated by male since its inception. This is evident from the following analysis on the trend of women's participation in the Councils since 1954 till the last election in 2009.

In the first Village Council election of 1954, from the 338 Village Councils, only two women were elected. They were from the Sawleng Village Council of Aizawl District. The two women, Ms. Kairumi and Ms. Thliahthangpuii, were from MHT Party.

In the Village Councils Elections of 1957 and 1960 (381 Village Councils), there was no woman Village Council member. In the 1963 (422 Village Councils) and 1975 elections, only one woman each, Ms. Kapchhingi, MNF party, of Rahsiveng (Lunglei District) and Ms. Zathuami, P.C. party, of Saron/Chhinga Veng (Aizawl District) got elected. In the 1982 election, only two women from the Aizawl District got elected, namely, Ms. Thangliani, Vaivakawn Village and Ms. Zathuami of Saron Village, of both the P.C. party. There were no women in 1983 election.

In the 1984 Village Council election, from the 412 Village Councils, only 6 women were elected, 5 and 1 from Aizawl and Lunglei Districts respectively.

In the 1987 Village Council election, from the 468 Village Councils, only four women got elected and that too only from Aizawl District. In the 1988 bye-election, from the 16 Village Councils, 3 women got elected. In the 1990 election, 18 women got elected and in 1994, 23 women got elected, 18 from Aizawl district and 5 from Lunglei district. In 1997, 15 women got elected and in 1999, 20 women, 16 from Aizawl district and 4 from Lunglei district got elected.

As per the record of 2002 Village Councils election, there are 532 Village Councils and only 54 women represent the 2339 members, 42 from Aizawl District, 2 from Mamit District, 1 each from Kolasib and Champhai Districts, 8 from Lunglei District and nil from Serchhip District.

The Village Council election of 2006 has 556 Village Councils. Out of 2036 seats, only 34 women got elected–25 from Aizawl District, 1 each from Serchhip, Kolasib and Mamit Districts and 6 from Lunglei District. No women got elected from Champhai District. Even in the bye-election held on 11th April, 2007 in N. Tinghmun and Sakawrdai, only males were elected (Evening Post, 13 April: 1).

In the 2009 election, for 555 village councils, there were 5258 candidates. In the election to the 554 village councils (excluding Serchhip IV), 78.27 per cent cast their votes, the highest was in Mamit district

(78.27%) and lowest, Aizawl district (67.56%) (Vanglaini, 27th February, 2009:1) Out of the 2071 elected candidates in 555 village councils, only 31 women managed to get elected, against 2040 men, which is comparatively very less. In Aizawl district, 22 women were elected, in Lunglei district 6, in Serchhip, Kolasib and Mamit districts 1 each and Champhai district no women were elected (GOM, 2009).

From the above, it is evident that women are rarely represented in the Village Councils of Mizoram. Even those elected are mostly from Aizawl district, seconded by Lunglei while in the remaining districts, they are almost invisible. Hence, in the rural areas of Mizoram, women do not enter the realm of politics. Among the elected, most of them held the post of just membership. From its inception in 1954 till 1988 elections, women's representation had not crossed 6. From 1990 till 1999, women did not cross 19. But we see much improvement in 2002 with 54 elected but declined again in 2006 with 34 only (Souvenir, 2004). Moreover, there is no provision of reservation for women in the councils and socio-economic development is beyond the scope of the Councils due to lack of financial and political power. There is no provision for bureaucracy as well to sit in the Village Council meetings and it is bureaucracy that decides occasional meetings with Village Council Presidents. Many Village Councils have not yet been provided with office accommodation by the government and District Councils. As such, the Village Council executives and members have no place to sit together, convene meeting, draw up plans and schemes for development and reconstruction, preserve records of meetings, case, and books/papers concerned with village administration (Prasad, 1995: 138).

Thus, political marginalization of women at the village level of administration has been prevailing in Mizoram. General masses consider women as inferior to men and do not expect them to get votes. Women also have inferiority complex and think of themselves as incapable of running the administration.[1] Besides this, people think that politics is for men alone and not for women. In the Mizo way of life, women look after the household and if they have to constantly go out, their husbands will not tolerate. They are too busy at home to go out. Right from the olden days men and women are not considered equal. But men can do as they like in the Mizo society.[2] Before the advent of the British, each village was ruled by a chief or Lal. When the chief died his wife to accede to the chieftainship in case of no eligible son or till the son becomes eligible only. With the abolition of chieftainship, this is not possible and there is very little possibility for more women to get elected at the decision-making bodies looking at the inferior status of women in Mizo society even today.[3] While the establishment of the new democratic institutions marked the participation of women in the decision-making bodies, which was traditionally the exclusive domain of men, the traditional value of gender inequality operating as a political norm in Mizo society seems to have prevented participation of women in larger number in politics (Haokip, 2009: 34).

Therefore, from the above analysis of the present position of the Village Councils, it is clear that the Councils in Mizoram are not intense its replacement with new PRIs will make the rural self-governance viable as well as in ensuring women's empowerment.

IV. Relevance of New Panchayati Raj Institutions in Mizoram

In India, the empowerment of women has been accepted as the essential subject in determining the status of women. Various legislations, development plans and policies have been made aiming women's development in all spheres. Setting up of National Commission for Women by an Act of Parliament in 1990 to safeguard the rights and legal entitlements of women, provision for reservation of seats in the local bodies of Panchayats and Municipalities by the Constitution of India 73rd and 74th Amendment (1993) which enables women's participation at the grassroots level and the proposed Bill of 33 per cent Reservation for Women in Parliament and State Legislatures if passed in the Lok Sabha will usher a new chapter towards women's participation in decision-making at all levels. The states like Rajasthan, Madhya Pradesh, Himachal Pradesh, Orissa, Tripura etc. already have made legislation giving 50 per cent of reservation to women in Panchayats.[4] It is time now for Mizoram to involve more women in decision-making especially at the village administration through the introduction of PRIs in ensuring the goal of women's empowerment. Reservation of seats in the Village Councils through legislation or introduction of Panchayati Raj is the only alternative in male bastion grassroots democracy in Mizoram. The PRIs and the local governments will play a central role in the process of enhancing women's participation in public life as well as in the implementation and execution of the National Policy for Women at the grassroots level. Introduction of PRIs in Mizoram will play a significant role to achieve the goal of National Policy 2001. The National Policy for the Empowerment of Women 2001 sets the goal to bring about the advancement, development and empowerment of women. The Policy disseminated so as to encourage active participation of all stakeholders for achieving its goals in creating an environment through positive economic and social policies for full development of women and to enable them to realize their full potential.

V. The Quality vs. Quantity Debate

The reservation of one-third of women in the PRIs largely increased the number of women and will drastically increase in Mizoram if PRIs being introduced. But the question is whether reservation for women only can bring in social change, lead women in shaping as better citizens? Are women of Mizoram ready for their position in local governance or will be dominated by men counterparts in decision-making? Here comes the debate of quality vs. quantity. Various studies in the States of India where new PRIs are in operation show that women representatives are yet to make qualitative participation.

Pathi, Srinibas (2007) in his study, 'Women Leaders and Panchayati Raj—A Micro Study' conducted in Satabadi Block of Puri district in Orissa found that in spite of the constitutional provisions, legal frameworks and structural arrangements most of the women leaders in the Panchayati Raj System have not participated in the working of the institutions effectively. They have played a very limited role in the policy formulation and decision-making stage. Most of the women representatives like their male counterparts too are more concerned with the implementation of government initiatives, but not with local level planning and resource management.

Poornima and Vinod Vyasulu (http://www) Mirror.undp) in their study "Women in Panchayati Raj: Grassroots Democracy in India: an Experience from Malgudi—Karnataka" that the experience of women in Panchayati Raj has been varied. Many are surrogates for husbands and fathers who could not contest because of the reservation. Some were put in place by the wealthy and powerful, for their malleability—a kind of puppet to serve the vested interest while appearing to be an elected representative. This has led to many problems that have been extensively discussed in the literature and form the basis for an excellent film, sponsored by UNICEF, called *Shansodha.*

Singh, Ajit Pal (2009) in his paper, "Women's Participation at Grassroots Level: An Analysis", revealed that women take up political career as an extension of their domestic role. While women have been active in mass movements, their presence is not felt in decision-making. The influence of the husbands and close relatives is quite palpable. This tendency is due to lack of confidence. This dependency is a stumping block in their empowerment. But the positive impact of the grassroots level experiment is the increase in the female literacy rate. Studies reveal that after two years of their election to PRIs, many women demanded literacy skills and also felt the need to educate their daughters. Issues in which women representatives generally take interest are drinking water supply, primary health, child care, public distribution system and environmental protection.

Bhatt, Dr. G.D. (2011) in his study, "Post-73rd Constitutional Amendment and Women Leadership in Sikkim", found that only those women leaders who had good educational backgrounds were in a position to influence the decision-making and those who had low educaational backgrounds were sitting silently and listening to the male members of the Zilla Panchayat meetings and not taking any active part in the decision-making process. The psychological factors that inhibited womens's active participation in the PRIs were shyness and submissiveness and lack of understanding of their roles and responsibilities. The low level of education can be treated as most inhibitor of women's active participation in PRIs.

From the above studies we can conclude that although women are empowered at the grassroots through legislation, they are either influenced by their male counterparts in decision-making or played marginal role in policy formulation. There is a tremendous relevance of PRIs in Mizoram not only to increase the women empowerment at the grassroots but also to make the local bodies viable. Howerver, mere increase of women in governance through reservation may not make any difference to the lives of women. Therefore, in the case of Mizoram too, the process of empowering women should be made by bringing self-confidence and independence among women first. Competence building training, inculcating the values of gender equality and independence in the courses of study at school and college levels should be made. The social mobilisation role of Mizo Hmeichhe Insuihkhawm Pawl (MHIP), the largest women's organization in Mizoram will also be crucial to mobilise public opinion in favour of the importance of women's participation in both decision-making and policy formulation especially at the grassroots level.

NOTES

1. Based on an interview with Ms. Sangliani, Lunglei, Mizoram on 18th July, 2010. She is at present Sethlun Village Council President, Lunglei.
2. Based on an interview with Ms. Zosangi, Lunglei, on 18th July, 2010. She has been the President of Sub-Headquarters MHIP, Lunglei.
3. Based on an interview with Mr. Thlengliana, Lunglei on 9th August, 2010. He is an Associate Professor, Deptt. of Mizo, Govt. J. Buana College, Lunglei and a Church Elder.

4. These states have agreed to the Union Cabinet's Amendment Bill of Article 243(D) of the Constitution to reserve 50 per cent of seats for women in Panchayati Raj Institutions (http://ssrn.com).

REFERENCES

Avasthi, A.P. (2002): "Indian Government and Politics", (New Delhi: Lakhsmi Narayan Agarwal Educationsal Publishers).

Bhatt, Dr. G.D. (2011): "Post 73rd Constitutional Amendment and Women Leadership in Sikkim", August (New Delhi: Kurukshetra).

Das, Kalpana (2004): "Rural Development in Mizoram" (New Delhi: Mittal Publications).

Government of Mizoram (GOM) (2009): Local Administration Department, Aizawl.

Haokip, T.T., (2009): "Traditional Self-governing Institutions and Democratic Governance in NE India", *Local Government Quarterly*, July-September, (Mumbai: All India Institute of Local Self-Government).

http://www.ssrn.com, viewed on 9th August, 2010.

http://www.en.wikipedia.org/wiki/History_of_panchayati_raj_in_India, viewed on 15th Oct., 2010.

http://www.mainstreamweekly.net, accessed 15th Oct, 2010.

http://www.en.wikipedia.com, accessed 15th Oct, 2010.

http://www.mirror.undp.org/magnet/events/gender/india/VYASULU3.htm, accessed 15th Oct., 2010.

Maheshwari, S.R. (2010–11): "Local Government in India" (Agra: Lakshmi Narain Agarwal).

Prasad, R.N. (1995): "Patterns of Rural Development in Mizoram: Restrospect and Prospect" in Datta P.S. (ed.) *North-East and The Indian State* (New Delhi: Vikas Publishing House Pvt. Ltd.).

Satpathy, R.K. (1995): "Local Government in Mizoram: Some Observations", in Prasad, R.N. and A.K. Agarwal (ed.) *Landmarks*: *A Study of Public Administration in Mizoram* (Aizawl: IIPA Mizoram Branch).

Singh, S.N., (1994): "Mizoram" (New Delhi: Mittal Publications).

Singh, Ajit Pal (2009):"Women's participation at grassroots level: An Analysis." *Mainstream* XLVII. No. 12, accessed 16th September, 2010. www.mainstreamweekly.net

Sinha, Harendra (2010): "Block Administration without Panchayati Raj Institutions: An Assessment in the Lunglei District of Mizoram", September, (New Delhi: Kurukshetra).

Sinha, Harendra, Irene Colbert (2011): "Women in Village Councils: Grassroots Democracy in Mizoram", *Local Government Quarterly*, Jan–March, (Mumbai: All India Institute of Local Self-Government).

Vanglaini (Aizawl), 27th February, 2009.

22

Gender Inequality in Contemporary Mizo Society

Andrew H. Vanlaldika

After the advent of the Britishers and the subsequent coming of the Christian Missionaries in Mizo hills the structure of Mizo society was altered tremendously. The contact of the Western civilization has had a profound and dramatic impact on Mizo society. In fact, it had brought about a considerable change in the ideological and value systems; and this had deeply affected the ethos of the Mizo. Furthermore, it had greatly facilitated the process of socio-economic and politico-religious transformation in the Mizo society. In short, Western civilization had played a crucial and significant role in bringing about social transformation in Mizo society.

Likewise, the arrival of the British and Christian Missionaries have had a profound and far-reaching impact on the status and position of the Mizo women. Moreover, after the attainment of independence, various policies undertaken by the government for the upliftment of the status of women have had a deep effect on the status and role of Mizo women. With independence, there has been a constitutional commitment to promote justice, liberty, and equality. The enactment of a number of laws specifically for the betterment and improvement of women greatly effected the status of Mizo women. In fact, different legislation emancipated women from various disabilities. Consequently, the status, position, and role of Mizo women had been altered considerably.

The main factors responsible for the progress of women in Mizo society are Christian Missionaries and their various activities specifically the introduction of *formal education*, British and their administrative policies like freedom, liberty, fraternity, democracy and equality and government of free India through its various constitutional provisions and legislation.

We can thus note that the three factors, which have significantly contributed for the emancipation and liberation of Mizo women, are the British administration, the Christian Missionaries, and the government of free India. These three factors constructively affected the status and role of women in Mizo society. The most significant impact of the Britishers and Christian Missionaries on the status of Mizo women was to be seen in the form of *mass education.* The spread of education amongst the women had made them enlightened and they are now increasingly participating in every walk of life.

Education greatly contributed for the improvement and advancement of women' status in Mizo society. The first school was started on 15th February, 1898 and it was a co-education school. In 1904, a separate school for girls was set-up. In 1901 Census, there were 25 women literate against 736 men. In the first Lower Primary School Examination commenced on June 1903, two females became successful amongst 19 successful examinees. In the subsequent year two more women passed the same examination and in 1927, one Mizo woman passed her Matriculation.[1]

After 1931, some girls began to study in the High schools. Since the establishment of the first High school in Mizoram in 1944, the number of Girl students in the High school increased progressively.

The progress accomplished by women in the field of education was spectacular. Statistic evidence shows that female literacy has been increased from 16.70 per cent in 1957 to 34.70 per cent in 1961. This was remarkable as compared to other parts of India. The progress of female education in Mizoram during 1901 to 2001 is presented in Table 22.1.

Table 22.1: Progress of Female Education in Mizoram (1901–2001)

Year	*Literate Person*	*Female Literacy*	*Percentage*
1901	295	14	0.14
1911	472	34	0.34
1921	743	106	1.06
1931	1,267	278	2.78
1941	2,312	844	8.44
1951	3,651	1,947	19.47
1961	5,124	4,034	40.34
1971	1,78,793	75,469	54.75
1981	2,92,638	1,28,852	68.60
1991	4,62,264	2,11,284	78.60
2001	7,88,497	6,79,132	86.13

Sources: Statistical Abstract 2001, C.S.O. Government of India.

The then Mizo hills had the lowest female literacy in 1901 amongst the eleven Districts of the state of Assam. During this period the United Khasi and Jaintia Hills had the highest with 401 female literate. However, the huge gap was made up within a period of five decades where Mizo hills topped the list in the Census of 1951. It continued to top the list in the subsequent Censuses. In 1997 along with Kerala, Mizoram achieved 86 per cent of female literacy, which was the highest in India. From Table 22.1, it can be safely stated that female literacy has grown much faster pace than male literacy since 1961. This indicated that educationally women are not much lagging behind men in the society. The speedy progress of women education also proved that intellectually there was no difference between men and women.

Similar to the women in contemporary Western world, the status of Mizo women in present day was based on equality, liberty, and co-operation. More and more women played important parts and significant roles in the socio-economic and political aspects of the society. In fact, their contributions in these fields were increasing day-by-day. In order to reinforce their status and role in the society certain voluntary organisations have been constituted by the Mizo women, prominent amongst them are given in Table 22.2.

Table 22.2: Women Associations in Mizoram

Sl. No.	*Name*	*Year*
1.	Hmeiche Tangrual Pawl	1946
2.	Mizoram Hmeichhia Insuihkhawm Pawl	1974
3.	Puitu Hmeichhia Pawl	1976
4.	Young Women Christian Association	1985
5.	Widow's Association	1987

Through the above organisations and other various NGOs, Mizo women of today involved themselves in one activity or the other in order to promote their status in the society. Through these voluntary organisations, they are contributing significantly for the welfare and betterment of the women folk. They also greatly promote and raised the status of women *vis-à-vis* man in the society. Accordingly, in present day Mizo society the position of women has improved and ascended to such an extent that they become part and parcel in the various aspects of the society. Nevertheless, empirical studies showed that in spite of the progress made by women in improving their status and role as compared with the past yet women still face discrimination in socio-economic and politico-religious spheres of the society. The mentality of the Mizo society was such that women are still considered as less intelligent and incapable of tackling a rather difficult and crucial problem or dilemmas. The values and norms of society viewed that women should be docile, timid, obedient, acquiescent, respectful, and live under the influence of the husband. This kind of attitudes was persisted amongst the male-folk of the society. Hence, myths based on gender inequality still continued in contemporary Mizo society.

Thus, it was felt that prejudiced and biased thinking towards women was still existent in present day Mizo society. Though in theory, socio-economically self-reliant women are appreciated or respected, nonetheless practically they are not much honoured and valued as compared to man. This was mainly because society was sceptical and suspicious towards higher educated women who are socially, religiously, politically and economically independent and self-sufficient. As a result of this, women with higher education and high government jobs found it hard to acquire married partner of their equal intellects. This was due to the fact that woman with high education and jobs are difficult to look after or handled, as they possessed their own independent attitudes and inclinations. It was argued that self-independent women take up and decided every family's problems and affairs without consulting the opinion of their husbands. This was greatly regarded as an insult to the manhood of the men-folk in Mizo society.

The still pertinacious notion was that '*Man is man, Woman is woman*', and they could not be equal in status. The basic duty of man was to look after woman in every aspect of lives and woman should admit her acquiescently and without question to man leadership. This means, in reality the mindset of the society towards the status and role of women was not structurally altered. Rather the kernel of gender inequality was latently continued. This differentiation between male and female could be discerned from the following observations.

Regardless of women increasing engaged in occupations other than traditional jobs, majority of them are employed mainly in low grade and low paid occupations like clerical jobs, school teaching, receptionists, nursing etc. This demonstrated that women are still incarcerated in certain kinds of works that are typically considered as female occupations. Consequently, women occupy low status due to their occupations in present day Mizo society. Thus, contemporary Mizo women are downgraded to the bottom of the occupational structure. The position they occupied in the office evinced the subordinate roles they played in traditional society. Empirical realities exhibited that increasing access of women in governmental jobs did not potently transpose their traditional roles and status. The housewife roles of women still lingered on. They are still assigned to do all domestic works, which are in conflict with her role as working women in the office. Accordingly, the entering of women in office works did not provide a significant impact on women status. It was also observed that despite a large number of female acquired governmental jobs the male dominates higher top jobs. Usually, the higher the level of authority of office, the lower the percentage of female in its personnel. This explicitly revealed the true nature of power relationship between men and women in Mizo society.

Religiously, it was observed that female are discriminated and dominated by the male. It was seen that almost all the religious denominations have biased attitudes towards the women. Almost all the Churches in Mizoram did not have women as '*Kohhran upa*' (Church Elder) and '*Rawngbawltu*' (Local Elder). The Mizo Church has a provision, which sanctioned that women cannot be elected as Elders. Furthermore, women could not be ordained as Pastor despite a large number of them having graduated in Theology. Rather women who hold the degrees of Bachelor of Divinity or Bachelor of Theology are usually given to office works in the Church offices. They never had the chance to get *Pastorate Circle* of their own. It was justified that women do not really possessed the energy and capacity to look after the entire members of one Pastorate Circle as men did.

This evinced that though women significantly contributed to the growth and speedy progress of each respective denomination they are definitely discriminated by the Church establishment. This indicated that the traditional unimportant religious role of women was still persistent in contemporary Mizo belief system. It seems 'Women *and a Crab did not have religion of their own*' still hold true in Mizo society.

As compared to their male counterpart, *politically* women stand nowhere in the Mizo society. Since the inception of District Councils right up to the attainment of Statehood, only one woman so far held the post of Ministership in Mizoram Legislative Assembly.[2] Moreover, of different political parties, whether national or regional, they have invariably elected male to be their leaders. Accordingly, various posts in a particular political party like President, Secretary etc., were predominated by the menfolk. Furthermore, the way varied political parties allocated seats to contest General Assembly and other related elections also manifested the unequal treatment faced by women. Unequal distribution of seats to be contested in the General election clearly exhibited how the womenfolk are politically marginalised in the Mizo society.

In theory, each and every political party supported *gender equality*, upliftment of women status, equal and just representatives of sexes and empowerment of women, but in practice, they hardly followed this rhetoric claimed. In this way, the legitimate rights of women to participate in the *decision making process* was greatly thwarted or defeated. Even though women actively participate in the electoral process, they are systematically marginalized at the higher level of political participation. At present (1999–2003), there is no women representative in the State Legislative Assembly. This was a clear indication of the marginal role played by Mizo women in decision-making processes.

The discriminatory position of Mizo women was more pronounced when the question of *Property's right* was taken into consideration. As said earlier. the Mizo custom did not provided possession of any property by women. Indeed, women themselves were regarded as valuable property owned by menfolk. Accordingly, Mizo women did not enjoyed the right to *inheritance* and made any stake on family's property. Unequivocally, this demonstrated the unequal relationship and positions of male and female in regard of property in the Mizo society.

Our study revealed that this custom still hold true in the present days Mizo society. It was noted that regarding right to inheritance of family's property, male members of the family are always favoured. Although rich parents might give some to their daughters, the lion's share was invariably given to the male children. The main and important properties were given to male members of the family. If the family possessed only one property, the question of female inheritance did not arise.

This shows the lower and inferior position of women in terms of *property rights* in the Mizo society. Implicitly, the traditional law of inheritance still persists which definitely favoured male groups of the society. Furthermore, the inferior status of Mizo women was evident from the fact that women alone could commit *Uire* (infidelity). Whereas male infidelity was never opposed by the society. This was a clear case of bias attitudes on the part of the society. Women who committed adultery were greatly looked downed, disgraced and despised. Accordingly, the husband was given the right to divorce his unfaithful wife according to his judgement and discretion. Conventionally, adulterer's women are deprived of all her belongings if her husband divorced her. She was compelled to go out from the house without her personal belongings except the one she was wearing. She did not had the right to claim her personal possessions after divorce.

The above findings clearly exhibited the low status and inferior role accorded to women in Mizo society. This still endured in contemporary Mizo society. The social mindset had been that of discrimination against women right from the beginning heretofore in Mizo society. In other words, the Mizo society in actuality did not change its attitude towards womenfolk of the society.

Therefore, consciousness amongst women about the reality of their situation and their solidarity are essential prerequisites for their liberalization. To realize the ideal of gender inequality in Mizo society, the following prerequisites are *de rigueure*:

(i) There should be mental revolution amongst the women.

(ii) Women should develop a sense of self-independence rather than dependent on men.

(iii) They should be self-reliant and develop self-confidence.

(iv) They should develop mobility both physically and mentally.

(v) The so-called men's roles and women's roles should not be differentiated.

(vi) The so-called masculine behaviour and feminine behaviour should be abolished.

(vii) The 'expected behaviour' for both male and female should be same.

(viii) Men and women should be considered as persons rather than male and female.

(ix) The 'fear psychosis' amongst the male groups should be abated by educating them that gender equality would not taken away their legitimate position and status in the society.

(x) The family, marriage, kinship systems and socialization pattern need to be redefined and remodelled.

(xi) Rationality and scientific temper should develop to do away the outmoded cultural myths and beliefs system.

(xii) Vocabularies, which differentiated male and female, present in the society, should be substituted.

The above measures could be accomplished through Cultural Revolution in Mizo society. Since we maintained that gender inequality was culturally constructed rather than biologically created, our hypothesis was that a *socio-cultural transformation* was imperative for the eradication of gender inequality. The societal values, norms, ideologies and beliefs system should be transposed in the right directions. Prejudices and predisposition attitudes against women should be removed from the society. The ideologies that legitimized gender inequality, the religious beliefs that sanctioned gender inequality and the values and norms that reinforced and justified gender inequality should be abjured.

Concluding Remarks

The complete transformation of the psyche of the society was very much required for the overall abrogation of gender inequality. Mizo society needs an ideological revolution, in which men and women might be seen as people not as gender. An individual should be given a chance to develop his personality and characters along lines best fitted to him, rather than being restricted and caged by the culturally defined labels–male and female. The gender inequality would end when women ceased to be slave of culturally defined labels. If there was no progressive transformation in socio-cultural spheres men groups would continue to rule the roost at home, in government and in fact every aspect of the society.

NOTES

1. Miss Nuteii was the first Mizo woman who passed her Matriculation in 1927.
2. Mrs Lalhlimpuii, belonging to MNF Party, held the post of Minister of State under the Chief Ministership of late Laldenga in 1984.

REFERENCES

Liangkhaia, Rev, *Mizo Chanchin,* Aizawl: Mizo Academy of Letters, 1938.

Lloyd, Meirion, J, *History of the Church in Mizoram (Harvest in the Hills),* Aizawl: Synod Publication Board, 1991.

McCall A.G., *Lushai Chrysalis*, London: Luzac & Co.

Parry N.E., *A Monograph on Lushai Customs* and *Ceremonies*, Aizawl: Tribal Research Institute, 1978.

Prasad, R.N., *Government and Politics in Mizoram,* New Delhi: Northern Book Centre, 1986

Sangkima, Dr, *Mizos: Society and Social Change*, Guwahati: Spectrum Publications, 1992.

Zawla, K., *Mizo Pipute leh an Thlahte Chanchin,* Aizawl: Gosen Press, 1989.

23

Women Prisoners in Mizoram:
A Case Study of Lunglei District Jail

Lalramdinpuii Chhangte

1. Introduction

Mizoram is situated on the North East of India covering a geographical area of 21,087 sq km. Mizoram is covered by international borders from three sides, Myanmar in the East and the South, Bangladesh in the West. The population is 10,91,014 according to the 2011 census and is 23rd state in India. In the last few decades, we never heard of Mizo women committing crime. But criminality arises among Mizo women now due to various reasons such as influence of the foreigners particularly who come from Myanmar in large number, product of modern civilization, growth of population and urbanisation, drugs abuse and influence by electronic media like television. The present paper focuses on the management of women prisoners in Mizoram. The researcher collected the opinion of 22 women prisoners lodged in Lunglei district Jail of Mizoram in order to assess the life of the women prisoners and the cause of criminality and to suggest some correctional measures. A simple tabulation method is made to analyse the data collected. This paper is organised from published works, web materials, apart from the field-work findings of the author which is required for the study. The present paper is organised as follows.

Section II presents the definition of prison, the purpose of imprisonment and the rights of the prisoners in India and the role played by the judiciary. Section III discusses the causes of imprisonment, occupational, educational, marital status of female prisoner in District Jail, Lunglei. In Section IV an attempt is made to know the problems and difficulties faced by the women prisoners. In Section V some measures are suggested for improvement of facilities for women prisoners.

II. Definition and the Purpose of Imprisonment

A prison, jail or correctional facility is a place in which individuals are physically confined or detained and usually deprived of a range of personal freedom. These institutions are an integral part of the criminal justice system of a country. There are various types of prisons such as those exclusively for adults, children, female, convicted prisoners, under trial detainees and separate facilities for mentally ill offenders. In this paper, "prisons" refer to only adult correctional facilities. Imprisonment is a legal punishment that may be imposed by the state for the commission of a crime or disobeying its rule. The objective of imprisonment varies in different countries and may be: (a) punitive and for incapacitation, (b) deterrence, and (c) rehabilitative and reformative (Scott C.L. & Gerbasi J.B., 2005).

The primary purpose and justification of imprisonment is to protect society against crime and retribution. In current thinking, punitive methods of treatment of prisoners alone are neither relevant nor desirable to achieve the goal of reformation and rehabilitation of prison inmates. The concept of Correction, Reformation and Rehabilitation has come to the foreground and the prison administration is now expected to function in a curative and correctional manner (Karnataka Prisons, 2009). The United Nations has also provided several standards and guidelines, through minimal rules or basic principles in the treatment of prisoners (United Nations, 1977). The State is under an obligation for protecting the human rights of its citizens as well as to protect the society at large, and is authorised to do so. To protect the citizens from any possible abuse of this authority, they are given certain basic privileges recognised by the Constitution of India as Rights.

Human Rights of Prisoners: National and International Instruments

In India, the idea of rights of prisoners was long suppressed under the colonial rule and has only recently emerged in public discourse. The Constitution of India confers a number of fundamental rights upon citizens. The Indian State is also a signatory to various international instruments of human rights, like the Universal Declaration of Human Rights which states that "No one shall be subject to torture or cruel, inhuman or degrading treatment of punishment" (UDHR, 1948). Also important is the United Nations Covenant on Civil and Political Rights which states in part: "All persons deprived of their liberty shall be treated with humanity

Table 23.4: Marital Status

Marital Status	*No.*	*Percentage*
Married	11	50
Unmarried	4	18.18
Widow	7	31.82
Total	22	100

Table 23.5: Educational Background

Educational level	*No.*	*Percentage*
Illiterate	1	4.45
Below Class V	4	18.18
Class VI to HSLC	17	77.27
HSLC and above	–	–
Total	22	100

I. Problems of Women Prisoners in Mizoram

Lunglei District Jail, Lunglei was set-up in the year 1977. At present the buildings are in an exhausted condition. There is only one small building to accommodate women prisioners resulting to congestion. There are only two bathrooms and two toilets because of that they face lot of problems. Mosquito nets are not supplied to the female prisoners, instead mosquito repellents are supplied which is also not regular. As the Lunglei is a malaria prone district, some of the women prisioners are suffering from malaria. There is no regular medical check-ups and no special care is given to those children staying with their mothers in the jail. Table 23.6 depicts the problems of the women prisoners in District Jail, Lunglei.

Table 23.6: Problems of Women Prisioners in District Jail, Lunglei

Problems	*Good No.*	*Percentage*	*Bad No.*	*Percentage*
1. Living situation (lack of mosquito net; cloths etc.)	9	40.90	13	59.09
2. Sanitary situation	8	36.36	14	63.64
3. Quality and quantity of food	19	86.36	3	13.64
4. Medical health check-up	8	36.36	14	63.64
5. Exercise facilities	0	0	22	100
6. Vocational and literacy training facilities	0	0	22	100
7. Facilities for reading newspapers, journals	2	9.09	20	90.90

The second and the last hypostheses that there is lack of adequate facilities for women prisoners in the jails and rectification measures are not being taken are also proved. The facilities meant for women prisoners in the jail are largely inadequate and correctional measures and vocational training facilities are not being made in Lunglei District Jail.

V. Suggestions

1. Setting up of distance education programme like IGNOU study centre at Lunglei District Jail should be provided to make the prisoners become a good citizen in the future.
2. Introduction of various programmes and recreational facilities inside the prison to achieve the purpose of imprisonment a correctional.
3. Subscription of newspapers and magazines for the prisoners to make their life connected with the outside world.
4. The present female prisoners building could not accommodate the female inmates. To avoid overcrowding new arrangement is required.
5. All facilities for exercise are in the male ward only, which is difficult for the female inmates to utilize it. Such facilities for women prisoners should be given to the female inmates.
6. Providing mosquito nets and appointment of regular doctor is necessary to check-up the health of the prisoners.

Though various rights have been granted to prisoners, in reality, they do not reach the prisoners. Imprisonment as punishment is now rethought of as rehabilitative punishment which involves a philosophy that individuals are incarcerated so that they have an opportunity to learn alternative behaviours to curb their deviant lifestyles. Correction, therefore, is a system designed to correct those traits that result in criminal behaviour. This direction of the Indian judiciary is not implemented in many of the Indian prisons. This is true in case of Lunglei District Jail also.

REFERENCES

Justice A.N. Mulla Committee, the All India Committee on Jail Reforms (1980–1985) under the Chairmanship of Justice A.N. Mulla.

Karnataka Prisons, 2009. Available online at http: Karnataka prisons. http//:Org pl.html. Accessed on 5-8-2011.

Mehta P.L., Neema Varma (1999), *Human Rights under the Indian Constitution: The Philosophy of Mandaring*. New Delhi. Deep and Deep Publication.

Nagla, B.K. (1991): *Women, Crime and Law*, Rawat Publications, Jaipur.

National Human Rights Commission (NHRC) 1993. Available online at http// :nhrc.nic.in. Accessed on 5-8-2011.

Sabita Mishra and Amarenda Mohanty (2007): "Administration of Women Prisoners in Orissa: Problems and Issues", in Lalneihzovi (ed.) *Women's Development in India*, Mittal Publication, New Delhi.

Scott, C.L., Gerbasi J.B. (2005): *Handbook of Correctional Menutal Health*, Washington American, Psychiatric Publishing.

Sree Kumar, R. 2003. *Handbook for Prison Visitors*. Pub: Commonwealth Human Rights Initiative, New Delhi.

Statistical Handbook, Mizoram 2010. Published by Directorate of Economics and Statistics, Govt. of Mizoram.

Sunil Batra *Vs*. Delhi Administration, AIR: 1978 SC. 1575.

UDHR: 1948. Universal Declaration of Human Rights, Article 5.

UNICCPR 1966, United Nations International Covenant on Civil and Political Rights, Article 10.

Index